Tributes for Widjojo Nitisastro
by Friends from 27 Foreign Countries

Tributes for Widjojo Nitisastro
by Friends from 27 Foreign Countries

Editors:
Moh. Arsjad Anwar
Aris Ananta
Ari Kuncoro

KOMPAS

Kompas Book Publishing
Jakarta, January 2007

Tributes for Widjojo Nitisastro
by Friends from 27 Foreign Countries

Published by Kompas Book Pusblishing, Jakarta, January 2007
PT Kompas Media Nusantara
Jalan Palmerah Selatan 26-28, Jakarta 10270
e-mail: buku@kompas.com

KMN 70007006
Editor: Moh. Arsjad Anwar, Aris Ananta, dan Ari Kuncoro
Copy editor: Gangsar Sambodo and Bagus Dharmawan
Cover design by: Gangsar Sambodo and A.N. Rahmawanta
Cover foto by: family document
Text lay-out: Ratno

The National Library: Cataloguing-in-Publication Data
    Tributes for Widjojo Nitisastro
    by Friends from 27 Foreign Countries,
    Jakarta: Kompas Book Publishing, 2007
    xviii + 382 pp; 14 cm x 21 cm
    ISBN: 979-709-292-5

Printed by PT Gramedia, Jakarta.
The printer does not assume any responsibility for the content of this book.

Table of Contents

Introduction

P rof. Widjojo Nitisastro was born on September 23, 1927.
In anticipation of his 70th anniversary, 71 friends from 27 foreign countries contributed tributes during the beginning and the middle of 1997. They include different periods of time as well as a variety of experiences.

Those tributes had not been published yet.

The compilation of tributes in honor of the 70th anniversary of Prof. Widjojo Nitisastro is for the first time published in this book.

We deeply appreciate the contributors of these tributes. We also would like to thank them for their extraordinary patience to wait for so long for the publication of their contributions.

Meanwhile, 12 of the 71 contributors have passed away. They are:

1. President Julius Nyerere of Tanzania (1999),
2. Prime Minister Noboru Takeshita of Japan (2000),
3. Lord Eric Roll of Ipsden of the United Kingdom (2005),
4. Dr. Dragoslav Avramovic, Governor of the Central Bank of Yugoslavia (2001),
5. Prof. Heinz W. Arndt of the Australian National University (2002),
6. Ambassador Masao Sawaki of Japan (1999),
7. Ambassador Marshall Green of the US (1998),
8. Dr. Pius Okigbo, Economic Advisor to the Federal Government of Nigeria (2000),
9. Mr. Derek Davies, Editor of the Far Eastern Economic Review (2002),
10. Prof. Guy J. Pauker of the University of California (2002),

11. Mr. John "Jack" Bresnan of the Ford Foundation and the Columbia University (2006).
12. Mr. Mitsuhide Yamaguchi, President & CEO, Tokyo Stock Exchange (2004).

We sincerely hope that this compilation of tributes in honor of the 70th birthday of Prof.Widjojo Nitisastro will be of benefit for the readers.

Jakarta, August 13, 2006.

Team of Editors:
Moh. Arsjad Anwar
Aris Ananta
Ari Kuncoro

Prof. Dr. Widjojo Nitisastro

B orn on September 23, 1927 in Malang, East Java.
Right after graduating from the Faculty of Economics, University of Indonesia with *cum laude* in 1955, he was appointed Director of the university's Institute for Economic and Social Research succeeding Prof. Sumitro Djojohadikusumo.

From September 1957 to March 1961 he continued his study in Economics and Demography at the University of California at Berkeley, California, USA. He received his Ph.D. in economics with a dissertation titled *Migration, Population Growth and Economic Development: A study of the Economic Consequences of Alternative Patterns of Inter-island Migration.*

He was only 34 years old when the University of Indonesia appointed him as full professor of the Faculty of Economics on June 1, 1962. The title of his inaugural was *Economic Analysis and Development Planning*, delivered on August 10, 1963. From 1964 to 1968 he served as Dean of the University of Indonesia's Faculty of Economics. In addition, he served as Director of the National Institute of Economic and Social Sciences of the Indonesian Council for Sciences. He was also an instructor at the School of Staff and Command of the Army and at the Military Law Academy. Cornell University Press published his book *Population Trends in Indonesia* in 1970.

In 1966 he was appointed Team Coordinator for Economy and Finance of the Staff of Personal Assistants of the Chairman of the Cabinet Presidium General Soeharto with the following members:

Prof. Mohammad Sadli, Prof. Subroto, Prof. Ali Wardhana and Prof. Emil Salim. In 1968 he was appointed to chair President Soeharto's economic advisory team with a larger membership.

When he was 39 years old he was appointed Chairman of Bappenas (National Development Planning Agency) on July 20, 1967 and retained the office for 16 years until 1983. In addition, on September 9, 1971 he became Minister of Development Planning and from 1973 to 1983 he was Coordinating Minister of the Economy, Finance and Industry.

From 1967 to 1983 he headed delegations to many international meetings, such as Inter-Governmental Group on Indonesia (IGGI), Paris Club (1967-1970), and others. Since 1983 he has been the government's economic advisor.

He was also member of the South Commission (headed by President Julius Nyerere) and the Policy Board of the Inter-Action Council (the Chairman of the Inter-Action Council was Chancellor Helmut Schmidt).

A Legendary Personality of Asia

Manmohan Singh *

The analysis of economic growth of nations has been a major concern of economists since the days of Adam Smith. Ricardo and Marx made important contributions to the economic literature dealing with the dynamics of growth processes. In the post-war period, the rivalry between the USA and the former USSR and the fears that the USA was lagging behind the USSR in the race for economic growth rekindled interest in the economics of growth. The decolonization process which began with the independence of India in 1947 and the ardent desire of the newly independent countries of the Third World to catch up with the developed countries in the race for social and economic development also provided a powerful stimulus to economic analysis of processes of growth and development. Economics being both a light bearing and fruit bearing science, the expectation has been that a scientific study of economic development will provide valuable inputs for policy formulation. As Professor A.C. Pigou pointed out in his classic work *The Economics of Welfare,* when we study economics "our impulse is not the philosopher's impulse, knowledge for the sake of knowledge, but rather the physiologist's knowledge, for the healing that knowledge may help to bring."[1]. Pigou went on to say, "Wonder, Carlyle declared, is the beginning of philosophy. It is not wonder, but rather

---

* Dr. Manmohan Singh (India) is Prime Minister of India (2004 - present). Member of Parliament and Finance Minister of India (1991-1996).

1   A.C. Pigou, *The Economics of Welfare,* London, 1920, p. 5.

the social enthusiasm which revolts from the sordidness of mean streets and the joylessness of withered lives, that is the beginning of economic science. Here, if in no other field Comte's great phrase holds good: It is for the heart to suggest our problems: it is for the intellect to solve them...The only position for which the intellect is principally adapted is to be the servant of social sympathies."[2]

Professor Dr. Widjojo Nitisastro belongs to that rare breed of economists who have distinguished themselves not only as great scholars but have also made outstanding contributions to the economic policy formulation and implementation in their respective countries. Professor Dr. Widjojo has lived up to ideals upheld by great economists like Pigou. Graduating from the Universities of Indonesia and California (Berkeley) he began his professional career as Dean of Economics Department, University of Indonesia. In 1967, he became Chairman of the National Development Planning Agency and subsequently rose to the powerful position of Coordinating Minister for Economy, Finance and Industry. *Indonesia's great success in the management of development, diversification of the economic structure and in poverty eradication is largely due to the wise economic policies pursued by the country under the far-sighted leadership of Dr. Widjojo Nitisastro.* In one of his recent writings, while summing up Indonesia's experience in poverty eradication, he has laid down guidelines which have almost universal validity. To quote him:

"Indonesia was able to reduce poverty rapidly, first, through sustained, broad-based and labour-intensive growth based on rapid growth of agriculture, and then through rapid growth of labour-intensive manufacturing exports. Second, the poor were able to participate in that growth because of substantial improvements in education and health and investments in infrastructure. Third, population growth fell sharply."[3]

Apart from being the architect of Indonesia's highly successful economic policies, Professor Dr. Widjojo Nitisastro has made powerful contributions to finding practical solutions to the debt crisis

---

2 Op.cit
3 Widjojo Nitisastro, "Reduction of Poverty: The Indonesian Experience" in *Fifty Years After Dretton Woods*, Washington DC; IMF pp. 176-182

of the developing countries. The report prepared in 1994 by the Ad Hoc Advisory Group of Experts on Debt of the Non-Aligned Movement entitled: *"The Continuing Debt Crisis of the Developing Countries" owes a great deal to the inspiration, guidance, expertise, wisdom and energy provided by Professor Widjojo Nitisastro.*

I was privileged to be associated with Professor Widjojo Nitisastro as a member of the South Commission. Although because of his other preoccupations he was able to attend only a few meetings of the Commission, his vast experience, knowledge, wisdom and his deep commitment to the cause of South-South cooperation and solidarity made a deep impression on the minds of all his colleagues. Personally, I shall remember forever the warmth of hospitality of Professor Widjojo and his charming and gracious wife Mrs. Tina Widjojo during the Jakarta meeting of the South Commission.

Indonesia is fortunate to have a person of the eminence of Professor Widjojo Nitisastro to guide the formulation and implementation of its economic policies. Although Dr. Widjojo left the front line of policy management in 1983 to become an Economic Adviser to the Government of Indonesia, his wealth of experience and knowledge is being put to effective use in guiding a new generation of government officials. He played an important role in drafting the Bogor Declaration adopted at the Asia-Pacific Cooperation Forum in Bogor, Indonesia in 1994. *He remains very active as a guiding star in the economic development of Asia as a whole, and of developing countries all over the world. The life and work of this legendary personality of Asia will continue to be a source of inspiration for scholars and policy makers for generations to come.* I join Dr. Widjojo's numerous friends and admirers in sending him my heartiest felicitation on the occasion of his 70th birthday celebrations. I pray to God to grant him a long life, good health and happiness so that he may continue to serve the Indonesian people and humanity at large for many years to come. ◆

16 July 1997

2

I Wished There Were More Widjojos in the South

Mwalimu Julius K. Nyerere*

I met Widjojo for the first time in 1986 in Indonesia, on one of my trips to different countries of the South to meet potential candidates for membership in the South Commission. When I invited him to become a member, I had already heard about his commitment to South-South cooperation and solidarity and his important role and involvement in North-South dialogue and negotiations over the years. I also knew of his reputation as one of the chief architects of Indonesia's economic success.

The real Widjojo I met when he began to attend the meetings of the South Commission. In his typically reserved and soft spoken style, he made very useful interventions at strategic moments, which contributed to the adoption of the report and fashioning of the final consensus in the Commission. I was struck by his precision and ability to articulate the consensus.

However, it was not until the Commission finished its work that the true importance of having chosen Widjojo to be a member became evident. Widjojo had grasped fully the importance of continuing the South Centre and of transforming it into a permanent institution. He played a key role, with the full backing of President Soeharto, in securing the financial and political support of Indonesia at a moment critical to the continuation and survival of the Centre. For this I am especially grateful to Widjojo. As a result, my task as

* Mwalimu Julius K. Nyerere (Tanzania) was President of Tanzania (1964 - 1985), Chairman of the South Commission (1986 - 1990) and Chairman of the South Centre (1990 - 1999). He passed away in 1999.

the Chairman of transforming the South Centre into a permanent intergovernmental organization was greatly simplified.

In the tribute to Widjojo in this volume by the Centre's staff, his contribution to the consolidation of the South Centre is described in greater detail. I want to conclude by saying that *I wish there were more Widjojos throughout the South, with the vision, leadership, professional competence and commitment that he has amply demonstrated during his long career, including through his association with the South Commission and the South Centre.*

I congratulate him on having reached his 70th birthday. I wish him good health and many more years of active life in the service of his country and people and their development, and in helping promote solidarity and cooperation among the countries of the South. *The young generations of leaders that are rising in the countries of the South can derive inspiration from his example and work.* ◆

One of the Most Respected and Influential Economists of the 20th Century in Terms of What He Accomplished in the Real World of Economics

Lawrence H. Summers*

As we celebrate Professor Widjojo Nitisastro's 70th birthday, I want to contribute some thoughts on the Professor's first 70 years. When I think of the Professor Widjojo's legacy, *three themes come to mind.*

First, Professor Widjojo has shown an extraordinary commitment to the welfare of his people. After studying economics in the United States many years ago, he returned to his native Indonesia to bring the economic ideas he had acquired abroad to bear on the economy of his homeland. Professor Widjojo's economic ideas have been a major force in helping Indonesia grow into the miracle economy that it is today. *His commitment to the welfare of his people is more than admirable.*

A second theme that stands out is Professor Widjojo's belief in the careful analysis of data. Not one to hold to ideas for their own sake. Professor Widjojo *has been careful to analyze what the data actually says, and not what he would like it to say. This trait has earned him the deep respect of his colleagues in the profession.*

Professor Widjojo is *one of the most respected and influential economists of the 20th century in terms of what he has actually accomplished in the real world of economics.* Generations of economic advisors for government–both domestic and foreign, have

---

* Prof. Lawrence H. Summers (US): President of Harvard University (2001-2006); Charles W. Elliot University Professor at Harvard; Secretary of the Treasury of the US (1999-2001); Deputy Secretary (1995-1999) and Under-Secretary (1993-1995) of the Treasury; Vice President, Development Economics and Chief Economist of the World Bank (1991-1998); Nathaniel Roper Professor of Political Economy, Harvard University (since 1987).

benefitted enormously from having the opportunity to work with him. In this way, the benefits from his wisdom and knowledge have been multiplied many times over through these contacts.

As he celebrates his 70th birthday, we look forward to another 70 years for Professor Widjojo. ◆

4

An Irreplaceable Friend For Advancing Friendly Relations Between Our Two Countries

*Noboru Takeshita**

I wish to extend my sincerest congratulations to the special advisor of the President of Indonesia, Prof. Dr. Widjojo, who has made such enormous contributions to promoting the national development of Indonesia, on his 70th birthday this year. As someone who has been privileged to enjoy a close relationship with this eminent advisor, I am very grateful to have the honor to contribute to this commemorative publication marking Dr. Widjojo's birthday.

As is well-known, Dr. Widjojo has played an extremely important role in the remarkable success of Indonesia's socio-economic development, which has been continuing over these past thirty years under the leadership of President Soeharto.

Indeed in 1996, in recognition of his contributions to the activation and stable growth of the Indonesian economy, Dr. Widjojo received from the Nihon Keizai Shinbun—a leading Japanese economic newspaper its Asia Prize, awarded to those who have made exceptional achievements in the economic field.

Earlier in his distinguished career, as Lecturer of the University of Indonesia, Dr. Widjojo sedulously trained many of the young economics specialists who are now behind Indonesia's present spectacular economic growth. In addition, while in the successive important cabinet posts he has held related to economic affairs, Dr. Widjojo has been able to solve, through his uncommon talents and

---

*   Mr. Noboru Takeshita was Prime Minister of Japan (1987-1989); Minister of Finance (1979-1980) and (1982-1986). He passed away in 2000.

abilities, numerous problems affecting Indonesia's national construction and development. He is truly someone who knows extremely well, and is deeply involved in, the history of Indonesia's economic development.

During these endeavors Dr. Widjojo deepened friendships with many governments and business leaders from around the world.

Of course in Japan as well, I know that Dr. Widjojo has made many friends from a very wide range of fields, including those from top political and business circles.

I myself have met Dr. Widjojo many times, as he has taken various opportunities to visit Japan, and I enjoy a deep friendship with him. The depth of Dr. Widjojo's knowledge and understanding of Japan and the wide range of his friends and acquaintances are astonishing. I also feel heartened and reassured by the fact that his very presence can and does play such a large role in the growth and strengthening of the bilateral relations between Indonesia and Japan. In particular I would like to take this opportunity to express my sincerest regards to Dr. Widjojo for the efforts that he has exerted towards the enhancement of mutual understanding between leaders from our two nations.

At present the relation between Indonesia-Japan has become extremely favorable for both countries. Though it hardly needs mentioning, it took a long time to develop the relations we now enjoy, a relationship in which we, as Asian countries, can understand each other and mutually offer a helping hand when the other is facing difficulty. *For Japan, which is intent on advancing the friendly relations between Indonesia and Japan, Dr. Widjojo is an irreplaceable friend.*

The 21ˢᵗ century, which for all of us will be the beginning of a new era, is looming just ahead of us, and in this continuously changing world I believed that the roles the international community expects both Indonesia and Japan to play, as well as our positions in the world, will continue to grow more prominent year by year. And as we head towards this new world, I have no doubt that *Dr. Widjojo's experience and efforts will certainly still be indispensable for further developing and strengthening our bilateral relations, which will have new significance in the future.*

Finally, on the occasion of the publication of this commemorative volume celebrating the 70th birthday of Dr. Widjojo, I would like to say that I sincerely hope for the lasting development of the Republic of Indonesia and for the good health and success of Dr. Widjojo and that we in Japan are eagerly awaiting Dr. Widjojo's continued guidance and advice for the enhancement of relations between our two nations. ◆

5

A Key Player in the Early Days of ASEAN Economic Cooperation

Goh Chok Tong *

I t is an honour for me to contribute a short essay to mark the 70th birthday of Professor Widjojo Nitisastro, one of Indonesia's illustrious sons.

I first met *Bapak* Widjojo in September 1977 when I attended my first ASEAN Economic Ministers (AEM) Meeting in Pattaya, Thailand. I had just been appointed Senior Minister of State in the Ministry of Finance. (A Minister of State in Singapore is a Deputy Minister, not a Senior Minister as in Indonesia.) I continued to attend AEM Meetings in this capacity and later as Minister for Trade and Industry until 1981 when I left the Ministry.

The AEMs then focussed on ASEAN economic cooperation through schemes like ASEAN Industrial Projects (an example is the ASEAN Ammonia-Urea Project in Aceh) and the Preferential Trading Arrangements, the forerunner of AFTA (ASEAN Free Trade Area).

It was extremely difficult for ASEAN to forge an agreement on those cooperation projects. Every country had tended to approach the projects from how much they could get out of them rather than how much they could contribute to the integration of the ASEAN economies. We were then less prepared to make short term sacrifices for longer term gains arising from economic integration.

---

* Mr. Goh Chok Tong (Singapore) was Prime Minister of Singapore (1990-2004); currently Senior Minister of Singapore and Chairman of the Monetary Authority of Singapore (The Central Bank).

A proposal would take several Economic Ministers Meetings to finalise, which meant one or two years as the meetings were held only six-monthly. In the slower moving, less competitive era of the late 1970s and early 1980s, that was acceptable. But I am sure it was frustrating and at times exasperating for all the people involved in the AEMs.

These meetings though paved the way for more fruitful co-operation in the later years. They enabled Ministers to understand each other better, their countries' aspirations and the constraints and challenges they faced. Over time, the Ministers built up trust and confidence in one another and approached ASEAN economic co-operation with greater openness and gusto.

Bapak Widjojo was regarded as a senior member among the economic ministers. He was highly respected for his ideas, contributions at meetings, and general leadership. He was patient and he always wore a smile when putting his point of view across. He was a key player in the early days of ASEAN economic cooperation.

I have fond recollections of working closely with *Bapak* Widjojo during an important phase of ASEAN's efforts at closer economic cooperation. In those crucial years, ASEAN required capable and decisive implementors. While the vision of intra-ASEAN economic co-operation was shared by all members, working towards this goal given our different stages of development proved more difficult. In this context, *Bapak* Widjojo made a significant contribution towards intra-ASEAN economic cooperation. Today's AFTA, Growth Triangles and other modes of intra-ASEAN economic co-operation are the result of the early efforts of many committed ASEAN Ministers, among whom *Bapak* Widjojo stood out.

Bapak Widjojo's contributions to Indonesia and the region have continued into the 1990s. When Indonesia assumed the Chairmanship of APEC in 1994, President Soeharto appointed *Bapak* Widjojo as his Special Adviser on APEC, a clear indication of his trust and confidence in the abilities of his economic doyen. *Bapak* Widjojo helped in Indonesia's successful hosting of the APEC Leaders' Meeting and launching of the Bogor Declaration, a landmark initiative of President Soeharto which set APEC on the road to trade and investment liberalisation.

Bapak Widjojo has served Indonesia with dedication in numerous capacities. In the late 1960s, *Bapak* Widjojo moved from quiet academia into the "front-line" of government as a member of President Soeharto's newly-created Economic Team. He faced an unenviable task then. The immediate problems facing President Soeharto, *Bapak* Widjojo and the Economic Team in those early years of the New Order included runaway inflation, unemployment and declining growth. *Bapak* Widjojo and his Team did not shrink from the tough challenge. They worked hard on President Soeharto's vision of transforming Indonesia into a strong and competitive economy. The result of their efforts is self-evident. In barely 30 years, Indonesia has succeeded in becoming one of the more open, dynamic and forward-looking economies in the Asia-Pacific region.

Bapak Widjojo continues to perform distinguished service to Indonesia with quiet determination and strong resolve. He has used his abilities to work for the prosperity and development of not just Indonesia but also ASEAN.

I extend my best wishes and warm regards to *Bapak* Widjojo on his 70th birthday. I wish him the best of health. ◆

6

I Admire His Great Capacity to Listen and His Dexterity in Molding Solutions to Complex Political, Economic and Social Problems

Cesar E. A. Virata *

Our generation—those born in the late 1920s to early 1930s—grew up in a region of disparate countries. The colonial experiences (or the lack of one) of Southeast Asian countries kept the countries of the region distinct and distant from one another. We did not trade with one another, our people rarely travelled to neighboring countries or communicated across borders. The members of our generation did not know each other.

After the Second World War, however, as each Southeast Asian country regained its independence, we soon discovered that our pre-colonial cultures and traditions were similar enough to define us as a distinct geographic and cultural region. This common thread of race, culture, and pre-colonial interaction had survived centuries of Western influence and domination. Even our separate struggles for independence from colonialism became part of our common background—an experience that most of us shared and all of us understood.

As our generation went through the school system we learned more about each other. In the 1940s, secondary school pupils (such as

* Dr. Cesar E. A. Virata (Philippines) was Prime Minister of the Philippines (1981 - 1986) and Minister of Finance (1970 – 1986). He held the positions of Professor of Business Administration and Dean of the College of Business Administration at the University of the Philippines (1961-1969). He was subsequently designated in concurrent capacities as Deputy Director General of the President Economic Staff in charge of investments, Undersecretary for industry, Director and Chairman of the Philippine National Bank (1967-1968). He was then appointed Chairman of the Board of Investments (1968-1970), Secretary/Minister of Finance (1970-1986). After his government services he resumed his consulting practice in 1986 and at present he is Chairman of the Rizal Commercial Banking Corporation (1995-present).

myself at that time) were taught the history of the Vijaya and the Madjapahit empire—an empire whose influence reached Philippino shores. After the World War II, as college students and newly independent Filipinos, we closely followed the Indonesian people's own struggle for independence. During the ECAFE meeting held in the Philippine city of Baguio in 1947 there was a dispute on who would represent Indonesia. In the early 1950s, before I graduated, there was also much discussion in the University of the Philippines (UP) whether President Soekarno should be awarded an honorary degree.

After graduated from UP in 1952, I became an instructor at the College of Business Administration and was sent to Wharton School in the United States under the auspices of the United States Agency for International Development (then known as MSA/ICA). Other Filipino graduates were sent to various American universities.

In Indonesia, graduates were being sent to the US under the Ford Foundation program. The Ford Foundation program was also established in the Philippines in the 1960s. It was also around this time that the Maphilindo grouping was formed with Malaya, the Philippines, and Indonesia as members. Maphilindo gave way to the formation of the Association of Southeast Asian Nations, or ASEAN in 1967.

In 1966 an economic seminar was held in Jakarta under the leadership of Professor Widjojo Nitisastro. This was closely followed by a seminar on Indonesian affairs held at the University of the Philippines with the support of the Rockefeller Foundation. As a professor and the Dean of the UP's College of Business Administration, I attended this seminar and for the first time learned of the issues Indonesians were facing at that time.

In March 1967 President Ferdinand Marcos designated me deputy director general for investments of the Presidential Economic staff, undersecretary of industry, and chairman of the Philippine National Bank. Therefore, in January of 1968, I had the opportunity of joining the party of Marcos' state visit to Indonesia. It was during this visit that I first met some members of the so-called "Berkeley Mafia" and other influential Indonesians with whom I have had long-standing friendships and working relationships. I call on them to this very day as friends and colleagues.

The Philippines actively strove to broaden the scope of intra-ASEAN trade and to make investments incentives as uniform as possible among ASEAN member nations. I attended a number of these ASEAN meetings on trade, investments, and development financing and extensively interacted with Prof. Widjojo Nitisastro and his colleagues in the cabinet. Whenever I visit Jakarta I make it a point to visit Prof. Nitisastro to share mutual experiences. We discuss the development process covering a wide range of socio-economic and political issues. During my terms as Philippine finance minister (1970-1986) I also met with Ali Wardhana several times.

In 1987 (I had retired from government in 1986), I was hired by the Asian Development Bank (ADB) as a consultant for Indonesia's financial institutional reforms and for promoting Indonesia's non-oil export sector. This effort resulted in ADB extending its first program loan—a major departure from the Bank's usual project loans.

Indonesia progressed very quickly around the time the program loan was approved and had less need for consulting services. The ADB therefore sent me instead to the Indochina countries of Laos, Vietnam, and Cambodia. I suggested to the Vietnamese authorities that they study the Indonesian approach to dealing with state enterprises.

Through the years I have had the occasion to witness the transformation of Dr. Widjojo Nitisastro, following the footsteps of Prof. Sumitro, into an accepted and well-respected leader. He has gained the trust and respect of President Soeharto and this relationship has resulted in consistent and stable government economic and social development policies. This stability has benefitted a great portion of the Indonesian population. Furthermore, Indonesia's step-by-step process in reducing the role of government in business has been so effective that it could stand as a model for transition economies the world over.

I have, through first-hand experience, become thoroughly cognizant of the various elements that influence decisions at the highest levels of government and the difficulties attendant to reconciling conflicting interests. *This is why I can truly appreciate*

Dr. Widjojo Nitisastro's ability to provide steady guidance and to formulate acceptable solutions through objective analyses and syntheses. I have observed and admired his great capacity to listen and his dexterity in molding solutions to complex political, economic, and social problems. I have no doubt that these abilities are product of his utmost dedication to his country and his steadfast commitment to serve the best interests of Indonesia. ◆

Not Only His Professional Achievements, but His Qualities as a Human Being Has Earned Him Wide Respect and Adulation

*Amnuay Viravan**

I t is my great pleasure to join the people of Indonesia in offering sincere best wishes to Prof. Dr. Widjojo Nitisastro on the occasion of his 70th birthday.

Long before Southeast Asia became the economic powerhouse as it is today, Prof. Dr. Nitisastro was at the forefront of the region's drive towards prosperity. As a leading technocrat and prominent intellectual, he has made an indelible contribution to the country's development. His far-sighted efforts in designing and implementing the Indonesian National Development Plan during 1967-1983 were instrumental in bringing about the economic success Indonesia now enjoys.

In addition his ideas have been influential in improving the living standard of the Indonesian people. His work on population trends in Indonesia reflected his concern for the welfare of the people and the future of the world's most populous Muslim nation. *A number of his recommendations have become guidelines not only for the economic development of Indonesia but also for other ASEAN countries.*

Impressive as they are, *it is not only his professional achievements, but his qualities as a human being that have earned him such wide respect and adulation.* I am honoured to have this opportunity to share my esteem for Prof. Nitisastro's dedication and the valuable work he has done over the past decades. I wish Prof. Nitisastro all the very best for his continued good health and happiness. ◆

---

* Dr. Amnuay Viravan (Thailand): Deputy Prime Minister (1995-1996 and 1992-1994); Minister of Finance; Minister of Foreign Affairs; Chairman, National Economic and Social Development Board (NESDB).

A Legend Who Fully Lives Up to His Remarkable Reputation

Stanley Fischer*

I am honored to have the opportunity to contribute to this publication on the occasion of Professor Widjojo's 70th birthday. I first met Professor Widjojo nearly a decade ago when I was at the World Bank. *At that time he was already a legend - and he fully lived up to his remarkable reputation. And our subsequent meetings and interactions have only confirmed those first impressions.*

We in the IMF—as in the entire international economic community—know well the outstanding role that Professor Widjojo has played in guiding the growth and development of the Indonesian economy for the past three decades. We are fully aware of the invaluable advice that he has consistently provided on a wide range of economic issues to many other countries. And we have all benefited from his original and thought-provoking—but always practical—views on key economic problems, whether in conversation or by reading his articles.

Professor Widjojo has always been able to react with remarkable clarity, as well as intellectual rigor, to new challenges throughout his career. His innovative work on poverty eradication beginning in the 1960s—which he outlined during the 1994 IMF—World Bank Conference on "Fifty Years After Bretton Woods" helped greatly to alleviate hardships and raise living standards in Indonesia. His untiring efforts to promote fiscal and monetary discipline and

---

* Dr. Stanley Fischer (US) was First Deputy Managing Director of The IMF (1994-2001); Vice President, Development Economics and Chief Economist, The World Bank (1988-1990); Killian Professor of Economics and Head of Department of Economics at MIT (since 1977).

deregulate trade and industry in the 1970s and 1980s have been amply rewarded by the subsequent strong performance of the Indonesian economy. His enthusiasm for the IMF-World Bank Initiative for the Heavily Indebted Poor Countries has been most useful in broadening the international support for this venture.

Professor Widjojo's talents and long experience continue to make him invaluable as an economic counselor. Recent disturbances in currency markets in the Asian region have demonstrated once more the vital importance for policymakers to develop forward looking and flexible responses to rapidly changing situations, with due regard for the implications of globalization. It is the possession of the entire combination of abilities needed to address such questions in an international context that has characterized Professor Widjojo's achievements. We hope that he will continue to influence events for many years to come, both in Indonesia and beyond. And we thank him for what he has done, both for his country, and for many others all around the world. ◆

July 1997

His Contributions to Food Security and Poverty Alleviation In Indonesia

Walter P. Falcon*

1. Introduction

F ew countries in the world have seen their food and agricultural sectors change to the extent that Indonesia's has been altered during the past 30 years. That this period also coincided with the era of Professor Widjojo's most important intellectual, policy, and operational contributions to Indonesia's development is not an accident. Although he is best known as a world-class macro economist (and also a very perceptive demographer), the commentary that follows indicates that Professor Widjojo also played a (perhaps the) key role in Indonesia's remarkably successful rural development program. He did not engineer this effort alone, but he was clearly the early leader in a group of stars that included, among others Professor Dr. Saleh Afiff, Professor Dr. Emil Salim, Bustanil Arifin, and, of course, President Soeharto, all of whom shared a remarkable interest in the plight of small farmers.

2. Early Recollections

My first visit to Indonesia and also my first encounter with Professor Widjojo was in 1968 at the very early stages of the New

* Professor Walter P. Falcon (US) is Helen Farnsworth Professor of International Agricultural Policy, Emeritus, at Stanford University; Chairman of the Board of the International Rice Research Institute. His specialties are food policy, commodity analysis, and rural development. He began working in Indonesia and with Professor Widjojo in 1968 as a member of the Harvard University Project in Bappenas. Since 1972 he has been at Stanford University, but he has continued to visit Indonesia twice annually for agriculturally related work at Bappenas, the Ministry of Finance, the Ministry of Agriculture, and Bulog. In 1992 Professor Falcon was awarded the Bintang Jasa, Medal of Merit, by the Government of Indonesia for his assistance with the country's economic development program.

Order Government. The country was desperately poor at the time—no one knew what per capita income was precisely, but probably less than $100. Nearly 80 percent of the nation was in poverty, and almost all of the population and the limited wealth of the country were in the rural sector. Jakarta had but three buildings—one of which was unfinished—of more than four stories. There was little foreign exchange to provide for food or capital imports, and even less international confidence in Indonesia's economy to permit much public borrowing from abroad. The few rice stocks that existed in the country were guarded zealously at the local level. Almost no rice moved across provincial lines, and multiple checkpoints were common even at short distances within islands—for example, between Jakarta and Bogor.

My overwhelming first memory of the time was of the Bappenas building—a slightly unkempt pair of low parallel structures—and of an incredibly intense small group pouring over the rice data in the most *minute* detail. Dr. Widjojo and Dr. Saleh Afiff, then Chairman and Bureau Chief of Bappenas, respectively, (and long before their rise to Senior Cabinet status) were worrying about each rain, each inbound ship, and almost literally, each grain of rice that existed or might exist in the next few months. Food security issues dominated the talk of Government and of the entire country, and at the very center of the analysis and action was Professor Widjojo and his younger colleagues. I can honestly report—and I hope he will forgive me—that he was not at that time a fully wise and self-confident food- policy specialist. But he may well have been the most savvy student who has ever entered the food-policy arena.

I vividly remember chatting with him about rice at his home one evening during an early visit. His question to me at the time was clear and straight-forward (It was important to him, I could tell, because as is his style, the more critical the issue, the more quietly he speaks!). He was leaving for Japan the next day he said, and wanted to know my views on what would be the most important thing he could ask for from the Japanese that would help with the food situation in Indonesia. After a moment's reflection, I replied that I thought that nitrogen fertilizer was the proper request. I will always remember his answer—"is that so; isn't that interesting"—a testament both to his openness and his breadth of interests. That reply began a four-hour conversation about the payoffs from increased use of nitrogen fertilizer—then being used at the rate of only a few pounds of N per hectare in Indonesia. He quizzed me about everything I knew (and much that I did not) about types of fertilizer, response ratios, fertilizer interactions with water and other inputs, and feasible mechanisms for making fertilizer available to poor farmers. It was that specific evening when I learned what a great agricultural champion Indonesia had as the head of its planning agency.

There are several endings to this vignette. First, fertilizer issues have been on Professor Widjojo's and my Indonesia agenda ever since then. What started as a four-hour discussion, ended up as a thirty-year seminar. Second, Professor Widjojo did go to Japan; he did ask for and receive a substantial amount of aid in the form of nitrogen fertilizer; and fertilizer later became, along with new rice-seed varieties, the major elements of an in-kind package of credit for small farmers (BIMAS). And the rest, as they say, is history—albeit with a large number of important chapters along the way. Professor Widjojo's early concern about farmers, coupled with his focus on *relevant* technology, incentives, infrastructure, and macro policy had major impacts on rural (and economy-wide) growth, economic stability, and poverty alleviation. Indonesia's small farmers and poor rice consumers clearly owe him a great debt of gratitude.

3. Incentives

Professor Widjojo, as most of the world knows, received his Ph.D. at the University of California at Berkeley. He has been the undisputed leader of the "Berkeley Mafia" in Indonesia, and it is ironic, therefore, that *some* of his views would have type-cast him early on as being from "Chicago". He often sounded more like Professor (and Nobel Laureate) T. W. Schultz on agricultural issues than did Schultz himself. Professor Widjojo, like Professor Schultz, had great faith in farmers.[1] He felt strongly that they were both more responsive and responsible than was generally thought to be the case—especially by economists who had worked in and on Indonesia,

---

1   See Schultz, T. W. *Transforming Traditional Agriculture,* Yale University Press (New Haven), 1964.

the key case country for much of the development literature on dualism.

The Widjojo Group thus worried much about the incentives faced by farmers. He was a strong advocate of a positive price policy for paddy *(gabah)* and for spending resources on rice-price stabilization to encourage on-farm investment and welfare. It is not surprising that he, Professor Afiff, and their long-term agricultural consultants—Professors Leon Mears and Peter Timmer among others—developed "the farmers formula" (the ratio of paddy to urea prices) as a central feature of Indonesian price policy for agriculture.

Professor Widjojo was clearly not from the Chicago school, however, in his views on subsidies. He was pragmatic not dogmatic, and he sometimes urged the use of input subsidies, as on fertilizer for example, to induce farmers adoption of it. He also went along with subsidies for pesticides, which in retrospect, turned out to have large negative consequences. The overuse of these chemicals disrupted prey-predator relationships among rice pests, which in turn caused a decade of increasingly resurgent problems with brown-plant hoppers. One lesson of development is clear—even great policy analysts sometimes are wrong on crucial issues. But a second lesson of development policy may be even more important. Professor Widjojo was "there" also to help Professor Dr. J.B. Sumarlin and Prof. Afiff with ending the subsidy when evidence from the field made it clear that a previous mistake had been made.

Professor Widjojo and President Soeharto were also great believers in deepening human capital in the countryside—another theme on which they and Professor Schultz were in complete agreement. Rural education for both boys and girls, rural health centers, and guidance centers on family planning were all a part of the "Widjojo lexicon" on rural development. The great lines from the opening of Professor Schultz's Nobel lecture might well have been penned by the Professor from Jakarta:

> "Most of the people in the world are poor, so if we know the economics of being poor, we would know much of the economics that really matters. Most of the world's poor earn their living from agriculture, so if we know the economics of

agriculture, we would know much of the economics of being poor."[2]

Professor Widjojo worked diligently as well at maintaining a rural flavor in Indonesia's public-investment program. In spite of a prevailing global view that industry was everything, he pushed hard for extensive rural investments. In the case of irrigation, for example, literally hundreds of irrigation projects were initiated or upgraded in the 1970s and 1980s. They were a major contributing factor in the doubling of paddy production from 20 million to 40 million tons in the 1970-85 period. It was also during this era that Indonesia went from being the world's largest importer of rice to being self-sufficient in rice on a trend basis.

4. Macro Policy

Impressive as the previous contributions have been, perhaps Professor Widjojo's greatest contribution to Indonesian food security has been his ever-present role as a formulator of a food-friendly macro policy. Many countries throughout the world, and especially those with oil resources, have learned the hard way that poor macro policy obliterates good agricultural projects and programs. From the outset, Professor Widjojo knew intuitively that balanced growth was needed. He believed strongly that exchange-rate and interest rate policies, if done poorly or wrongly, would mean the downfall of the food and agricultural sectors.

The macro management of Indonesia's foreign-exchange system during the New Order Government is known throughout the development community as one of the most impressive performances in *any* country's development experience. Professor Widjojo, working typically with his strong colleague and ally, Professor Dr. Ali Wardhana, seemed to perform best when the stakes were the highest and the circumstances were most grim.

Such were the situations both during the years in which oil prices rose substantially (1973-1980) and also those in which they fell precipitously (1981-1986). During the rising-price period, Indonesia

---

2   From Schultz, T. W. *The Economics of Being Poor,* Nobel Lecture (Stockholm), Decembers, 1979.

faced a serious threat of Dutch Disease. (This affliction had nothing to do with Indonesia's colonial heritage, but rather refers to a situation, taken from the Dutch experience with natural gas, when the balance of payments is healthy and foreign exchange reserves are large, but when producers of non-resource tradeables [such as agricultural products] are caught in a familiar cost-price squeeze).

Unlike Nigeria, Venezuela, Mexico and a number of other oil countries, the Berkeley Mafia realized that a devaluation was nevertheless called for in spite of Indonesia's strong reserve position. On November 15, 1978 the country devalued the rupiah (not re-valued as many thought likely because of the size of the foreign-exchange reserves) from Rp 415/$ to Rp 625/$ in what is still regarded as one of the boldest and wisest macro-policy decisions made in the post World War II period. This action helped to prevent the widespread destruction of the rural economy that would have almost surely occurred—as it did in most other oil-rich countries whose governments had less vision.[3]

During the later era of sharply falling oil prices, Professor Widjojo also acted in important ways to protect the rural economy.

With reduced oil prices, government revenues were also con-comitantly decreased. It would have been very easy *not* to have cut back on big industrial projects, to have induced a rapid inflation, and to have again neglected agriculture. That this did not happen, in the face of powerful pressures to maintain the large, show-case projects, is a great tribute to the watchful eye of Professor Widjojo and his reasoned concern for the well-being of farmers and poor consumers.

5. The Bottom Line

Because of his enlightened views about farmers, and because of his concerns with agricultural technology, agricultural investments, incentive and human-resource policies, and macro-policy ma-nagement, Professor Widjojo's contributions to the country and to the countryside are almost incalculable. He clearly had help from strong and able colleagues, and from a President who was

---

3 For a much more detailed version of this story, see Scott R. Pearson, "Exchange Rate Policy in Indonesia, 1968-1994", in Subiakto Tjakrawerdaja, *Bustanil Arifm 70 Tahun: Beras, Koperasi, Dan Politik Orde Baru*, Pustaka Sinar Harapan (Jakarta), 1995.

sympathetic and wise about food-security issues. But it is also true that issues which now seem clear after the fact were murky and controversial during the policy process in real time. That, of course, is the nature of the "policy game" in all countries, and the real heroes are those who understand the difference between the truly important issues versus those that are merely interesting, and who have the courage and capability to see that key policies are implemented into practice. By that standard Professor Widjojo is indeed a national hero, and especially so with respect to food security and agricultural development issues within Indonesia.

The evidence on this point is unambiguous. Between 1970 and 1990 rural poverty, for example, fell from 58 percent of the rural population to 14 percent. In spite of Indonesia's much larger total population in 1990, the absolute decline in numbers of people in rural poverty over this twenty-year period declined from 56 million to 18 million persons.[4]

Perhaps even more surprising, given the traditional Geertz[5] view of Java's countryside, real rural wage rates for both men and women began rising in the 1980s at a significant pace.[6] It was only 30 years previously that everyone, and I mean *everyone*, simply knew unequivocally that Java could not rid itself of surplus rural labor in the 20th Century! But the rate of per capita income growth during the 1970-90 period was almost 5 percent annually; moreover, it had a rural bias to it. Largely as a consequence of this concern for agriculture, the ratio of incomes for the richest 20 percent of the population relative to the poorest 20 percent actually fell from 7.5 to 4.9.[7] Few other countries can claim results as impressive as these for expanding agriculture and improving food security; and perhaps no individual has greater claim to that history or to those rural results than does Professor Dr. Widjojo Nitisastro. ◆

June 1997

4   Naylor See Rosamond L. and Walter P. Falcon, "Is the Locus of Poverty Changing?". *Food Policy*, Volume 20, Number 6, December 1995, pages 501-518.
5   Geertz, See Clifford. *Agricultural Involution: The Process of Ecological Change in Indonesia*, University of California Press (Berkeley) 1963.
6   Naylor, See Rosamond L. "Wage Trends in Rice Production on Java: 1976-1988, "*Bulletin of Indonesian Economic Studies*, Volume 26, Number 2, August 1990, pages 133-154.
7   Falcon, See Walter P. *Food Policy Analysis, 1975-95: Reflections of a Practitioner*, Lecture Series, Number 3, International Food Policy Research Institute (Washington, D.C.), November 29, 1995, 16 pages.

10

I Will Always be Proud
of Having His Friendship

Nathan Keyfitz*

S cholar, teacher, administrator, international negotiator, Prof. Widjojo Nitisastro has been an outstanding public official and a devoted servant of Indonesia for a good part of the last half century.

Pak Widjojo, as I later always addressed him and now think of him (even though he protested that the *Pak* was not necessary) was first known to me in the year 1952-3, when I arrived from Canada as consultant on population in the *Biro Perantjang Negara*, the State Planning Bureau. The founder and Director of the Bureau was the economist Professor Sumitro Djojohadikusumo, then Minister of Finance, whose colorful career was well under way. It was he who turned the wheels that got me out of the Dominion Bureau of Statistics in Ottawa for a year and so gave me my first taste of Indonesia.

Pak Widjojo taught me the newly established *Bahasa Indonesia*, brought me abreast of Indonesian culture insofar as a foreigner can know it, introduce me in Dutch scholarly circles. The Keyfitz's got to know Widjojo and his wife Ibu Darsih very well during that time, a charming young couple if ever there was one.

Widjojo, still a student, arranged field trips to East Java where a group of us went to live with the then Head Man of the village of

---

* Prof. Nathan Keyfitz (US) is Professor Emeritus of Population and Sociology at Harvard University. He was born in Canada, studied at McGill University in Montreal and the University of Chicago, where he received the doctorate in 1952; since then he has taught at the University of Chicago, at the University of California at Berkeley, and has been at Harvard since 1972. His first visit to Indonesia was in 1953, for a year, in which time he was associated with Professor Widjojo, then a graduate student. He has visited Indonesia at intervals of about five years ever since that time and never lost touch.

Balearjo, and spent our days examining how the villagers made a living. (We must have made an impression on the villagers because when I revisited in the late 80s the new Head Man said he remembered us from when he was a boy in 1952. And he proved it by telling me facts about myself and family that he could not possibly have known except for having talked to me 35 years earlier.)

The members of our team included young men who went on to big things—I recall especially Dr. Permadi who became the Director of the Bank Rakjat Indonesia and did much to spread the small savings practices that have helped Indonesia accumulate capital for industry.

Widjojo first thought of himself as a demographer, and that indeed is how he was trained, first at the University of Indonesia, then at Berkeley, where he was a student of the already famous Kingsley Davis, deceased in the last few months. His particular subject, suggested by the title of his thesis, was *Migration, Population Growth, and Economic Development in Indonesia*. That thesis, accepted in 1961, was updated and published in 1970 as a book: *Population Trends in Indonesia*. I reviewed it enthusiastically in *Economic Development and Cultural Change* (20(3): 604-606, 1972), praising, among other features, the scholarly way it corrected early census figures, whose understatement had contributed to exaggerated estimates of the colonial power's favorable effect on population growth.

Widjojo and I together wrote the first text book on population in the national language, *Soal Penduduk dan Pembangunan Indonesia*, published in 1954 by P.T. Pembangunan in Jakarta. The title translates as "Population Problems and Indonesian Development". It was published under both our names and went through at least four editions that I know of, selling tens of thousands of copies—far more copies than I had ever expected. No book I have been associated with since has been nearly so popular.

After that our paths separated, but I managed to find an excuse to visit for longer or shorter periods every three or four years since. I had gotten to love Indonesia, its language and culture more than its politics. The bottom politically was in a visit of 1964, when the country was in complete disarray. There were indeed some border infiltrations into Malaysia, but with the change of government the undeclared war was brought to an end in 1966, and one year later the close alliance of ASEAN (Association of South East Asian Nations, that included Malaysia) was founded.

I met him once at the Kemajoran Airport, on his way to Beijing as a member of a group of research scholars responding to an invitation of Chairman Mao's government. I was envious because as an American citizen I would not at that time have been permitted to make such a trip.

I was away for a few years after President Soeharto took over, and when I returned I was told by Widjojo about various measures he had promoted on behalf of the peasantry. Among other help was a subsidy to each village to build roads and other public works. That and similar measures *made the villages that I saw in the 1980s very different from those of the 1950s—instead of naked boys in the muddy waters watering their buffalo there were boys in neat school uniforms riding their bicycles up and down the paved main streets of the villages. Schools were everywhere and the country was on the way to universal literacy.* Though all spoke Javanese at home, everyone under 45 knew the National *Bahasa Indonesia.* Higher education still had some way to go but the instruction in reading and writing was very effective, as I found when I met some elementary classes.

No one was more aware than Widjojo of the need for education if Indonesia was to take its place in the world economy and the society of nations. Sales of oil, gas, and timber were going well and bringing lots of money into the national treasury, but there were several things wrong with depending so completely on these staple exports. The first was the uncertainties of the oil market, the second that it did little for employment, the third that with the economically efficient but ecologically damaging way it was carried out, it was denuding large areas of forest cover.

Widjojo with his training in economics at Berkeley was the most influential of the senior administrators who were aware that the country needed jobs above all, jobs for the millions of young people coming out of the schools. Without jobs there would be neither continued prosperity nor a stable society. Widjojo contributed very substantially to the successful transformation of Indonesia's economic and social policies, so that now it has a proud manufacturing sector, on a track with rapid and seemingly automatic growth.

That growth track, whose success we can observe in retrospect, was in considerable part formulated, planned in its detail, and then put into effect by many people, but Widjojo was at every stage the coordinator, and it is not too much to say the leader, among the numerous officials whose cooperative involvement was required. It was an elaborate process, and hardly to be described in this brief and modest note. However we have the help of a magisterial address by Widjojo to the World Bank and IMF in 1994. It may be appropriate here to include a summary of the address, a summary of Widjojo's summary.

The first step in the Indonesian development track was concentration on agriculture. The individual peasant could not be very productive on his small plot—after all he had been growing rice and vegetables on small plots for countless ages, and had always remained poor—but the policy did what it could to support him. It stabilized the prices he received, and distributed fertilizer and superior rice varieties. The outcome was an increase of nearly 5.3 percent per year in agricultural output between 1971 and 1983. At the same time the rate of growth of population slowed due to a highly successful family planning policy associated with the name of Haryono Suyono. The rate of population increase was 2.5 percent in 1970 and now is 1.7 percent and still falling. The combined effect of changes in agriculture and population resulted in output per head showing an increase where up to the 1960s it had been going down. As Widjojo says "This early emphasis on agriculture played a decisive role in breaking the downward cycle of poverty, population growth, and environmental degradation."

With increased efficiency in agriculture fewer hands were needed in the rice paddies. A substantial part of the rural population became available for other work. Whether they remained in the villages or flowed into the cities those unemployed needed jobs, and the provision of these became the chief object of policy. The answer was "labor intensive manufactures, which generated employment growth of about 7 percent per year after 1985." The large amount of capital for these was beyond Indonesia's capacity—especially after the fall in oil prices about 1986—and foreign direct investment was required: suitable policies succeeded in attracting it. Distributional effects were favorable to the poor. That the poor were able to participate in the growth was deliberate policy just as the virtual exclusion of the very poor from the gains in the United States in the 1980s and 1990s was brought about by the policies followed in that country.

Widjojo's activities were by no means confined to the pure economics of Indonesian development. He used his great powers of diplomacy to give moral support to those thinkers and writers who were less diplomatic. Soedjatmoko will always be remembered among Indonesia's all-time greatest scholars. He was not one to hide his thoughts, however unpopular with the authorities they might be. When he was in trouble, he never lost the friendship of Widjojo, who took him on as advisor to Bappenas (the Government Planning Agency of which he was Chairman) but unfortunately could not prevent a period of house arrest. I visited Soedjatmoko more than once at times when he could come into the front garden to greet me or say good-bye, but not go beyond the front garden gate. And I feel sure—though no one has told me this—that Widjojo's voice was raised to have Soedjatmoko appointed Ambassador to the United States, and later helped to put him up as candidate for President of the United Nations University.

When we see how widespread corruption is in the modern world, not excepting the United States, it is remarkable that I have never heard a whisper of a rumor that Widjojo was anything but incorruptible. He has evidently played by the rules; with him everything has been transparent, everything above-board. Such a model of integrity is rare.

I will always be proud of having the friendship of Pak Widjojo. Now he is passing another milestone, but I cannot imagine that it is an ending. I foresee him spending his time and effort pushing for employment-creating industry, foreign investment, better education at the college level, perhaps in an official capacity, perhaps as a private citizen. If he decides to retire he will be an honored elder statesman providing ideas and advice to younger men, like Vice President Hatta to whom he introduced me. *Pak* Widjojo is the person, among all those I know, who is most aware of the vital importance for Indonesia of a labor force that is not only literate but that knows computers, is skilled in electronics, that includes many with advanced bio-technology and such other applications of science as the modern economy requires. 1 hope that he will remain healthy so that he may continue to press these and other good causes for many years to come. ◆

11

I Marvel at His Accomplishments and Salute a Model Economist: An Example to All Developing Countries

Henry Rosovsky*

I met Professor Widjojo in the fall of 1958 on the beautiful campus of the University of California at Berkeley. The now so distinguished Professor, advisor to heads of state and internationally famous planner was-at that time—a graduate student in economics. I was an acting assistant professor (the lowest of all conceivable academic ranks), just back from two years of research in Japan. We were both very young: I am twenty-two days Widjojo's senior. *Even at that time he seemed to me to be a mature and experienced person who had already seen much in his life.*

The late 1950's and early 1960's were an unusually happy and positive period in American history. Our victory in World War II remained a national inspiration; the stalemate in Korea did not seem to matter; and, of course, in 1961 the election of John F. Kennedy created an all too brief euphoric mood especially among young people.

During these years there were similar feelings of optimism and empowerment among economists. Economic development was a favorite subject among graduate students because we had a genuine concern about world-wide poverty and combined this with a belief in the capacity of economic science to provide solutions. Compared to today, it seems to me that the cutting edge of economics was more

* Prof. Henry Rosovsky (US) is Geyser University Professor Emeritus, Harvard University. At Harvard as Professor of Economics since 1965. Professor of Economics and History at the University of California at Berkeley (1958 -1965). He was consultant to DAS and HIID in Indonesia in early 1970's and again in early 1990's. Special fields: Japanese economic history and higher education.

concerned with the problems of the real world. It was a good time to be young, and an especially good time to be a student of economics.

The University of California—and Berkeley in particular—also felt on top of the world. Berkeley was the flagship campus of the flagship public university located in the most trend-setting state of the Union, and many believed that private higher education had seen its best days (They were wrong!). The economics department at Berkeley was also in one of its particularly strong phases. Elder statemen included famous names like Gordon, Bain, Ellis, and Condliffe. Rising stars included Leibenstein, Landes, Jorgenson, Caves. I hope that I am not forgetting too many important names.

In retrospect, one of the more noteworthy aspects of Berkeley economics in the late 1950's and early 1960's was the presence of Indonesian graduate students. I write " in retrospect" because none of us could anticipate the momentous events of 1965/66 that would catapult a group of young men into leadership positions of such great and unexpected importance. I do not now recall the exact number of these students and wish to avoid—once again—the trap of naming names. I do remember that the Ford Foundation had made available funds to train fledgling economists from the University of Indonesia and that Berkeley had the good fortune to become the chosen institution. *The Indonesians were among our most stimulating students.*

My own relatively close relations with these students no doubt had something to do with my interest in and knowledge of Japan. The Japanese economy was my special subject at a time when few in the West had any interest in the matter. Remember we are back in 1958: Japan had not yet fully recovered from World War II and the impressive economic achievements of an earlier era were virtually unknown in the United States. At that time I was offering a course on Japanese economic history from the Meiji Restoration to the present, and I believe that it was the first such course offered in any American University.

This course was unusually popular among our Indonesian visitors for fairly obvious reasons. Unlike their American or European conterparts, they knew that Japan was the first-and at that time the only-non-Western country to have achieved advanced levels of industrialization. To be sure, their feeling about Japan were ambivalent. They and their parents had frequently been victims of Japan's brutal military occupation. Yet they knew that Indonesian independence was greatly aided by Japan's initial successes against the colonial powers, and they suspected that the "Japanese model" might have relevance to their own country.

These suspicions proved to be entirely correct. Writing in 1994, Widjojo noted that: "... Indonesia was able to reduce poverty rapidly, first, through sustained, broad-based and labor-intensive growth based on rapid growth of agriculture, and then through rapid growth of labor-intensive manufacturing exports. Second, the poor were able to participate in that growth because of substantial improvements in education and health and investment in infrastructure." (Reduction of Poverty: The Indonesian Experience, a presentation at IMF-World Bank Conference in Madrid, September, 1994.) These sentences could have been taken from a textbook on Japanese economic history !

Before turning more closely to Prof. Widjojo, I want to offer a few more personal observations concerning the Indonesian group. Their physical stature was, in general, quite small, especially compared to that tall race of Californians who seemed to populate the Berkeley campus. I often had the feeling that our Indonesian friends felt a bit chilly in the climate of northern California, that they yearned to return to the tropics and sometimes suffered from homesickness— not unusual emotions among foreign students. *But this group was more mature than our average graduate students: many were veterans of Indonesia's War of Liberation; some were married; all had a strong sense of duty. For them the study of economics and especially economic development were not matters of theoretical niceties.*

I left Berkeley for Harvard in 1965 and did not make my first visit to Indonesia until 1973. That is when I again encountered the young men from Indonesia, and by now they had been transformed into ministers, bureau chiefs, senior professors, etc. The economic fate of the nation was in their hands and they seemed to be doing very well indeed. *Their transformation from students to responsible leaders was exceedingly rapid and astonishing,* but for a former teacher it was also extremely satisfying. Certainly a very proud moment for Berkeley economics.

Finally, a few words specifically about Professor Widjojo whom we are honoring in this volume. *He was and remained the intellectual and moral leader of the Berkeley group—its most influential leader. This was no accident. His thesis, for which I had the privilege of being a reader, was a major piece of economic-historical-and demographic research. The late Professor Harvey Leibenstein was its main sponsor, and Widjojo's work undoubtedly was one of the very best pieces of research produced under his direction during a long career. Quite a few of us would have been happy to keep the young Widjojo at Berkeley as a faculty member, and there were not many graduate students from abroad or from the United States who achieved that level of intellectual recognition.*

Upon his return to Indonesia in the 1960's, aside from his many specific assignments, Widjojo also became the principal philosopher of Indonesian economic development, as demonstrated by many writings, speeches, and conversations. He achieved this standing because the term "technocrat" does not describe him at all. All the necessary techniques were at his command, but he added vision, a feeling for all his compatriots, and courage.

I briefly worked with the old DAS in the 1970's and the newer HIID in the 1990's. My first assignment related to Indonesia's relations with Japan, and the second assignment involved the future of higher education. I reported to Professor Widjojo and sought his advice. *His wonderful and very special personality always came through unambiguously calm, trustworthy, and understated. I marvel at his accomplishments and salute a model economist: an example to all developing countries.* ◆

12

The Japanese Team of Economists at Bappenas

Shinichi Ichimura*

1. Introduction

My first meeting with Dr. Widjojo Nitisastro was initiated by his personal telephone call to my hotel room in 1969 when I visited Indonesia for the first time. He was well known as a leading economist of the new Soeharto regime after the 1965 political upheaval as well as an upcoming demographer worthy of academic attention in Indonesia. Even now I do not know how he found out my visit to Jakarta at that time or why he knew my name. I had heard of the names of Dr. Widjojo and other economists in Indonesia when I was a visiting professor at the University of California, Berkeley in 1965–66. I was delighted to have the opportunity of meeting him in person at his office in Bappenas the next day. My visit to Indonesia then was primarily to set up a research project in Indonesia as the newly appointed Director of the Center for Southeast Asian Studies at Kyoto University.

There was an increasing recognition or serious concern in Japan as well as in the United States that the necessary studies of contemporary economic and political conditions of Southeast Asian nations are missing among the specialists on Asia. Many new nation-

---

* Professor Shinichi Ichimura (Japan) was Professor of Economics at Kyoto University (1968-1988); Director, the Center for Southeast Asian Studies, Kyoto University (1969-1979). After retirement in 1988 he became Professor Emeritus of Kyoto University and the Vice-Chancellor of Osaka International University newly established (April 1988-June 30, 1995). Then, he took the position of Director at the International Center for the Study of East Asian Development, Kitakyushu, Japan in July, 1995. He is the President of the East Asian Economic Association which is the only regional economic association in East Asia. Now he is Director of International Center for the Study of East Asian Development.

states were established but colonial days were not yet over. New political order of Southeast Asia was yet to come. Anyway I chose to come to Jakarta and met my old friends whom I had met in Japan and the United States and tried to see what we could do. After a serious talk with Dr. Widjojo on these matters, he suggested me to see his successor at Leknas, Dr. Harsja Bachtiar, for my purpose.

2. The Regional Economic Survey of South Sumatra Province

I had a long discussion with Dr. Harsja about what to do. After an intensive discussion, we agreed that the most urgently needed for scientific studies as well as practical policies for development in Indonesia was the better statistics for Indonesia, particularly those of outer regions. Dr. Harsja suggested to choose the Province of South Sumatra for our regional survey. This led to the organization of our first project in Indonesia; that is, the South Sumatra Project to estimate Regional Product and Income Accounts in the Province of South Sumatra as a model case to consolidate the foundation of National Income Accounts in Indonesia. The outcome of this project was made available as: *The Regional Economic Survey of South Sumatra, 1970 - 77*, LIPI, Jakarta, 1971 edited by Dr. Thee Kian Wie and me.

To undertake this survey was not easy. First of all we had to explain the field work approach to conduct the statistical surveys in the urban and village areas in developing countries. In any country were available very few experts with needed experiences. As soon as I came back to Japan, I consulted with Dr. Minom Tachi, Director of the Bureau of Statistics, Prime Minister's Office at that time. He recommended with no hesitation Mr. Hiroshi Mizuno in his office. He was a short but stout man, and having served at the ECAFE for many years, he was already a world-famous expert on statistical surveys. I still remember what Dr. Tachi told me about Mr. Mizuno: " he has a strong character but if you trust him, he can do anything difficult in statistical surveys anywhere in the world. Perhaps he is the only one in Japan who can be trusted in that kind of work." I still cherish his friendship and I must say that the success of our survey in South Sumatra owes 99% of it to his devotion. I myself learned a great deal from the experiences of this survey. I am grateful for having this chance given to me by Dr. Widjojo and Dr. Harsja.

3. A Training Course On National Income Accounts in Japan

A few months after completing the South Sumatra survey and of course reporting it to Professor Widjojo, I received a telephone call again to my office at Kyoto University, Japan. He requested me to organize a training course on National Income Accounting at Kyoto University, Japan to a group of Indonesian economists and statisticians. Our survey for South Sumatra may have impressed him and persuaded him to recognize the need for improving the national income statistics in Indonesia. Immediately accepting his request, I began to prepare a program of the course by asking some friends for lectures and arranging the visits to government offices of statistical bureaus. A trouble occurred, however, that I did not hear anything further from Dr. Widjojo after completing the preparation. Finally I had to make a telephone call myself to his office in Indonesia and make sure that he was really sending the Indonesian team.

They came in June 1971 and spent almost a month with us. They included such as Ms. Tjahajani, Dr. Soedradjad Djiwandono—who became governor of the Bank of Indonesia in 1993 and others. They played an essential role in improving the national income data and their applications in Indonesia later. Toward the end of the training period I took them to a resort in the Japan Alps area for recreation and visited a small primary school there for international exchange. I thought that this would give them a pleasure of meeting innocent Japanese children. Maybe it did but the children also reminded some members of their own children and moved them to tears. This impressed my wife and me of the similarity of our sentiments to families. An unforgettable memory!

4. Japanese Econometric Team At Bappenas

Dr. Widjojo told me at our first meeting that corresponding to a significant contribution of Japanese economic cooperation, he and Dr. Saburo Okita agreed to have a Japanese advisor at Bappenas. Mr. Koichi Baba, government economist of the Economic Planning Agency was there at that time. When I came home and met Dr. Okita at the Economic Planning Agency, he earnestly requested me to cooperate with Dr. Widjojo and maintain the advisory service at Bappenas. About a year later when Mr. Baba returned to Japan, I had to find his successor for a project of the Kyoto University Center for Southeast Asian Studies. I asked Professor Kazumi Kobayashi (Kyoto Sangyo University), Professor Tsuneo Lida (Nagoya University; now at the International Center for Japanese Culture in Kyoto) and then Mr Kinoshita (Electric Power Development Co.) and others to serve as advisors at Bappenas.

These Japanese economists often told me that in their capacity they were not sure of what they should do in their office. Dr. Widjojo himself and his team must have been extremely busy in designing the fundamental direction of their macro-policies for Indonesian economy. As Professor Lida told then that in 1970-71 the weight of the oil sector was steadily declining and was expected to be as small as 15 percent of GDP soon. It was the oil booms of 1973/74 that rescued the Indonesian economy from its crisis in 1972. I still remember that Dr. Mohammad Sadli, the Minister of Mining then asked me what I would recommend to do with half a million dollars bonanza.

For one or two years, there was an intermission in sending Japanese economists to Bappenas, during which time my main efforts was in the fields of non-economic but related fields in Indonesia.[1] One day after a while when I had some discussions with Dr. Sumarlin, Deputy Minister of Bappenas then, I suddenly came to realize that Indonesia was ready for constructing an econometric model and making the forecast and policy simulations by the use of such model. By 1973 the national income data of Indonesia have improved thanks to the efforts of the Central Bureau of Statistics

---

1 The main findings of our studies were published in Indonesian as well as in Japanese and English. The interested reader may be able to find them in an Indonesian book: *INDONESIA - masalah dan peristiwa bunga rampai*, (ed.) S. Ichimura and Koentjaraningrat published by Obor, Jakarta and Center for Southeast Asian Studies, Kyoto University, Kyoto, 1976. The contributions include the excellent papers by leading scholars in Indonesia, Japan and other countries. Many of them are no longer with us. Akira Nagazumi (University of Tokyo), Kenji Tsuchiya (Kyoto University), Masashi Nishihara (Kyoto Sangyo University and now National Defense College), Koentjaraningrat (University of Indonesia), Shinichi Ichimura, Koichi Mizuno, Yoshihiro Tsubouchi, Toshio Asano (Kyoto University), Prasert Yangklinfung (Chulalongkorn University), Akin Rabibhadana, Yut Sakdejayoni (Thammasat University),Mubyarto, Masri Singarimbun (Gadjah Mada University), Thee Kian Wie (Leknas).

with some Japanese economists from the Institute of Developing Economies.

Moreover, Professor Yukio Kaneko, one of our team members, have completed the very first tentative Input-Output Table of the Indonesian Economy. Time was ripe to construct an econometric model of the Indonesian economy and make the full use of modern techniques for the development of this young promising country. Immediately I requested to have a meeting with Dr. Widjojo, but as usual it was not easy to have a chance of seeing him at Bappenas. I had to keep requesting his secretary many times a day. Waiting a long time, I finally had an important meeting with him and proposed to undertake a project of constructing Indonesian econometric models. He immediately agreed and promised to request the Japanese International Cooperation Agency for this purpose.

Clearly it was no longer possible to support such a large scale project by Kyoto University Center for Southeast Asian Studies alone. More budget and more human resources were needed. With his strong support I moved to contact JICA in Tokyo and requested the full support for a team of experts to come to Bappenas and work there in cooperation with Indonesian experts. In the foreword to the book mentioned below, Mr. Hiroaki Tamamitsu, Executive Director of JICA in 1988 wrote: "The technical cooperation for the development of Indonesian economy was planned between Mr. Saburo Okita, ex-minister of Foreign Affairs of Japan and Professor Widjojo Nitisastro, the first Chairman of Bappenas in 1968. Until 1980 the cooperation had been conducted by dispatching only a few experts. However, since 1981, full technical cooperation in its quality and quantity was developed by dispatching a total of 37 experts until 1987 to support the preparation of the fourth 5-year plan, with the econometric technique under the guidance of Professor Shinichi Ichimura of Kyoto University. The cooperation covered project planning in various fields such as regional development, banking and financing, population, labor, and industrial development."

There were, however, several worries to start this large scale of economic cooperation. The first was whether I could find and persuade any excellent econometrician to come to Jakarta and stay at least one year and produce a workable econometric model of the

Indonesian economy or not. The second was whether we could set up a computer system with adequate programs under the conditions in Jakarta. I could only rely on some of my personal friends and get their help. As for the first, my friend at EPA, Japan, Professor Shuntaro Shishido recommended Mr. Sei Kuribayashi of EPA Institute. He and my colleague at Kyoto University, Professor Mitsuo Ezaki were the ones who really produced the first outstanding econometric models of the Indonesian economy and laid the foundation of econometric works in Indonesia.

The second worry was solved by the voluntary offer of co-operation of my friend, Professor Ippei Sugiura of Wakayama University then. He chose a set of PCs and gave his own programs for econometric models to the Japanese team. Many experts came from Kyoto University and other universities as well as the Economic Planning Agency, Japan. Many experts who participated in our project have occupied the key positions in the EPA later and become famous economists in Japan.

By the time that this new team began its works in full swing, Deputy Head of Bappenas had changed from Dr. Sumarlin to Dr. Adrianus Mooy. It was Dr. Mooy who really tried to advocate the usefulness of econometric models and its applications to Indonesian policy issues by encouraging us and organizing many meetings with participants from important other ministries as well as Bappenas. He gave a room to the Japanese team equipped with a set of best PC's available then. The trust between the members of the Japanese team and the Indonesian economists at Bappenas may be a model case of the success of international cooperation. It was Dr. Widjojo after all who took the initiative for all these works toward the end of the 1970's.

5. Achievements of the Japanese Team

The cooperation of Japanese economists was by no means limited to model works. It was gradually extended to many related areas. Not only those mentioned here but also many others participated in our work at Bappenas at one stage or another or in one way or another. The whole range of our work were reported in our

Indonesian Economic Development – Issues And Analyses

Chap	Titles	Author
1	An Overview of Indonesian Economic Development	Shinichi Ichimura,Adrianus Mooy,and Soedrajad Djiwandono
2	A Medium- term Marco econometric Model for Economic planning	Sei Kuribayashi
3	A Revised Marco Model and Policy Simulation	Nobuhiko Kosuge & Yasumi Matsumoto
4	Agricultural Development	Yonker Tamba & Hirosi Nishimura
5	Energy and Mineral	Yoichi Kaya &Hismaryanto, Suriadi & T. Imoto
6	Manufacturing Industry: Analysisand Policy	Yukio Kaneko & Hasudungan Tampubolon
7	Government Budget and Taxation	Dono Iskandar & Sumimaru Odano
8	Financial Development	Sumimaru Odano, Syahir Sobirin & Soedrajad Djiwandono
9	Population and Economic Development	Kazumasa Kobayashi, KeiichiroMatsusita & Prijono Tjiptoherijanto
10	Labor Force and Employment	Payaman J. Simanjuntak & Yasuhiko Torii
11	Education and Manpower Training	Hiromitsu Muta & Boediono
12	Price Changes	Boediono & Takabumi Kaneko
13	Regional Economic Development	Soeroso, Soedibyo, Tatsuhiko Kawashima & Takahiro Akita
14	Private Sector and Public Sector	Mohammad Sadli, Dorodja-tunKuntjoro-Jakti & Toshihiko Kinoshita
15	Income Distribution	Sugito & Mitsuo Ezaki
16	Foreign and Domestic Capital inIndustrialization	Thee Kian Wie & Kunio Yoshihara
17	The Role of Non-Economic Factorsin Economic Development	Selo Soemardjan
18	Statistical Notes	Yasumi Matsumoto & Nobuhiko Kosuge

comprehensive report, edited by myself and published by JICA, Jakarta in March, 1988 (see list).

Its contents clearly shows the coverage of our works and the contributors in each area, so that they are reproduced here.

I have made an effort to make the main contents of this report available in Indonesian as well, and at the suggestion of Dr. Widjojo it was published by the University of Indonesia Press as: *Pembangunan Ekonomi Indonesia–Masalah dan Analisis*, (ed.) Shinichi Ichimura, UI Press, 1989. It was widely used by many universities as a text book or reference book for undergraduate and graduate courses. It is my great pleasure that I have had this opportunity to work together with Dr. Widjojo himself and many of his colleagues at Bappenas and have been in association with them since 1969 until now.

Finally I have always been under the impression that he is younger than I. Now I am very much surprised to discover that my impression was wrong. Nobody told me until very recently. Good luck and good health, more and more to him ! I wish him to make all the more contributions to the development of the Indonesian nation into the 21st Century. I am sure that many colleagues of mine in Japan and my family join in this prayer. ◆

13

Our Highest Admiration for His Tireless Efforts to Help Other Countries Realize Better Living Standards

Michel Camdessus *

It is a great honor to have this opportunity to pay tribute to Professor Widjojo in this valuable collection of papers commemorating his 70th anniversary. In a remarkable career devoted to public service, including in high offices of state, Professor Widjojo has provided exemplary leadership both in formulating economic policy in Indonesia and in addressing the challenges of global economic cooperation. Few leaders have had a greater impact on economic development in the developing countries and their integration in the world economy. I count myself among those fortunate enough to have benefited from his counsel over many years.

Professor Widjojo's contribution to Indonesia's economic success needs little elaboration. Together with his colleagues in government, he has been instrumental in the steadfast implementation of prudent macroeconomic policies and outward-oriented trade and exchange regimes that have laid the foundation for the virtuous circle of high saving, high investment and sustained high economic growth. *The impressive reduction in poverty since the 1960s provides strong testimony for the virtues of Indonesia's development strategy— growth based on sound economic policies has benefited all sections of the community and sustained the widespread consensus for market structural reforms.* Strong leadership in steering economic policy

---

* Mr.Michel Camdessus (France) was Managing Director, International Monetary Fund (1987-2000); Governor of the Bank of France (1984-1987).

and strengthening public institutions has perhaps been the most important ingredient in this achievement and I am certain no one will disagree that it is difficult to overestimate Professor Widjojo's contribution in these areas.

A growing number of countries are seeking to replicate the successful experience of Indonesia and other Asian countries and they continue to benefit from Professor Widjojo's guidance. Policy makers in many African and other developing countries are indebted to him for sharing with them his invaluable experience and wisdom, especially on economic policy challenges during the early stages of development and how policy reforms can best be sustained over the long term.

I would like to express my strong appreciation for Professor Widjojo and Indonesia's support - in the context of the Non-Aligned Movement—for the joint IMF—World Bank Initiative for the Heavily Indebted Poor Countries.

Constructive interest and support from Indonesia represents an important part of the international consensus which is a crucial underpinning to this historic initiative to lower the debt burden of the poorest countries.

Professor Widjojo's intellectual discipline, vision, and tireless efforts to help other countries realize their potential for better living standards deserve our highest admiration. ◆

14

May a Second
and Third Widjojo be Born

*Akira Nishigaki**

The sixth meeting of the Consultative Group for Indonesia (CGI) was held in Tokyo on July 16 and 17, 1997. In closing the two-day meeting, the donor countries and international organizations which commended Indonesia's progress pointed out that much remain to be done to address remaining economic and social challenges. They pledged a total of US$5.3 billion for aid projects and programs, larger than last year's US$ 5.26. Thus Tokyo CGI meeting was successfully concluded. H.E. Prof. Widjojo Nitisastro, Advisor to the Government of Indonesia, joined by his colleagues H. E. Prof. Saleh Afiff, Coordinating Minister for Economy, Finance and Development Supervision and H.E. Dr. Ginandjar Kartasas-mita, Minister of State for National Development Planning and Chairman of Bappenas, contributed to the success of the meeting. As I was not present at the meeting, Prof. Widjojo requested an OECF participant to convey to me his appreciation for the OECF's contribution.

In reviewing the economic development of Indonesia to date and the relationship between Indonesia and the OECF which has

* Mr. Akira Nishigaki (Japan) was President, Chairman of the Board ,The Overseas Economic Cooperation Fund (since 1990). He Joined the Ministry of Finance and assigned to the Overall Co-ordination Division Minister's Secretariat (1953); Executive Assistant of the Prime Minister (1971-1972); in the Ministry of Finance respectively as Director of Allowance Control Division, Budget Bureau (1972-1974); Budget Examiner (Construction, Public Works), Budget Bureau (1974-1977); Director of the Secretarial Division, Minister's Secretariat (1977- 1979); Deputy Director General of Budget Bureau (1979-1982); Deputy Vice Minister, Economic Planning Agency (1982-1983); Director General, Financial Bureau (1983-1984); Deputy Vice Minister, Ministry of Finance(1984-1986); Director General, Budget Bureau (1986-1988); Vice Minister for Finance (1988-1989); Senior Advisor to the Institute of Fiscal and Monetary Policy (since 1989).

supported its development, I cannot but recognize an essential role played by Prof. Widjojo. Indonesia has achieved economic growth at an annual rate of more than 6.0% for the past 30 years and its current GDP per capita exceeds US$1,000. In contrast to a number of developing countries in which economic growth benefits only limited groups of the nation thus aggravating the problem of income gaps, it should be highly appreciated that in Indonesia benefits of economic development have been widely distributed , resulting in the reduction of poverty from 56% in 1970 to 11% in 1996 or the decrease of the number of people below the poverty line from 70 million to 22.5 million. Moreover, the progress of social development is also remarkable, as demonstrated by the data on the substantial increase of life expectancy (from 46 years in 1970 to 63 years in 1995) and the improvement of literacy rate (from 61% in 1970 to 84% in 1995). These are the results of the efforts of the Government of Indonesia for development, which is based on long-term and medium-term development plans commencing in 1969.

Japan has been extending ODA loan to support development of Indonesia since 1968. As of March 31, 1997, the cumulative total of the OECF loan commitments to Indonesia was Y2,900 billion, for 565 projects. This sum accounts for about 20% of all OECF loans committed to foreign governments. In recent years OECF loans (about Y195.2 billion for FY1997) account for about one third of the total CGI financing (about US$ 5.3 billion for FY1997). In other words, Indonesia is the largest recipient country of OECF loans, and regarding the scale of loans Japan is the largest donor to Indonesia.

The history of OECF loans to Indonesia is naturally interrelated to the history of economic development of Indonesia. In the mid eighties, Indonesia faced balance of payment difficulties caused by the sharp fall of the oil price. Prof. Widjojo, former Coordinating Minister for Economic, Financial and Industrial Affairs, had assumed the post of Advisor to the Government of Indonesia. To address the situation, Prof. Widjojo and other Indonesian government officials concerned and their Japanese counterparts consulted and considered measure to be taken in a constructive manner. As a result, the Government of Japan decided to extend to

Indonesia a series of special assistance such as local currency finance, commodity loans, and sector program loans in the latter half of the 1980's. At that time I was in the Ministry of Finance and I participated in the decision making thereof.

As President of the Overseas Economic Cooperation Fund I met Prof. Widjojo several times. One of the meetings that I remember very well was when Prof. Widjojo visited Japan as Special Envoy of President Soeharto in May 1995. At that time many developing countries faced the risk of massive foreign capital movement in the wake of the Mexico crisis as well as the suddenly increased burden of debt repayment due to sharp appreciation of the Yen. The government of Japan, having seriously considered Prof. Widjojo's explanation, decided to extend another round of balance of payments support loans and increased the amount of the 1995 OECF loan package from the previous year's level.

The Indonesian economy has recently achieved a sound development, utilizing among others, the special assistance from Japan, and graduated from such special assistance in 1997. Indonesia is thus one of the most successful countries in utilizing foreign assistance from Japan and other donors for economic development and economic structural adjustment, while many developing countries continue to face balance of payments difficulties and other economic problems. I, having been involved in the cooperation with Indonesia, am very pleased with the success of Indonesia.

Although my contacts with Prof. Widjojo are limited, he has already impressed me with his ability and personality. First of all, he is a statesman and economist who seeks most appropriate solutions to issues based on the deep understanding of the Indonesian economy. Hence he is a leading figure in the Indonesian administration. Also impressive is the fact that his remarks and behavior imply his commitment not only to the Indonesian national interests but also to economic development and poverty alleviation of all developing countries. Furthermore, Prof. Widjojo very well understands Japan and Japan's policy in economic cooperation and he is a very good friend of Japan. His sincerity in listening to what I said struck me deeply.

On the occasion of the 70th birthday of H.E. Prof. Widjojo Nitisastro, I wish His Excellency continued health and contribution to address remaining challenges and thus further develop the economy of Indonesia. *May a second and third Widjojo be born.* ◆

15

Highly Competent, Never a Prisoner of Intellectual Dogmas and Ideological Posturing, Indefatigable and Persevering, but Warm Personality and Soft Spoken Manner

*Gamani Corea**

I am indeed grateful for this opportunity to pay tribute to Prof. Widjojo Nitisastro on his 70th birthday. Ours has been a long acquaintance. We first met in the early 60s at an expert group convened by the Economic Commission for Asia and the Far East-as ESCAP was then called. Some years later, I learnt from many sources of the pivotal role he was playing in building up the economy of Indonesia. At that time I was serving in the Central Bank of Ceylon and in the Ministry of Planning and Economic Affairs. The Government of Ceylon had launched an economic recovery programme to restore growth after a period of relative stagnation. The experts I met from the international financial institutions and from academic advisory groups abroad often pointed to the positive example of Indonesia and the outstanding economic leadership of Prof. Widjojo Nitisastro. In subsequent years our paths crossed from time to time. I particularly recollect meeting him on a visit to Jakarta to acquaint some of the Asian countries of the preparations for the 1972 Stockholm Conference on Environment and to underline aspects of the environment issue that were crucial to developing countries. On that occasion he assisted me in making many contacts and also helped to make my mission a success.

*   Dr.Gamani Corea (Sri Lanka) was the Secretary—General of UNCTAD from 1974-1984. He was a member of the South Commission (1987-1990) and is presently a member of the Advisory Board of the South Centre. In Sri Lanka he is currently Chancellor of the Open University, Chairman of the Institute of Policy Studies, and Senior Adviser to the Ministry of Foreign Affairs.

It was, however during my term of office as Secretary General of the United Nations Conference on Trade and Development (UN-CTAD) that I came to be especially grateful for his interest and assistance. The major initiative of UNCTAD during that period was the launching of the Integrated Programme for Commodities. My colleagues in the UNCTAD Secretariat and I were convinced at the time of two things. First, that weak and unstable commodity prices were major deterrents to the development efforts of the many developing countries dependent of the export of primary products; and second, that the piece-meal, case by case, approach to international commodity policy needed to be reinforced by an overall and integrated framework with common principles, common instruments, and a coordinated programme for negotiations. Accordingly, UNCTAD proposed the Integrated Programme for Commodities with the establishment of a Common Financing Fund for buffer stocks as its centre piece.

It was at UNCTAD 4 in Nairobi in 1974 that the battle was fought to gain acceptance of the Integrated Programme. The Conference virtually broke down in the final stages. But, fortunately the heads of key delegations from both the developed and the developing countries agreed to come together for informal consultations in my hotel suite with a view to breaking the deadlock. Prof. Widjojo was one of the central figures in this crucial process who contributed strongly to bringing about the consensus that was eventually reached. In fact, even prior to Nairobi, it was he who first flagged the commodity issue and the Integrated Programme at the ongoing Paris Conference on International Economic Cooperation (CIEC) to which the term "North-South dialogue" was first applied. In the negotiating processes that followed UNCTAD 4, the consistent support of Indonesia, a major commodity producer, was a vital factor that gave strength to the UNCTAD initiative. Indeed, Mr. Ali Alatas, then Indonesia's Permanent Representative to the UN in Geneva, was the spokesman of the developing countries throughout the negotiations on the Common Fund. Prof. Widjojo's part in all this was of central importance.

I remained in contact with Prof. Widjojo in the years that followed the end of my UNCTAD role. We were both members of the

South Commission in the late 80s. When the work of the Commission was completed both Prof. Widjojo and I were among those who felt that the Secretariat that had been established to support the Commission should continue and be transformed into a permanent body. Prof. Widjojo's role in helping to bring this about was particularly important, and the support of the Government of Indonesia was a crucial factor in ensuring the eventual conversion of the Secretariat into the South Centre. The assumption by Indonesia of the Presidency of the Non-Aligned Movement over the years 1992 to 1995 gave a new impetus to the South Centre. Once again, it was Prof. Widjojo who was the catalyst. NAM needed to respond to the vast changes in the global economic scene by updating and recasting its economic platform. Prof. Widjojo secured the support of the South Centre to establish a group of economists, with whom he worked closely, to address this issue. The group's report was published and distributed widely by the Government of Indonesia in time for the NAM Summit in Jakarta and became the basis for the identification of issues for further work.

Another major initiative was soon to follow. The problem of external indebtedness had assumed serious proportions for a growing number of developing countries and the Government of Indonesia felt the need for NAM to highlight the issue. Once again, Prof. Widjojo asked the South Centre to help organise a study with the help of knowledgeable experts. A group was accordingly set up to which Dragoslav Avramovic of Yugoslavia made a particularly valuable and comprehensive contribution. Nevertheless, the process of merging views and texts was taking much time and Prof. Widjojo decided to take the matter in hand himself. He joined me—since I was, thanks to his persuasion, the Chairman of the Group—in Colombo and set himself to work on the document in his hotel. The task was completed within a few days and we were able, soon after, to get the endorsement of the Group. All this, I am convinced, would not have been possible without the special effort of Prof. Widjojo. The report, in many ways, helped to break new ground. It underlined the importance of arrears in debt servicing as a yardstick to help identify countries in difficulty, a yardstick additional to the conventional criteria in common use. But more significantly, it pointed to the growing importance of developing country debt service obligations to the multilateral financial institutions such as the World Bank and the Regional Development Banks and the need to extend debt relief measures to this category of debts. Up to then the multilateral institutions were treated as preferred creditors whose rating in the world's capital market should not risk impairment through participation in programmes of debt rescheduling and debt cancellation. The report of the group on debt was printed and distributed widely. It became the focus of a special ministerial meeting of African countries in Jakarta convened by Indonesia that held the chairmanship on NAM at that time. Since then there has been progress on this front and a recognition of the need to find acceptable ways of providing relief to debts owed to multilateral institutions. Prof. Widjojo can draw some satisfaction from the emerging developments in this field.

Prof. Widjojo's contributions in both the national and international fields over his long period of service have been outstanding on any reckoning. But those who have been privileged to know him and to work with him cannot help underlining the personal qualities that went to shape this record. His intellectual abilities were a powerful force in moulding his career and in forging his leadership role. From his earliest days in public service he won recognition as a *highly competent economist.* But he was practical in his approach and *not a prisoner of intellectual dogmas and ideological postures.* He was sensitive to the wider processes at work in society and to the realities that conditioned the path to development. He was also *keenly aware of the international dimensions of the development process* and of the *importance of dialogue and negotiation in the multilateral arena.* He was, at the same time, a man of action. He was *indefatigable and persevering* in his effort to get things done and in following an initiative to its conclusion. These were qualities that helped achieve results.

But there was also *the warmth of his personality* and his *soft spoken manner* that specially endeared him to those who came to be acquainted with him. I myself have known him for long as a friend, a working colleague, and a hospitable host. However, at the level of personal relations, I cannot separate his warmth and personality from the supportive qualities of his wife Tina. During the years of Indonesia's leadership of NAM I had many opportunities to visit Jakarta and other parts of the country. On each of those visits I was privileged to be entertained at their home and to enjoy the relax atmosphere of those surroundings. I was able to meet them both in Geneva. On all those occasions I came to know and admire the support they gave each other. My good wishes to Prof. Widjojo extends, therefore, to both of them. I feel privileged indeed to have this opportunity to put on record these words of appreciation and to extend, on his 70th birthday, my warm congratulations on an outstanding career. ◆

Geneva, 25 June 1997

16

His Friends Who Know Him Should Tell the World about His Achievements, Since He is a Modest Person and Does Not Talk about His Accomplishments

Vicente T. Paterno*

I knew Dr. Widjojo Nitisastro from a number of official ASEAN meetings and socials we both attended during the 1970's. He was then head of Bappenas and Coordinating Minister for Economic and Financial Affairs, one of the most senior positions in the cabinet of Indonesia. My responsibilities then in the Philippine government were as head of Department of Industry and of Board of Investments. My government designated our Minister for Planning and myself its representatives at meetings of ASEAN Economic Ministers (AEM). Dr. Widjojo attended AEM meetings, with H.E. Radius Prawiro, then Minister of Trade and who had been Central Bank governor.

From conversations with Indonesian government officials and private sector, I gathered that Dr. Widjojo was regarded in Indonesia as a leading technocrat and a highly respected economist. He was a principal architect and indefatigable overseer of the plans which led the country to economic recovery from its almost bankrupt and precarious position in the 1960's. By the mid 70's the Indonesian economy was well on its way to full health and high growth. After successfully overcoming the difficult problems that the economy

---

* Dr. Vicente Paterno (Philippines) was Minister of Industry and concurrent chairman of the Board of Investments, Republic of the Philippines. After leaving the Cabinet in 1980 he engaged in private business, but returned to government service briefly in 1986 as President of Philippine National Oil Company. He was elected nationally to the Philippine Senate in 1987, serving a 5-year term till 1992. He is now back entirely in the private sector, where he is chairman and director of several companies, including Philippine Seven Corporation (7-Eleven convenience stores). He is currently chairman of BIMP-East ASEAN Business Council, the private sector organization of the BIMP-East ASEAN Growth Area (BIMP-EAGA).

faced in the early to mid 1980s, Indonesia has managed to maintain the economic growth to the present day.

Two of Dr. Widjojo's concerns in the '70's on which he often sought information from us on what Philippines was doing were on increasing farmer productivity in rice production and developing handicrafts and other labor intensive exports. He regarded progress in these two fronts as important in his country's struggle to reduce poverty. I was also aware of his continuing efforts to ensure that his government's budget allocated enough funds for rural infrastructure and for social development, such as health and education, in the face of all the other demands for funding. I thought this was probably an important reason why he could not fully delegate the administration of economic planning in Bappenas though he was already Co-ordinating Minister for Economic and Financial Affairs. With the multiplicity of his tasks, we knew he worked long hours indeed.

We admired his dedication to fostering North-South dialogue and South-South cooperation, and his steadfast conviction in the potential of these activities for contributing to progress of the Third World and to world peace. We shared his strong belief in ASEAN and in the advantages of regional economic cooperation to all participants. We now share his sense of fulfillment that reality in the 1990's confirms our faith in ASEAN of the 1970's.

There are a number of developing countries especially in Asia which have experienced steady and strong growth in the last two to three decades, but none match the success of Indonesia in achieving economic growth and in reducing poverty—a great distinction and a very worthy achievement. That success has been attributed to correct policies. But there is not enough mention of those who conceived, advocated, and implemented the policies in the face of all odds in their way. Much of this economic success we ascribe to the foresight and consistent course of Indonesia's economic plans over two decades of Dr. Widjojo's cabinet stewardship, as well of course to the vision and support of its political leadership.

Dr. Widjojo Nistisastro is a modest and humble person. He does not seek publicity, nor talk about his accomplishments. Yet I believe that his friends who know him should be obliged to tell both his countrymen in particular and the world in general about his achievements.

I am glad to have been given the opportunity on the occasion of his 70th birth anniversary to express my admiration for and contribute my thoughts about my friend Dr. Widjojo, this exceptional talented economist technocrat, who has dedicated his whole life and being to the development of his country and upliftment of the poor among his countrymen. ◆

17

Holding a Unique Team in the World Which Has Completely Turned Around the Economy of the Fourth Most Populous Nation

*Edward Masters** *

I have known and respected Dr. Widjojo for more than 30 years, and it is a pleasure for me to join his many other friends and admirers in congratulating him on his seventieth birthday and wishing him many more years of productive service to Indonesia. His contributions to the nation and the Indonesian people have been impressive indeed.

I first met Dr. Widjojo in 1964 during the first of two tours with the American Embassy in Jakarta. At that time he was a young and enthusiastic Professor of Economics at the University of Indonesia. He had returned only two or three years earlier with his Ph.D. Degree from Berkeley. Our association at that time was social. From time to time Allene and I invited Dr. Widjojo to join us in our home to see American movies which were not then being shown commercially in Jakarta. On occasion we talked about the economic situation, and I recall thinking at the time that this was a man who had an unusual grasp of Indonesia's economic problems and practical ideas on what needed to be done if the opportunity should arise. Fortunately it did arise and Widjojo rose fully to the challenges.

---

* Mr.Edward Masters (US) was President of The United States-Indonesia Society, a private organization devoted to expanding understanding of Indonesia in the United States. He served as Counselor of the US embassy in Jakarta from 1964-68; as Director of Indonesian Affairs in the Department of State from 1968-70; and as US Ambassador to Indonesia from 1977-81. Since leaving government, he has served as Senior Vice President of the Natomas Company, President of the Washington-based National Planning Association, and Adjunct Professor of Southeast Asian Studies at the Fletcher School of Law and Diplomacy.

It was fascinating from my position in the Embassy in the 1960s and later as Director of Indonesian Affairs in the Department of State to watch and, in ways in which he wanted our help, to support his efforts. But it was clear from the outset that Indonesia was in charge and that foreigners should curb their tendency to take control; Widjojo would let us know when and what type of assistance was required. This was a sound policy indeed, and I have long felt that Indonesia's economic outcome would have been far different without Widjojo's firm hand in setting priorities and channelling the exuberance of Americans and others in directions set by Indonesia— not the other way around.

I was pleased during the late 1960s to have played a small role in the rescheduling of Indonesia's massive foreign debt in an operation in which, once again, Widjojo as a key member of President Soeharto's team set the guidelines. Under the direction of US Deputy Assistant Secretary of State, Robert Barnett, we were pleased to work with Widjojo and his colleagues in what I still believe was one of the most imaginative and successful operations anywhere to reschedule the debt of a developing nation. *Similarly, we were pleased to support his views and work with him in establishing a multilateral consortium of economic aid donors. These two actions under Widjojo's leadership, plus his success in rejuvenating Bappenas, set the stage for the nation's spectacular economic growth.*

During my tour as US Ambassador (1977-81) I had the opportunity to work particularly closely with Dr. Widjojo in his dual capacity as head of Bappenas and Coordinating Minister for Economic, Financial and Industrial Affairs. We had our differences reflecting the different positions of our respective governments, but I always found him a tough but fair negotiator.

Usually we were in strong agreement. Two attributes impressed me particularly. First, Widjojo *has an over-riding interest in meeting the basic needs of the Indonesian people. His first priority was always insuring adequate food supplies followed closely by good health care, education and jobs.* Secondly, he has a deep sense of political reality—of what is possible and what is not. This has been essential in mobilizing support not only from the governmental leadership but also from interested private groups. His understanding of his people and their needs and their hopes is, in fact, one of Dr. Widjojo's real strengths.

Dr. Widjojo *has for more than 30 years headed an economic team which is unique in the world and which has completely turned around the economy of the fourth most populous nation.* A generation ago Indonesia was described as a "chronic dropout." Today it has one of the fastest growing economies on earth. *This dramatic success has been a collegial effort, but it clearly would not have happened without the leadership and foresight of Dr. Widjojo.* ◆

18

Never Before Had Five University Professors Done So Much in So Short a Time To Resurrect The Economic Fortunes of a Great Nation

John Bresnan*

Widjojo Nitisastro and I first met in Jakarta in 1961, when we were both 34 years of age. He was fresh from his doctoral program in economics at the University of California at Berkeley, and I was newly appointed as assistant representative in Indonesia of the Ford Foundation. It was our joint interest in the Faculty of Economics of the University of Indonesia that brought us together initially. Later on we were brought together by our joint interest in Indonesia's economic and social development, he as head of Bappenas, later as Coordinating Minister of Economic Affairs, and more recently as an adviser to President Soeharto, and I as representative in Indonesia and later as a senior executive of the Ford Foundation in New York, and more recently as a research scholar at Columbia University. In spite of these shared interests, we have met only from time to time over the years, although I think it is only fair to say that we have been friends as well as professional associates since we first became acquainted.

Professor Sumitro Djojohadikusumo had approached the Ford Foundation as early as 1951 in search of help for the new Faculty of Economics. He envisaged the Faculty as an Asian version of the

---

* Mr. John Bresnan (US) was an executive of the Ford Foundation for many years, serving as its assistant representative in Indonesia from 1961 to 1965, representative in Indonesia from 1969 to 1973, and head of its Office for Asia and the Pacific from 1973 to 1981. He has been a senior research scholar of the East Asian Institute of Columbia University since 1982, where he also was professor in the School of International and Public Affairs. He was the author of, among other works. *Managing Indonesia: The Modern Political Economy* (Columbia, 1993), on which he had drawn in preparing the present memoir. He passed away in 2006.

London School of Economics, one that would provide leadership to national development by training government and business leaders in rational economic principles, providing experts to consult with the government on economic policies, and conducting research on the country's principal economic problems. But it took several years for the Faculty to decide to ask Ford for comprehensive assistance to all aspects of the Faculty's needs, and it took Ford, which for all practical purposes was, like the Faculty, founded in 1950, several years to define its interest in Indonesia and in development. The University of California at Berkeley became involved because it was meanwhile seeking Ford support to expand its research and teaching on Southeast Asia, with an emphasis on Indonesia. Agreements among these three parties were concluded, and the first grants of funds made, in 1956. The main goal, accepted by all, was to develop the Faculty of Economics and its Institute for Economic and Social Research in as short a time as possible to the point where both institutions could function effectively without further major foreign assistance.

Much has been made of the fact that Widjojo was the "heir apparent" to Professor Sumitro as leader of the Faculty. It is not always appreciated that this position made its own demands. Initially there was a disinclination within the Faculty of Economics to adopt the American pattern of graduate training. The initial Faculty plan was that its personnel should go abroad for a year or two of non-degree study, on the grounds that they would already have completed the *sarjana* degree, and were already qualified to write a dissertation and receive the doctorate. The earliest story I remember hearing about Widjojo was that, on a visit to Berkeley, he had been impressed with the depth and breadth of graduate training available there. In fact he was one of the first members of the Faculty staff to go abroad for a degree with Ford financing, in 1957, and returned with a doctorate in 1961, after an astonishingly rapid progress through the requirements of one of the strongest departments of economics that the United States had to offer. He was soon first deputy dean, and director of the Institute of Economic and Social Research, and from such positions played the principal role in setting the standards for the subsequent training of Faculty personnel. By 1965, fully 47 members of the Faculty and Institute staff had received fellowships for training abroad, almost all for programs leading to graduate degrees. Widjojo had paved the way by doing it himself.

Indeed, Widjojo's respect for economics as an intellectual discipline was evident even much earlier. In 1955, the year he graduated from the Faculty, he had undertaken to debate Wilopo, the National Party leader and former prime minister, on the issue of whether cooperatives should be the dominant form of economic organization in Indonesia. He did so in a classic statement in support of the modern mixed economy, which Indonesia under his considerable influence has since become.

Widjojo's devotion to his profession also set him markedly apart from President Soekarno, whose impatience with economics was well known. In his Independence Day address on August 17, 1963, Soekarno expounded on the subject in characteristic terms: "I am not an economist. ... I am a revolutionary, and I am just a revolutionary in economic matters. My feelings and ideas about the economic question are simple, very simple indeed. They can be formulated as follows: If nations who live in a dry and barren desert can solve the problems of their economy, why can't we? ... I have already issued the Economic Declaration known as *Dekon,* and fourteen Government Regulations are also out. Now I say only: be patient a while longer, be patient, wait and see!" One week earlier, in his inaugural lecture as professor of economics, Widjojo had vigorously defended the role of economic analysis in development planning, and argued that if Indonesia was to break out of its stagnant economic situation, a process of planning and policy-making was required in which efficiency, rationality, consistency, clear choices among alternatives, and attention to prices and material incentives all would play a central role. It is important to recall these events because they remind us that Widjojo's development as an economic thinker was already focussed on institutional and policy issues from his earliest public appearances.

Widjojo's devotion to the intellectual life did sometimes cause him to forget temporarily the demands of politics in the life of anyone who takes a serious interest in policy. By 1965 Indonesian-American relations had become highly politicized. Dr. Subandrio, the foreign minister, issued instructions in that year that Indonesians should no longer be permitted to go to the United States to study. The families of Indonesians already studying abroad were beginning to express concern that their young relatives should come home "while there is still time." The Ford Foundation staff was ordered by its management in New York to leave Jakarta, in part out of concern for our safety. In the middle of the year, Dr. Sjarif Thajeb, Minister of Higher Education, quietly arranged for Widjojo, after a visit to Eastern Europe, to visit the United States with a message: Indonesian students should concentrate on their studies; finishing their academic programs was the best thing they could do for their country.

I was not long back in New York before I received a cable from Ali Wardhana. Widjojo was needed back urgently, the cable said. I was astonished to receive this news that Widjojo was not long since back in Jakarta. I telephoned around the country and found him at Cornell University, where he was at work on the manuscript for what was to become the first comprehensive book on the demography of Indonesia, *Population Trends in Indonesia,* which appeared in 1970. One has to ask: Given political turmoil in one's own country at all approximating that in Indonesia in 1965, would I have thrown myself into a work as abstruse as demographic history? And why? Perhaps it was essential to Widjojo's moral balance in the midst of impending adversity. What I remember about the incident is that he was not at all apologetic about his immersion in scholarship at a time of political crisis.

In a note of acknowledgments in the *Population Trends* volume, Widjojo expressed gratitude to his colleagues at the Faculty of Economics for "the intellectually challenging climate they have been able to preserve during years of mounting problems and difficulties." That note serves to remind us that, as exceptional as Widjojo's intellect was demonstrated to be very early on, he was also a member of a group that played an essential role in sustaining him.

Indeed, the years of problems and difficulties were not few. The Faculty found itself in an emergency situation in 1957 and 1958, following the departure of its founding dean from Java in May, 1957.

Widjojo was about to leave for Berkeley. The effective leadership of the Faculty rested on two men, only marginally older than he, who had received foreign training under earlier fellowships from sources other than the Ford Foundation, Subroto and Mohammad Sadli. The Faculty was able to function in part because Berkeley recruited and fielded temporary teaching staff to man the curriculum.

But the dangers to the Faculty were not professional. The political environment was threatening from 1957 on. A political crisis developed over the teaching of "liberal" economics in 1961, and while the Faculty of Economics in Jakarta was not the object of direct attack, the effect was extremely unsettling. The professorial lecture by Widjojo in 1963 made it clear, moreover, that the Faculty was not going to bow to presidential preferences. One of the reasons why this was possible was that older men of prominence protected the young members of the Faculty, including Dr. Soedjono Djuned Poesponegoro, who was rector of the University from 1957; Dr. Sjarif Thajeb, who was rector from 1962; and Professor Soeriaatmadja, who was dean of the Faculty from 1961. But the young leadership group of the Faculty was shaped principally by the very difficulties that threatened them. Shortly before Widjojo became Acting Dean in 1965, an internal Ford Foundation report described the Faculty's young leaders as "proud, resourceful, and self-reliant."

How Widjojo and four other UI (University of Indonesia) economists became the economic policy advisers to the government of Indonesia in late 1966 is worth recalling, because the process says much not only about their self-confidence and professionalism, but also about their persuasiveness as tutors to the national elite.

The Indonesian economy in 1965 produced the lowest average per capita income of any economy in Asia. The situation was explored in analytical terms and in public for the first time on January 10, 1966, at a conference organized by the students of the Faculty of Economics. The event was notable chiefly for an address by Mohammad Sadli, who offered a wide-ranging critique of the causes of Indonesia's crippling hyper-inflation. The basic problem, he said, was "the state of mind". The government had spent the nation into bankruptcy, and the economy was without savings. The "only way out" was to restore the good will of the international community and seek new credits abroad. This was unfamiliar advice to an audience accustomed to the revolutionary rhetoric of Soekarno, who, at this point, continued to hold office as President. A major psychological boundary was crossed with this public break with the President.

On April 12, 1966, one month and a day after the transfer of power from Soekarno to General Soeharto, the Sultan of Yogjakarta issued the new government's first formal report on the state of the economy. Widjojo, Sadli, Subroto, Ali Wardhana and Emil Salim all participated in the drafting. The picture they drew was one of widespread economic deprivation, moving one foreign observer to remark that the situation was "without parallel in modern times except in the immediate aftermath of war or revolution".

From May 4 to 9, 1966, a second symposium was held at the University of Indonesia on the full range of economic, political, social and cultural problems confronting the country. Ali Wardhana was chairman of the event, and Emil Salim was rapporteur. Subroto made a slashing attack on the policies of Guided Democracy. It was time, he said, for the government to use its funds to rehabilitate the economy instead of paying for political luxuries like helicopters and the Asian Games. Every effort would have to be made to bring into balance the entire array of monetary and fiscal policies, foreign trade, prices, civil service salaries, and production.

In June the Provisional People's Consultative Assembly, meeting for the first time since the political crisis began the previous October, approved a lengthy statement on the economy, written by the same five UI economists who drafted the April statement by the Sultan. This time, the economists acted on their own initiative and lobbied the Assembly for support. The government was to play the central role in guiding the course of economic development, the statement said, but private business would be encouraged to play an active role. The government was to adopt a drastic austerity program at once. In the longer term, the economy needed to be developed, with agriculture as the first priority. Foreign borrowing was approved, provided the funds were used for the essential purposes of stabilization and rehabilitation. Legislation was to provide for foreign private investment as well.

At this point, the economists still had not met General Soeharto. That occurred only in August at a seminar held at the Army Staff and Command School in Bandung. The seminar was held in order to develop a consensus among the army's commanders behind a course of action for the new government. Colonel Suwarto, who was the organizer of the seminar, arranged for the senior UI economists to meet with the army commanders and argue in person for their ideas. Evidently Soeharto, among others, was favorably impressed. He began calling the economists in for discussions; before long he appointed them members of his Team of Economic Advisers, with Widjojo as chairman. One of the economists later recalled: "It was a step by step process. The Assembly statement was clear, but it needed to be worked out, to be made more operational. It had to be accepted by the army leadership as a whole, not just Soeharto. And he, of course, was not a vacuum into which we could just put our ideas."

On October 3, guided by his new advisers, Soeharto announced a sweeping program of economic policy reforms. Taken together, the measures constituted the single most significant statement of economic policy of what was to become the long Soeharto presidency. Several steps were taken to decontrol the economy, eliminating the system of multiple exchange rates and import-export licensing controls from a large portion of the country's international trade. Budget control was restored to the Ministry of Finance, and spending was halted on most public works pending formulation of a program of priority projects. In December Indonesia's Western creditors, meeting in Paris, agreed to a moratorium on payments on Indonesia's national debt, and committed themselves to a program of economic assistance that was soon to become—and long remain—the largest in Asia.

Thus in the months from January to December of 1966, the UI economists, under the leadership of Widjojo, completed the extraordinary task of analyzing the problems of Indonesia's economy, designing a comprehensive program of radical reform, persuading the civilian and military elite of the nation to accept the program, and then persuading the governments of the wealthy industrial democracies to support it as well. Even if Widjojo and the others had made no further contributions to Indonesian public policy, they would have earned a notable place in Indonesian history by their actions during the twelve months of 1966. *Never before had five university professors done so much in so short a time to resurrect the economic fortunes of a great nation.*

The extraordinary accomplishment of the university economists during 1966, not to mention their subsequent rise to even greater influence, has caused some to search far and wide for explanations. *I want to say here that, to the best of my knowledge, there was never any more to the rise of Widjojo and his associates than meets the eye.* The Ford Foundation never sought any more than the building of a Faculty of Economics at the University of Indonesia, much as it did at other universities in Indonesia and in other nations. The University of California at Berkeley stood for no more than a mainstream approach to the predominant economic issues of the time. The International Monetary Fund had worked out a stabilization program with Indonesia as recently as 1963, much as it had with other nations. All these, and the other international actors, behaved very much as one might have expected them to behave in the circumstances. There is no reason to attribute to any of them any more of the Indonesian accomplishment than could be attributed to the successes and failures of policy makers and advisers in many other countries of the world at the time. In my opinion, *the critical difference that set the Indonesian case apart lay in the exceptional personal abilities of the Indonesian economists, their unusual history as a group of nationalist intellectuals under pressure from the political left, and the unexpected readiness of then-General Soeharto and the army officers around him to assimilate the economists way of thinking and commit themselves to the course of action the economists espoused. That combination was not matched anywhere in the world in the decade of the 1960s, nor, so far as I know, in the second half of the twentieth century.*

In any event, the UI economists began in 1967 to move into new roles as the heads of government agencies. Widjojo in that year was appointed chairman of the National Development Planning Agency, and he soon turned to Harvard University and the Ford Foundation for assistance. This was not surprising. The Indonesian Academy of

Science (LIPI) had created an Institute of Economic and Social Research (Leknas) in the early 1960s, and the Ford Foundation had agreed in 1963 to provide funding for the training of its staff. The Foundation engaged the Development Advisory Services of Harvard University to help arrange the training. Selo Soemardjan, the long-time secretary to the Sultan of Yogyakarta, along with several of the UI economists, had meanwhile been appointed to the Leknas staff, pending the training of its own permanent cadre. As a result, Widjojo and his colleagues were already acquainted with the Harvard group, and in late 1967 or early 1968, Widjojo opened the question of Harvard's providing advisory services to Bappenas. Harvard services were available from mid-1968.

The relationship between Bappenas staff and their Harvard advisers was very close. At the outset, the Indonesian and foreign personnel shared offices. The relationship also was completely confidential. Bappenas described the sorts of expertise it needed; Harvard proposed personnel to meet the Bappenas specifications; Bappenas made the final personnel decisions; and Bappenas evaluated the results. Although I was an executive of the Ford Foundation during the entire period of Ford funding of the Harvard advisory services to Bappenas, and recommended some of the funding during my own years as representative of the Foundation in Jakarta from 1969 to 1973, I never read a single piece of economic analysis that Ford funds paid for. My only involvement, as Ford representative, was to agree to the nature and number of full-time Harvard positions, agree to the number of months of short-term consulting services, negotiate the financial terms, and exercise the right of veto over the choice of the Harvard chief of party. This might seem irresponsible to some, but I was concerned above all to protect both Bappenas and Harvard from potential political attack.

In time, political attacks did occur. On one occasion, Widjojo sent word to me conceding that I had been right in anticipating this—but adding that he had been right about the need for professional help in the first place. Looking back, with the benefit of distance, I have to say I still think Widjojo was right. The recruitment and training of professional economists in Indonesia has not even yet been sufficient to catch up with the initial absolute shortage of personnel and the later rising demands of economic growth and development. Moreover, experienced economists such as David Cole, well known for his work on the economy of Korea, and Malcolm Gillis, well known for his work on public finance in Latin America, were undoubtedly valuable to Bappenas in part because of their detailed knowledge of what had worked well elsewhere. Others, such as Peter Timmer, an authority on food policy, and Richard Patten, an authority on rural banking, are today best known for their work on Indonesia, in part because they devoted many years to it. The quality of the Harvard contribution also was measurable in the respect in which they held their Indonesian colleagues, which was uniformly high.

My own association with Widjojo took a new form in 1983 when I began work on a book on the political economy of modern Indonesia. He had by this time just finished a decade as Coordinating Minister for Economic, Financial and Industrial Affairs. I found him as full of youthful enthusiasm as ever when it came to matters of policy. I also found him as modest as ever when it came to attributing responsibility for success. He was particularly strong in his praise of two institutions that had much to do with implementing government policies that have earned much international praise: the National Family Planning Coordinating Board (the BKKBN) and the program of government intervention that contributed to a reduction in the rate of growth of the Indonesian population (without the high level of economic development often considered a necessary precursor); and the Logistics Agency (Bulog) and the program to stabilize the price of rice and make Indonesia self-sufficient in this most significant food grain. The lesson that successful policy requires strong institutions for its implementation is one that many national societies have still to learn, and Indonesia should remain a model for many for some time to come.

The role of Indonesia as a significant actor on the international stage has been at the center of my recent conversations with Widjojo. The successful meeting of the Asia Pacific Economic Cooperation forum (APEC) in Bogor in 1994 is widely attributed around the region to the leadership of President Soeharto and Widjojo Nitisastro. That was, of course, the meeting that set the target of free and open trade and investment in the Asia Pacific by 2010 and 2020. Those I know who were personally involved in the process credit Widjojo with having had more to do than any other individual with the drafting and acceptance of the APEC leaders' eight-page Declaration of Common Resolve.

The debt crisis that continues to afflict many poor countries has been perhaps the single most significant topic to engage Widjojo in recent years, if I can judge from my conversations with him. Based on a resolution approved by the heads of the governments of the Non-Aligned Movement in Jakarta in 1992, the government of Indonesia took the initiative to establish a Group of Experts on Debt, of which Widjojo was an Indonesian member. President Soeharto, speaking as chairman of the NAM, presented a memorandum proposing urgent actions of debt relief to the leaders of the Group of Seven industrialized nations in 1993. The Group of Experts lobbied representatives of the World Bank, the IMF and other institutions. The Group of Experts also completed a report. *The Continuing Debt Crisis of the Developing Countries* in 1994. On that occasion, Gamani Corea, chairman of the group, wrote in a foreword that the members were all "specially indebted to Professor Widjojo Nitisastro who inspired and guided us in our work, and who also gave us the benefit of his immense expertise, wisdom and energy."

So the Widjojo story continues. One looks forward to the next chapters with high expectations. An Indonesian poet once remarked to me that what has made Widjojo so influential has been "the purity of his language." He was speaking of his use of the Indonesian language, of course. That quality attaches to Widjojo's work in English as well; he writes with great clarity and simplicity. As one who follows Indonesia today from a distance, I am highly sensitive to the quality of the written word. And I look forward to reading what Widjojo has to say on the economic issues that engage him for many years to come. ◆

19

The Man Behind the Gigantic Development Effort of His Country With a Real "Human Face"

Victor Soler-Sala *

O n my arrival in Indonesia in 1978, I was well aware of Bappenas excellent reputation both in the country and abroad. I had spent many years as a planner, first at UNICEF Headquarters and then in India. When one of the members of my team in New Delhi went to Jakarta as a consultant, the feedback he sent was most exciting. I saw this as a great opportunity to cooperate with the planning body in Indonesia.

One of the "Sages" I met immediately was Prof. Soedjatmoko, at the time an adviser on social affairs to Bappenas and he referred with great respect to the Chairman of that Institution. In my conversations with him it became clear that the man at the top did indeed support and encourage the human aspects of development. Work on the preparation of the new PELITA was in full swing and we had submitted a position paper reflecting UNICEF parameters to develop a joint strategy addressing the urgent survival and development needs of children. Everybody warned me of the tough "Berkeley Mafia" and their hardnosed attitude towards the social dimensions of development.

The day came when I was invited to meet the leader of Bappenas and I had to accept that I felt somewhat uneasy. My fears were quickly put to ease as he greated me warmly with his customary unassuming manner. Prof. Widjojo went over the accomplishments

---

* Dr. Victor Soler-Sala (Spain) was UNICEF Representative in Indonesia (1978-1981); UNICEF Regional Director for the Middle East and North Africa; Vice President UNICEF-Comite de Catalunya.

made so far by the prior development plans and then he focused on the still pending severe problems to be addressed. He was aware that the focus had to move from the center to the regions and to simplify the somewhat cumbersome bureaucracy. He also favored the basic services approach which included the participation of the people themselves. Infant mortality was still a major problem and the success of the family planning program was jeopardized by it. He realized the importance of linking and consolidating services at the *Desa* and *Kampung* levels. In order to do that he was willing to assign the necessary resources and political support at the highest levels. The State of the nation speech of President Soeharto started to include references to infant mortality rates and other social indicators and progressively this became an important part of that document.

Prof. Widjojo was always available when necessary and if serious bottlenecks appeared he was ready to provide a solution.

During the six Consortium meetings that I attended, his performance was masterful and encouraged me to share with the major donors the very creative activities which were being tried in Indonesia. A number of these received important financing from these donors. With his very *halus* manner, but sharp and well informed presentations, Prof. Widjojo convinced and charmed his audiences and needless to say that the great success of Indonesia's economic and social plans are due to his unique blend of Indonesian leadership and professionalism. *For me he was and will always be the man who was behind the gigantic development effort of his country with a real "human face".*

I cherish the years I had the honor and pleasure to be associated with him and believe that UNICEF, in Indonesia and worldwide, owes a great deal to his leadership. I am certain that many, many Indonesian children, who have benefitted from the policies and programmes that he supported will be available on September 23rd to wish him long life and say *TERIMA KASIH PAK WIDJOJO.* My heart and my spirit will be with those children. ◆

20

The Key Role He Played in the Remarkable Social Achievements of Indonesia

Anthony A. Kennedy*

I first met Professor Widjojo Nitisastro at the June 1989 meeting of the Inter-Governmental Group on Indonesia (IGGI) in The Hague, three months after I had taken up my assignment as the UNICEF Representative in Indonesia. Over the next six years, as the donor consortium changed from the IGGI chaired by the Dutch, to the Consultative Group on Indonesia (CGI) chaired by the World Bank, I came to know and admire this gentle, firm persuader who was Indonesia's senior economic adviser at those meetings.

His deep concern for the social consequences of economic development was evident in our first meeting and later he could only have felt great satisfaction when, in 1992 at the first CGI meeting, a World Bank Vice-President cited as evidence of the effectiveness of the management of its development process the fact that over the previous 25 years, Indonesia had achieved the fastest rate of the reduction of poverty of any developing country for which the Bank had statistics.

This long term record of poverty reduction was achieved through unyielding resolve and an ability to question conventional wisdom. Indonesia's approach was not the norm. Several years earlier, through the publication of *Adjustment with a Human Face*, UNICEF had invited attention to the unjust paradox that while the poor were never the direct beneficiaries of loans that stretched national

---

* Mr. Anthony A. Kennedy, (US) is at present Director, Programme Funding, UNICEF; was Unicef Representative in Indonesia (1989-1995).

economies, in times of contraction, they were most often visited early with the direct negative consequences of economic adjustment through the reduction of social program budgets that for them were vital. In contrast to this dismal norm, *Indonesia was among the few, if not the only country that protected the poor from the worst ravages of adjustment policies then popular in much of the rest of the world. In reviewing Indonesia's performance, the World Bank's study of poverty pointed out that while Indonesia was not alone in suffering deep economic difficulties in the mid-1980s, it did enjoy the singular performance of continuing to reduce the poverty gap while weathering the storms of a sharp drop in oil prices and debt problems made more difficult by the strengthening of the US dollar when much of its indebtedness was held in other currencies.*

Prolonged and strong concern for the social impact of its economic growth policies, continued in difficult as well as good times, is close to the top of the list of Indonesia's most impressive achievements. It was only some time after our first meeting that I learned that this concern was crafted and maintained by a group led by Professor Widjojo. In fact, I came to know more about the man through the results of the policies he championed than I did from our periodic, warm and friendly personal contacts as his deep intelligence and the iron will and drive that accompany it were masked by the self-effacing manner with which he expressed himself and a luminous smile that started in his eyes.

The spread of Posyandu (Integrated Service Post), the improvement of child nutrition, the drop in infant mortality which helped pave the way for the drop in the fertility rate, and the achievement of the 1990 goal of Universal Child Immunization by overcoming a slowing coverage trend which indicated that goal would not be met, are a few of the major social advances facilitated by national economic policies and social values underlying the Repelita crafted by Bappenas. But, to sustain progress made and to lay the foundation for further growth, primary education deserves special mention.

In all Asia, Indonesia earned a place high among the early leaders in recognizing the wisdom of investment in primary education. In 1972, during my first visit, though the focus of the mission was on urbanization and the urban poor, the dinner table opinion of the economists with whom I was travelling was that Indonesia could not possibly sustain the cost of a conventional solution of government provided schooling to meet its primary education needs. It was felt that another and perhaps more effective solution would have to be found, such as a massive informal education system. But *those informal chats could not have reckoned with the twin benefits of the oil profits that were about to come and the ability of Professor Widjojo and his Bappenas collaborators to enlist and maintain a willing President's resolve to achieve universal primary education.* The approach coupled a massive expansion of the formal system with a giant and highly effective non-formal effort aimed at older children and adults that has since earned a UNESCO prize. It is perhaps too easily forgotten that *there was heavy competition for the funds that went to schools. To meet that competition, the economic team led by Professor Widjojo provided the welcome but necessary arguments that enabled the President to maintain the push for primary education, while at the same time maintaining and even increasing an emphasis on the importance of education for girls.*

While the remarkable social achievements of Indonesia are the fruits of the labours of many and no one person deserves credit alone, it is evident that Professor Widjojo Nitisastro has played a key role. It's pleasing to know his role has been recognized. ◆

21

One of the Most Effective Anti-Poverty Programs Ever Implemented In Any Country in the World

Peter McCawley*

1. Introduction

The essential facts about the remarkable team of Indonesian economic technocrats who became known as the Berkeley Mafia are well-known inside Indonesia. But the key role that Professor Widjojo Nitisastro and his colleagues played in the economic recovery of Indonesia after 1965 is not as well-known as it should be overseas. In recalling the role that Widjojo and his closest colleagues have played since the mid-1960s then, I will first note some of the key achievements of economic policy in Indonesia during this period, then consider what lessons might be drawn from the Indonesian experience, especially for policy-makers in other developing countries.

2. The Record

Briefly, the main facts about economic performance in Indonesia since the mid-1960s are the following. In 1966, when President Soeharto effectively assumed power, the Indonesian economy was close to collapse. Anwar Nasution recalls that Benjamin Higgins described Indonesia at the time as "the number one failure among the major underdeveloped countries" (Nasution 1992). In what

---

* Dr.Peter McCawley (Australia) was Deputy Director General of AusAID, the Australian Agency for International Development. Excecutive Director of the Asian Development Bank (1992-1996). He was a lecturer in the Faculty of Economics, Gadjah Mada University, Yogyakarta, in the early 1970s. He is co-editor, with Anne Booth, of *The Indonesian Economy during the Soeharto Era*, and has been a student of economic policy-making in Indonesia for almost 30 years.

turned out to be a remarkably far-sighted step, the new President chose to draw on the advice of a small team of economic technocrats. The team became the economic *juru masak* (chefs) of the New Order Government (Thee 1992). The President listened to the policy suggestions of this group carefully, and in economic matters he generally accepted their advice (Sadli 1993). Throughout the whole period, he gave his strong support to the broad set of policies which Widjojo and his colleagues recommended.

The result of this alliance between the economic technocrats and the President was, in short, an amazing success. President Soeharto and his economic advisers produced *one of the most effective anti-poverty programs ever implemented in any country in the world.* Indonesia's average economic growth in the 25 years to the mid-1990s was close to 7% per annum. There was a sharp drop in the proportion of the Indonesian population living in measured poverty (Widjojo 1994). There were large increases in welfare for the great majority of the population. As Professor Sadli recently observed, "The Indonesian people are now better fed, better housed and better educated than at any time in their history" (Sadli 1996). And he could easily have added that they are better clothed and have better medical care as well. Important microindicators show dramatic improvements as well: as an example, the proportion of girls going to school has risen sharply in recent decades, which means that millions of young women have benefited greatly from the economic improvements in Indonesia in recent decades. This, surely, is a wonderful thing.

Australian economists with a close interest in Indonesia such as myself have largely been no more than spectators of this dramatic economic performance. But simply to watch this Asian drama unfolding, and to follow both the successes as well as some of the severe difficulties, has been immensely exciting. Much has depended on the success of economic management in Indonesia. Apart from the importance of success for the Indonesian people, Australia, as well as all of the countries of Southeast Asia, has had a great stake in the process of successful development in Indonesia. And on a personal level, to have met and worked with Professor Widjojo and some of the other members of the Berkeley Mafia team as well as their colleagues has been very rewarding.

One of the main aspects of economic performance in Indonesia which has been so encouraging in recent years has been the impact on poverty across the country. It is true that the record has not been perfect. And as Professor Emil Salim recently noted, many younger Indonesians who know little of the chaos of the 1960s are quite dissatisfied with the gains that have been made (Salim 1997). But the record is very impressive nevertheless. If one believes, as I do, that the persistence of mass poverty in developing countries is the single most important economic problem of the planet, then the role that Widjojo and his closest colleagues have played in Indonesia since the mid-1960s is of great significance. It is useful, therefore, to consider what lessons can be drawn from their experience. Can nearby countries in Asia -especially those, such as Vietnam and Cambodia, which are in an early stage of the development process—learn from the successes of Indonesia? And might Indonesia's experience also have relevance for other developing countries further afield, such as in Africa?

3. Lessons

Perhaps the most important lesson of the Indonesian miracle is that, as former Trade Minister Billy Joedono has pointed out, it was not a miracle at all - not, at least, in the economic sense. Rather, the success reflected the steady application of well-known economic principles designed to help preserve economic stability and encourage economic growth. Nevertheless, there are a number of more specific observations which can be made. Four general lessons, in particular, stand out.

First, the Indonesian experience suggests that an essential precondition for successful economic development is a reasonable degree of stability. At the broadest level, it is important that overall law and order be generally maintained. Sustained development can scarcely take place when there is chaos and disorder at home. A reasonable degree of political stability is helpful as well so that political leaders have the opportunity to formulate and then implement reform policies.

Many of the kinds of public policies needed to tackle difficult problems in developing countries (as well as in developed countries) are unlikely to be implemented if governments have but a tenuous hold on office. In Indonesia, for example, when the Pertamina crisis emerged in 1976, Widjojo was instructed by President Soeharto to manage the financial aspects of the crisis (Sadli 1993). The succeeding period was a difficult one for the economic technocrats as they carefully moved to strengthen government control over Pertamina (McCawley 1978). But in the end they won.

Sadli has attributed the success, in part, "to the persuasive power of the technocrats, particularly Widjojo, in being able to convince the President that he had to act as the head of the government, as well as to Soeharto's ability to see the country's long-term interest" (Sadli 1993). In retrospect, of course, it is clear that it would have been better to have had in place policies to control Pertamina's borrowings before the problems occurred. But once the crisis emerged, the position of the technocrats was greatly strengthened by firm political support from the President.

A second lesson of the Indonesian experience is that once the basic conditions of domestic security and political stability are in place, sustained growth is largely dependent on the consistent application of good macroeconomic and microeconomic policies. Firm macroeconomic settings, which Widjojo and his colleagues were generally able to persuade the President and the Cabinet to maintain, are a key part of the overall enabling environment needed for strong economic growth. Inflationary fiscal or monetary policies, or destabilising fluctuations in foreign exchange rates, can do much to harm a nation's growth prospects. With this fact in mind, Widjojo led the Indonesian economic policy-making team through the oil shocks of 1970s and into the 1980s with the aim of always maintaining, as far as possible, the main macroeconomic settings within acceptable bounds.

Widjojo and his colleagues also emphasised the need for good microeconomic policies to act in tandem with macroeconomic policy. Whilst good macroeconomic policies act to underpin a favourable overall enabling climate for economic growth, a constant process of microeconomic reform is generally needed to encourage constant improvements in national productivity. Productivity improvements are central to the growth process. Widjojo and his colleagues supported the key reforms to the Indonesian rice sector during the

1970s, took a close interest in the formulation of sound foreign investment policies, promoted change in the manufacturing sector, and during the 1980s strongly supported the historically important thrust towards economic deregulation in Indonesia.

Throughout this process of macroeconomic and microeconomic reform, the general approach of Widjojo and his colleagues was to support high growth pro-market policies which generated strong employment growth. The inner group of economic technocrats had, as Sadli has put it, "a real commitment to political security and economic development along rational non-ideological lines". It is hard to imagine how the Indonesian success story could have occurred without this sustained program of imaginative reform.

A third lesson is that while constant productivity improvements are crucial to economic success in developing countries, so are policies to improve the supply of factor inputs—especially labour and capital. The economic technocrats gave much attention to this aspect of the growth process as well. It is, of course, hardly surprising that Widjojo himself emphasised the importance of labour force factors—his professional training as a demographer at Berkeley in California in the 1960s encouraged him to pay close attention to the link between demographic changes and economic growth. In his own observations on the Indonesian experience, he has often emphasised the links between rapid economic growth and the qualitative and quantitative changes in the labour force. Widjojo has recently summarised the key elements of the Indonesian strategy as follows (Widjojo 1994):

"What explains the sharp drop in poverty in Indonesia? The most important factor seems to be sustained rapid economic growth, which was broadly based and labor intensive. The effects of this growth were reinforced by an array of policies that improved the health and education of the poor, reduced population growth to manageable levels, and provided infrastructure. In economic terms, the rate and pattern of growth generated a strong demand for labor, while the policies in education, health and infrastructure enabled the poor to take advantage of this demand to improve their incomes."

Widjojo and his colleagues rightly emphasised the major importance of capital accumulation as well. While Sadli concentrated on formulating appropriate policies to encourage foreign investment, Widjojo spent much time dealing with bilateral donors, the World Bank, the IMF, and in working with IGGI, the Inter-Governmental Group on Indonesia (Sadli 1993). More recently, Widjojo has continued to be a regular participant in the annual Consultative Group on Indonesia (CGI) meetings which replaced IGGI in 1992. It was my personal pleasure in Paris in 1996, as leader of the Australian delegation to the CGI, to be able to officially acknowledge the presence of Widjojo at the annual meeting, and to take the opportunity to pay tribute to his role as one of the outstanding economic policy-makers of Asia in recent decades.

A fourth lesson concerns foreign aid. The international donor community has provided strong support to Indonesia for almost 30 years since the first IGGI was convened in the late 1960s. In current prices, although hard to measure accurately, the total flow of international assistance to Indonesia over the period must be well in excess of $80 billion. It seems clear that this assistance has been both quantitatively and, especially, qualitatively important. Perhaps the central lesson of the experience is that provided the conditions are right, international aid can be very helpful in promoting the development process.

What, then, are the right conditions which might help improve the effectiveness of international assistance? Indonesian experience casts some light on this matter. One important characteristic of the aid relationship between donor agencies and Indonesia since the late 1960s has been *the strong involvement of Indonesian policy-makers themselves in the aid process*. Widjojo's own close work with the IGGI is, perhaps, the clearest example of this. In the current jargon, it is very clear—and very significant -that senior Indonesian policy-makers themselves had strong ownership of the aid process to Indonesia. In other words, aspects of Indonesian nationalism have (rightly, in my view) always been clearly evident in the relationship between donor agencies and Indonesian recipients. *This arrangement has contributed to quality improvements in the design of the international aid program to Indonesia.* It has also helped to ensure that there has been genuine commitment on the Indonesian side to the success of the aid effort.

Another important characteristic of the aid relationship between donors and Indonesia is the volume of assistance. For better or for worse, it is a basic fact of life that money talks. For close on 30 years, the international donor community has maintained a volume of aid to Indonesia which has been large enough to ensure that donors, as a group, have had a role in the policy-making process in Indonesia. To be sure, the key economic policy-makers in Indonesia such as Widjojo have always been ready to listen carefully to the views of donors. But on the other side of the table, for 30 years donors have always been prepared to support their policy dialogue with significant amounts of assistance. The main lesson to be drawn from this experience seems to be that the volume of assistance counts; if donors want to retain the option of casting a vote on policies inside developing countries, they need to be prepared to support their representation with taxation.

4. Conclusion

The four main lessons listed above, drawn from the experience of Widjojo and his colleagues in Indonesia during the past three decades, are perhaps not especially surprising. They are very important, nevertheless. The application of these lessons has underpinned a dramatic period of economic growth in Indonesia which has, in turn, had a striking impact on the incidence of poverty in the world's fourth largest nation.

But the most important implication of the Indonesian experience is a most significant one: it is that provided proper policies are followed, most developing countries should be able to achieve sustained economic growth rates of 7% per annum for several decades or more (with the 7% made up of perhaps half from increases in factor inputs, and the rest from improvements in total factor productivity).

Developing countries which are not achieving sustained growth rates of around 7% per annum are not fulfilling their potential. And the key policy settings, which we know from the experience of Widjojo and his colleagues, are these: first, *reasonable security and* stability at home underpinned by, second, good macroeconomic and microeconomic policies. Simple though these lessons may be, not nearly enough developing countries follow them. These lessons are the key to further progress in eliminating mass poverty in developing countries during the first few decades of the next century.

The key economic technocrats in Indonesia have consistently worked as a highly effective team to implement these principles for three decades. But for most of this time, the acknowledged leader of the team was Widjojo. One of his closest colleagues, Professor Emil Salim, has recently provided an affectionate summary of Widjojo's special role within the Berkeley Mafia (Salim 1997):

> "Looking back on my experience as a cabinet minister for over two decades, I would like to point out that it was Widjojo who was the real architect of the economic policies of the New Order. He was the dalang, or puppeteer, who directed the play, while we, the other economic technocrats, were the players, the wayang. We used to call him lurah (village head), and we still do. Widjojo was able to carry out his economic policies because Soeharto trusted him; the President knew that he did not have a 'hidden agenda'. Widjojo was also able to rely on us, his fellow economists, because we all shared similar views on the need to pursue sound economic policies."

Professor Widjojo Nitisastro has provided outstanding service to his nation. And he has done more besides. *In making a major contribution to development in Indonesia during the past 30 years, he has made a major contribution to peace and prosperity across the whole of the Southeast Asian region.* Thus in working to be a good Indonesian nationalist and to serve his own country, Widjojo has served the interests of many other nations too. Because of this, *my own country, Australia, as well as other countries further afield, owes an important debt to Widjojo for his work in promoting development and prosperity in Asia.* ◆

REFERENCES

Anwar, M. Arsjad, Thee Kian Wie, and Iwan Jaya Azis (Editors) (1992), *Pemikiran, Pelaksanaan, dan Perintisan Pembangunan Ekonomi,* Jakarta, PT Gramedia Pustaka Utama in cooperation with the Fakultas Ekonomi Universitas Indonesia.

McCawley, Peter (1978), "Some Consequences of the Pertamina Crisis in Indonesia", *Journal of Southeast Asian Studies,* IX(1), March.

Nasution, Anwar (1992), "Demokratisasi Ekonomi di Sektor Industri Manufaktur", in M. Arsjad Anwar et. al., *op.cit.*

Nitisastro, Widjojo (1994), "Reduction of Poverty: The Indonesian Experience", paper prepared for the IMF-World Bank Conference *Fifty Years After Bretton Woods: The Future of the IMF and the World Bank,* Madrid, September.

Sadli, Mohammad (1993), "Recollections of My Career", *Bulletin of Indonesian Economic Studies,* April, 29 (1).

Sadli, Mohammad (1996), "Introduction", in Hollinger, William C., *Economic Policy Under President Soeharto: Indonesia's Twenty-five Year Record,* Background Paper Number 2, The United States-Indonesia Society.

Salim, Emil (1997), "Recollections of My Career", *Bulletin of Indonesian Economic Studies,* April, 27 (1).

Thee Kian Wie (1992), "Pendahuluan", in M. Arsjad Anwar et. al., *op. cit.*

22

Indonesia's Economic Crisis Management
1966 - 1969

*Kemal Siber**

1. Introduction

I t is a privilege and a duty for me to review the Indonesian experience to combat the economic crisis at the early stage of the new
order government of the Soeharto regime, on the occasion of the
commemoration of the 70th birthday of Prof. Widjojo Nitisastro.

The stabilization and rehabilitation policies of Indonesia during
1966-69 have been studied by several developing countries and
constituted a model for formulating their policies. It is noteworthy
that after three decades, the success of Indonesia in bringing down a
hyperinflation to one-digit level in a short period drew the attention
of Turkey, a more developed country, recently. A high-level
Indonesian delegation headed by Prof. Widjojo met with the Turkish
Prime Minister, economic ministers and senior officials in January
1997 to exchange views on economic stabilization policies and
measures, upon the invitation of the Prime Minister.

At the outset, I wish to indicate that it is important to examine
the role of Prof. Widjojo Nitisastro as the chairman of the economic
team in the formulation and the implementation of the stabilization
and rehabilitation policies and the relations of Indonesia with the

---

* Mr. Kemal Siber (Turkey) was the first Resident Representative of the IMF in Jakarta (1969). During his
three-and-half year mission in Indonesia, he actively participated in the preparation and implementation
of the stabilization programs, for which he was decorated by the Indonesian Government in 1981 (after his
retirement from the IMF). In 1984 he was engaged by the Ministry of Finance of the Republic of Indonesia
until 1988 to serve as an economic adviser to the Minister and was re-engaged in 1991 to assist the Central
Bank to introduce a monetary program scheme. He completed his assignment in 1995.

International Monetary Fund (IMF) during that period (1966-69). As the first IMF resident representative in Jakarta during that period I had a historical opportunity to witness the developments at a vintage point.

I believe it is necessary to set the records right in this field for the benefit of the new generations of Indonesia as well as for the outside world, especially for those countries examining Indonesia as an economic model.

In this context, I recall the visit of a young Indonesian lady from one of the Universities in Surabaya, in 1991 when I happened to be in Jakarta on a temporary mission as a Harvard Institute for International Development (HIID) consultant. She was referred to me by Prof. Arndt from the Australian National University. She said that she was even prepared to fly to Istanbul, Turkey to meet me. She was preparing a dissertation on "the Indonesian stabilization programs and the role of the IMF".

I had to spend several hours with her in agony. Her views, assessments and information were completely wrong. In brief, she was arguing that the stabilization measures of Indonesia were entirely formulated and dictated by the IMF.

I tried to explain to the young academician that the chief architect of the Indonesian stabilization program was Prof. Widjojo. The main components of the stabilization policies, namely, (a) the containment of the monetary expansion, the main source of hyperinflation, by eliminating huge budget deficits swiftly, (b) the liberalization of foreign exchange and foreign trade systems by removing exchange restrictions and licensing and (c) the elimination of price distortions by allowing free market mechanism to operate and raising fixed prices of essential commodities to realistic levels were formulated as guidelines by Prof. Widjojo and supported by the President consistently all through the stabilization period.

The role of the IMF during the period was to assist the Indonesian authorities initially to translate the stabilization policies as adopted by Indonesia into specific measures and programs, and later on to provide financial support under stand-by arrangements to facilitate the implementation of the adopted policies.

At this date, I have no information whether the young lady was able to finalize her dissertation and receive her doctorate degree.

I recall another incident concerning the so-called role of the IMF dictating economic policies to Indonesia.

Rice pricing, procurement, distribution and intervention policies were important components of stabilization programs of Indonesia. Such policies were under a close supervision of the economic team, headed by Prof. Widjojo and they were submitted for the approval of the President.

The Bulog rice operations based on the policy guidelines adopted by the Indonesian government were incorporated in the stabilization programs, supported by the IMF stand-by arrangements. In this context, special domestic credit allocations were provided for Bulog operations under the stand-by arrangements.

Prof. Widjojo and the chairman of Bulog, General Achmad regularly requested from the resident IMF staff to assist in the preparation of rice programs on the basis of adopted policy guidelines, even prior to entering formal stand-by arrangements with the IMF.

In 1968, a senior economic advisor from a prominent institution, attacked arrogantly the IMF resident representative in a meeting organized by Prof. Widjojo and Prof. Ali Wardhana, to discuss a rice program prepared by the IMF resident staff. Unaware that the paper was reflecting policies adopted by the Indonesian government, he stated bluntly that policies in the paper were wrong and that the IMF staff were not qualified to advise on rice policies.

It was an embarrassing situation for the advisor who was newly appointed to head an important advisory group in Jakarta. He might have thought that by challenging the policies dictated by the IMF, he would draw the attention of the economic team and strengthen his position.

Prof. Widjojo who is well-known for being open to advise and regularly consult with different institutions before making a final decision, ignored the comments of the advisor. The advisor was transferred from Jakarta after a short period.

In a different context, the role of the IMF in Indonesia had come out as a significant topic during the recent visit of an Indonesian delegation to Turkey, headed by Prof. Widjojo.

While senior Turkish officials and economic ministers responsible for IMF relations were experienced and knowledgeable about the role of the IMF, the political leaders and cabinet members of the conservative Welfare Party wing of the coalition government had misgivings about entering a financial arrangement with the IMF in support of the economic policies of the new Turkish government.

Following a lengthy meeting with Prof. Widjojo on economic stabilization policies and the Indonesian experience concerning the IMF (and the World Bank), the Turkish Prime Minister authorized a Turkish delegation visiting USA—consisting of a senior minister and the central bank governor—to request the assistance and financial support of the IMF in January 1997. Since then negotiations / discussions are continuing between the Turkish authorities and the IMF on a possible financial arrangement. Although prospects for reaching an agreement at this stage are uncertain, it was an important breakthrough for the new government to initiate discussions with the IMF. The information received by the Prime Minister from Prof. Widjojo on the nature of the IMF support of the Indonesian economic programs was an important factor for removing reservations and misgivings of conservative Turkish political leaders concerning the IMF.

2. Economic Crisis

Indonesia survived a communist coupe d'etat crashed by the military under the command of General Soeharto in September 1965. Uncertainties in domestic politics were settled by the transfer of the executive power from President Soekarno to General Soeharto in March 1966.

The new government under the leadership of General Soeharto had to deal with an economic crisis. The annual inflation rate of over 600 percent in March 1966 had reached to a record level of 1524 percent in June 1966.

Government budget revenues were less than half of government expenditures. The budget deficit financing by the central bank credit was a dominant factor responsible for an excessive increase in money supply for over 700 percent.

Foreign debt payments due in 1966 (about $475 million) were larger than total export receipts in 1965 ($460 million).

The legacy of the former President Soekarno regime was leading the country to an economic collapse.

3. Economic Team

As a first and most important step to combat the economic crisis, General Soeharto appointed Prof. Widjojo as Chairman of an Economic Team (1966). The team consisted of Prof. Mohammad Sadli, Prof. Ali Wardhana, Prof. Emil Salim and Prof. Subroto. This economic team was responsible for the formulation of economic policies to solve the problems of the economic ills of Indonesia.

The members of the team originally had no ministerial rank, but the policy recommendations of the team were directly reported to the President for approval. Economic departments such as finance, industry, agriculture and trade were under ministers responsible for the implementation of the economic policies and daily operations.

As a formal set-up, however, all economic units were under Sultan Hamengku Buwono IX as the Minister of State for Economics, Finance and Industry.

It was well-recognized at the IMF and the World Bank quarters that the economic team, a unique set-up, was the most powerful body in economic policy-making in Indonesia during the stabilization-rehabilitation period (1966-69).

The team enjoyed an unqualified support of President Soeharto. During my three-and-half year mission in Jakarta as the IMF resident representative, I can not recall any incident in which a proposal for decision submitted to the President by Prof. Widjojo, as the head of the economic team, was turned down by the President.

On this occasion, I would like to repeat a memory that I had disclosed during a seminar held at the Atma Jaya University, Jakarta in September 1996 on the occasion of the commemoration of the 70th birthday of the former Finance Minister Drs. Frans Seda.

The World Bank President Mc Namara visited Jakarta in June 1968. The purpose of the visit was to examine the developments under stabilization and rehabilitation efforts and to determine whether the conditions were suitable for the World Bank to play a more active role in Indonesia.

The IMF had already opened a resident representative office in January 1967 and had played a more active role due to the nature of the economic conditions in Indonesia at that time. President Mc Namara thought he had to open a resident mission in Jakarta to provide more actively technical and financial assistance for development efforts, if Indonesia had made sufficient progress in the stabilization and rehabilitation field.

During his visit, he informally asked my opinion whether the Indonesian stabilization program supported by the IMF would succeed and a development period would start in a foreseeable future.

However, a more significant question President Mc Namara raised was whether the Indonesian leadership would continue to support the economic team led by Prof. Widjojo, or whether the team was going to remain in power, indicating the rumors and some foreign press reports that Prof. Widjojo would be replaced. As for the first question, I reiterated the IMF views that the stabilization program was progressing successfully. As for the second question, I expressed my personal view that Prof. Widjojo who was getting the full support of the President, would remain in power, for at least five more years (I could not give assurances for another 15 years, as it happened).

President Mc Namara accelerated the opening of the resident World Bank mission in Jakarta following his visit which was very much welcomed by the Indonesian authorities.

4. External Debt

Recognizing the urgent need for debt relief and fresh foreign aid in addition to economic measures to be introduced by Indonesia in order to succeed in combating the economic crisis, Prof. Widjojo gave a high priority at the very beginning of his work to open up to the outside world and face creditor countries.

In this context, the Indonesian authorities decided to rejoin the IMF and the World Bank and benefit from the support of such international financial institutions in their relations with the creditor/ donor countries.

The decision of the Soeharto's new order government was significant, reversing the unusual action of the Soekarno regime of resigning from the United Nations as well as the IMF and the World Bank.

The first international meeting on Indonesia was a debt conference in Tokyo held in March 1966 attended also by a high level IMF mission. The meeting was followed by a second debt conference in Tokyo in September 1966 and a third debt conference in Paris in November 1966.

The Indonesian government debt rescheduling requests were discussed in several international conferences under the so-called Paris Club during the stabilization-rehabilitation period. Temporary debt reliefs were gradually provided by creditor countries, facilitating the Indonesian efforts to combat the economic crisis. However, a long-term settlement of the Indonesian external debt awaited for about four years. In April 1970, creditor governments finally agreed to enter debt rescheduling agreements with Indonesia, on favorable terms.

The Indonesian delegations led by Prof. Widjojo consistently requested long-term settlement of debt problems, rather than temporary debt reliefs in order to avoid frequent debt rescheduling. It is noteworthy that, once a long-term settlement was agreed in April 1970, Indonesia never requested more debt rescheduling from creditors under any circumstances in almost the following three decades.

5. Foreign Aid

In addition to debt reliefs, fresh aid was needed to support the Indonesian efforts to overcome the economic crisis.

In an environment of uncertainties and reluctance of donors to provide foreign aid generously to support Indonesia, an informal aid-group, called IGGI (Inter-Governmental Group on Indonesia) was set up under the chairmanship of the Netherlands to coordinate foreign aid to Indonesia.

The first IGGI meeting was held in February 1967. The aid-group met three times in 1967 and twice in the following years during the stabilization-rehabilitation period, to follow the progresses made under the Indonesian stabilization programs, based on economic reports prepared by the IMF staff (the World Bank also attended the meetings, but during the stabilization -rehabilitation period the IMF played a more active role).

Prof. Widjojo as the head of the Indonesian delegations in all these meetings favored open discussions on the economic problems of Indonesia and welcomed the IMF staff reports and presentations, providing information and assessments on the Indonesian stabilization policies and developments.

The IGGI played an important role as a forum to follow up the progresses in the Indonesian economy.

Friendly countries matched the efforts of Indonesia by raising their assistance progressively as the Indonesian economy improved as a result of self-help measures taken by Indonesia in a close cooperation with the IMF.

During the first year (1967) of IGGI meetings, total foreign aid commitments amounted to $176 million only. However, in the second year foreign aid commitments amounted to $362 million or twice of the first year.

In the third year (1969) representing the end of the stabilization-rehabilitation period and transition to the development period, coinciding with the introduction of the first development plan (REPELITA), donors raised their aid commitments significantly to $550 million. The increase reflected larger project aid commitments from donors, particularly from the World Bank (IDA), to finance Indonesian development efforts under the Repelita I.

Major donors during the first three years of the IGGI were the USA and Japan, representing about 40 percent and 27 percent of total commitments respectively, including food aid generously extended by the USA to meet rice shortages during the period. Excluding food aid, the USA and Japan aid commitments were approximately equal under a matching principle between the two major donors.

Foreign aid obtained during the first two years were mainly in the nature of quick-disbursing program loans, facilitating the Indonesian stabilization and rehabilitation efforts. Foreign aid disbursements during the three year stabilization-rehabilitation period (1967-69) financed about 35 percent of total Indonesian imports, providing a significant balance of payments support. They also financed all of the government budget development expenditures during the first two years and about 75 percent in the third year, mainly through the counterpart proceeds generated from the sales of program aid receipts.

Undoubtedly, the IGGI played an effective role in facilitating the flow of foreign aid to Indonesia during a difficult stabilization-rehabilitation period. Also, it was an important forum of communication between the friendly countries and the Indonesian authorities. As the donor government representatives in the meetings appreciated the Indonesian government efforts and observed significant progresses in the economy, as presented by Prof. Widjojo and his delegations, the willingness of donor countries to meet foreign aid requirements of Indonesia increased significantly.

The IGGI was a unique informal aid group, with no official status. Normally such aid coordination activities were under the jurisdiction of the World Bank. However, under the existing conditions (economic crisis, urgent situation) in a non-member country (Indonesia was not yet a member of the World Bank) and the enthusiasm of the Dutch government to chair such an informal aid group was welcomed by Indonesia and major donor countries.

During the stabilization-rehabilitation period the aid group was chaired by an able professional, Mr. Everts, the director general of the economics ministry, brought Holland prestige and appreciation of Indonesia, irrespective of its minor aid contributions (the Dutch aid commitments during the first three years of the IGGI amounted to $67 million or 6 percent of total commitments).

However, it was regrettable that following a 25-year successful operation based on non-political discussions on the economic issues and development policies of Indonesia, a Dutch minister, Chairman of the IGGI, attempted to bring non-economic policy issues and tie foreign aid to such policies. His efforts amounted to an intervention to domestic policies of an independent country by a former colonial power.

It was ironical that Prof. Widjojo, the mid-wife of the IGGI who contributed substantially to its success and prestige, was instructed by the President to arrange the cancellation of the IGGI and its replacement by a formal aid coordination set-up under the chairmanship of the World Bank.

In retrospect, the incident was a blessing in disguise giving opportunity to form a Consultative Group for Indonesia (CGI) under the chairmanship of the World Bank. Prof. Widjojo as the mid-wife of the CGI also should be proud of its establishment in view of its more effective and successful operations than the IGGI. It is noteworthy that, as far as I know, Prof. Widjojo, despite his present status (economic advisor to the president) and his major occupations (including to assist non-aligned member countries to solve their external debt and other economic problems), maintains the CGI meetings as a top priority in his work agenda.

6. Self-Help Measures

In addition to debt relief and foreign aid from foreign countries, it was the utmost important for Indonesia to introduce the so-called self-help measures, immediately, in order to overcome the severe economic crisis.

The foundation of stabilization-rehabilitation policies were laid down by Prof. Widjojo and the economic team in mid-1966. The main ingredients were a free foreign exchange system and a balanced budget.

The stabilization-rehabilitation policies were translated into specific measures in the course of the second half of 1966 and were introduced as an exchange reform in October 1966, and a balanced budget for 1967, in January 1967.

The stabilization-rehabilitation measures were strengthened progressively in the three-year stabilization period (1967-69) as described below.

7. Foreign Exchange Policies

An important component of the stabilization—rehabilitation policies of Indonesia was the measures in the field of exchange rate and exchange system.

As a first major step, an exchange reform was introduced in October 1966, allowing the foreign exchange rate to find its level in a free foreign exchange market (BE market).

Under the existing export bonus (BE) system, a substantially larger portion of export proceeds (ranging according to export categories, from 50 to 90 percent) were exempted from surrender requirement at an artificially low official exchange rate (The 50 percent rate for major exports category was further increased to 75 percent in July 1967). Such export proceeds were freely sold in the exchange market (BE market) to finance imports, under a free import list.

Thus, a small export bonus market was transformed into a primary exchange market based on a floating exchange rate. (Although a parallel exchange market was maintained for financing less essential imports and other payments, the size of this so-called DP market was small.)

The exchange reform of October 1966 amounted to an instant sharp devaluation of local currency (Rupiah) from 10 to 100 per US dollar in the primary exchange market.

In addition to its positive balance of payments effect, such as encouraging exports and liberalization of imports, the exchange reform played a major role in increasing the government budget revenues.

Based on a realistic exchange rate, import duties and foreign aid counterpart revenues increased sharply. Also, the exchange reform produced an export tax (a new budget revenue) amounting to 12.5 percent of total budget revenues in the first year of the stabilization period (1967).

Exchange rate developments were a major concern of the Indonesian authorities during the three year stabilization -rehabilitation period (1967-69). They fluctuated abruptly and depreciated sharply at periods of political uncertainties and rice shortages. Nevertheless, a free exchange rate system was maintained under all circumstances.

The primary exchange rate (BE) depreciated moderately during 1967 (from Rp 100 to Rp 150 per US dollar). However, it depreciated sharply during the first half of 1968 (from Rp 150 to Rp 300 per US dollar), associated with an upsurge of inflation caused by a severe food (rice) shortage. As the speculative demand for foreign exchange subsided, as a result of improvement in food supplies and reinforcement of stabilization measures, the exchange rate became stable in the second half of 1968 and remained unchanged (at Rp 326) during 1969, the last year of the stabilization—rehabilitation period.

In support of the free exchange rate policies, the exchange system was maintained free of exchange restrictions. In the primary exchange market, exporters were authorized to sell a large portion of their export proceeds for financing of imports under a free import list, as indicated earlier. The size of the primary exchange market was widened step by step by reducing export taxes (from 50 percent on major exports in October 1966 to 15 percent in 1969).

In a parallel official exchange market (DP) all other payments for so-called non-essential imports, services and private capital transfers abroad were financed mainly by private capital inflows, without any restrictions.

The free exchange system was simplified and improved further shortly after the stabilization-rehabilitation period. Under a major exchange reform of 17 April 1970, the exchange markets were merged. A unified rate was applied for all trade, service, and private capital receipts and payments.

The unified rate was set at the level of the parallel secondary market rate (Rp 378 per US dollar), rather than the less depreciated primary market rate (Rp 326 per US dollar).

The maintenance of a free exchange system, accompanied by free exchange rates, encouraged the inflow of private capital to Indonesia. It is noteworthy that a significant amount of private capital (corresponding to about 20 percent of foreign aid) repatriated to Indonesia during the stabilization-rehabilitation period, representing the return of capital that flew out from Indonesia during the Soekarno regime.

The significance of foreign exchange policies during the stabilization-rehabilitation period of Indonesia is that the exchange rate was allowed to depreciate sharply in free exchange markets. It is important to note that the exchange rate stability was maintained during the end of the stabilization period only after the inflation rate was brought down to near one-digit level, as a result of successful monetary and fiscal policies.

The role of Prof. Widjojo in the introduction and maintenance of a free exchange system in Indonesia was significant. He has been a strong supporter of realistic exchange rates and free exchange systems since the beginning of his career in the government as the head of the economic team. As generally known such policies are conditions for the IMF support of stabilization programs. But, in the case of Indonesia these policies, although incorporated in the stand-by arrangements at a later stage, were not dictated by the IMF; they were initiated by the Indonesian authorities, under the leadership of Prof. Widjojo, and gladly supported by the IMF.

I recall a conversation with a chief economist of the World Bank resident mission in 1985, when I was economic advisor of the Finance Minister Radius Prawiro (as an IMF retiree, not connected to the IMF).

The World Bank economist who was the chief author of several World Bank economic reports submitted to the IGGI and had a close association with Prof. Widjojo, was puzzled with the introduction of an unusually free exchange system during the stabilization period, allowing even free private capital in-and-out transfers with no restrictions, a system freer than in some developed economies.

My response to the chief economist was as follows: Prof. Widjojo did not believe that exchange restrictions could be implemented effectively in Indonesia. Also, he feared that they could encourage corruption. More importantly, he believed that exchange restrictions could conceal economic illnesses and mismanagement, such as excessive monetary expansions and faulty interest and exchange rate policies. Accordingly, private capital transfers could be used as an indicator and warning concerning the weaknesses in the economic policies.

It is noteworthy that large private capital transfers abroad in 1990, five years after our conversation, played an important role to convince the Indonesian authorities that the economy was over-heated, credit expansions were excessive and interest rates were artificially low. As a result, shock-measures were introduced to cool down the economy.

During the stabilization-rehabilitation period, a free exchange system allowing the capital transfers abroad with no restrictions, contrary to fears of some critics who were afraid that it could cause capital flights, had resulted in a significant repatriation of private capital to Indonesia, as indicated earlier.

Concerning the exchange rate policies, Prof. Widjojo was the main force behind all sharp devaluations in the history of Indonesia. During the stabilization-rehabilitation period, the first important measure was the introduction of a floating exchange rate system, allowing the exchange rate to be determined by market forces.

The action amounted to an initial sharp devaluation of the Rupiah by thousand percent (from Rp10 official rate to Rp100 BE rate, per US dollar) as indicated earlier. The devaluation was made at a period of hyper-inflation, inflation rates running over 600 percent, contrary to fears of the critics that sharp devaluations would cause hardships and push the inflation further as a result of raising import prices (cost-push effect). Exchange rate depreciations during the period played an important role to achieve the balanced budget objective, facilitating the deceleration of inflation rates sharply, as described below.

It is noteworthy that under different conditions and in a different capacity (economic advisor to the president) Prof. Widjojo was again the main force behind a sharp devaluation (31 percent) of Rupiah in September 1986. The historical devaluation of 1986, a surprise action for many circles, was an important component of a chain of structural reform measures. They prevented an exchange and debt crisis in Indonesia, at that period, as a result of external shocks, namely sharp fall in oil prices and revaluation of Japanese Yen. In the longer run the reform measures played an important role to reduce the dependence of Indonesia on oil revenues.

Concerning the stabilization-rehabilitation period, I recall an incident reflecting significantly the role of Prof. Widjojo, the President and the IMF in the field of exchange rate policies. Following the successful implementation of the stabilization policies in a three-year period, and bringing the inflation rate to one-digit level (9.9 percent) at the end of 1969, the IMF encouraged the Indonesian authorities to aim at a single exchange rate system, and indicated its willingness to support the unification of two exchange markets, the so-called BE and DP markets, under a third standby arrangement. Initially the unified exchange rate was considered at a level between the primary BE rate of Rp. 326 and the parallel secondary market DP rate of Rp.378, per US dollar. The IMF had no objection to the mid-level rate under consideration by the Indonesian delegation. Prof. Widjojo, personally was in favor of an initial unified rate at the more depreciated DP rate level of Rp. 378, but before a commitment to the IMF, he decided in a close meeting of the economic team to leave the decision to the President.

A paper was prepared by the team indicating two alternative unified rates (mid-rate, and DP rate) and pros and cons for each alternative. The paper was presented to the President for decision. The choice of the President was the more depreciated DP rate of Rp.378, on the grounds of—among others—exchange rate stability. The Indonesian exchange rate decision was welcomed by the IMF and the exchange reform of 17 April 1970 concerning the unification of exchange rate was supported with a stand-by arrangement.

8. Budget Policies

The most important component of the Indonesian stabilization programs was the balanced budget policies.

The dominant factor responsible for the hyper-inflation in 1966 was an excessive monetary expansion (700 percent) caused by a huge budget deficit (56 percent) financed by the central bank credit (accounting for two-third of money supply increase).

In order to lower the inflation rate swiftly, the Indonesian government adopted a balanced budget policy and prepared the first period for budget stabilization for 1967, in balance. The target was of course ambitious, requiring the elimination of a budget deficit of 56 percent (budget revenues in 1966 were only 44 percent of budget expenditures). While budget revenues were projected to increase six-fold, budget expenditures were planned to increase less than three-fold in 1967.

An important factor responsible for budget deficits was large budget subsidies, arising from administrative low prices for essential goods and services. In order to eliminate budget subsidies, prices of several sensitive items were increased sharply in February 1967. For example, gasoline and kerosene prices were increased by 700 percent and 500 percent, respectively. Electricity and city water prices were increased by 1100 percent and 400 percent respectively. Postal rates were increased by 1600 percent.

These drastic price increases were politically difficult and bold decisions for a new government; but they were considered by the outside world as a sign of determination of Indonesia to seriously implement a stabilization program. Sharp price increases did not only eliminate subsidies but also generated significant revenues for the budget. Prior to price increases in petroleum products, oil revenues collected from foreign companies were not transferred to the budget, but kept by the state oil company (Pertamina) to meet losses from domestic petroleum product sales at low prices (hidden subsidy).

As from 1967, oil revenues from foreign companies started to flow to the budget. Oil revenues from foreign companies transferred to the budget in 1966 were zero (0); they amounted to 9 percent of total revenues in 1967, exceeding every tax category in the budget except import and export duties.

As indicated earlier, exchange rate depreciations played a major role in increasing the budget revenues. Taxes on foreign trade (import and export duties) increased sharply. Also sales of program aid receipts for financing essential imports at realistic exchange rates generated significant counterpart funds for the budget.

The negative effect of devaluations on the budget was small, mainly due to the postponement of foreign debt payments. (In 1967, budget external payments amounted to only 8 percent of total expenditures). Despite very favorable developments in budget revenues, the most effective budget policy to achieve the balanced budget objective was on budget expenditures side. An austerity budget was implemented, restricting the budget expenditures severely.

Salary increases of civil servants were initially kept below inflation rates (about 100 percent in 1967). However, as the inflation rate was lowered, and the balanced budget objective was achieved, salary increases were accelerated considerably on selective basis (about 200 percent in 1968, 120 percent in 1969).

A quarterly budget program was introduced to keep budget expenditures at the level of actual revenue receipts. Expenditure ceilings allocated to each department were monitored closely. If revenues fell shorter than quarterly estimates, the following quarterly expenditures were reduced to accommodate revenue losses, thus maintaining the balanced budget objective. An overall budget balance was the initial policy objective. Accordingly, a part of foreign aid was utilized to finance routine expenditures in 1967.

In the second year of the stabilization—rehabilitation period a more ambitious balanced budget policy, namely routine budget balance was introduced. Routine budget expenditures were programmed within the limit of domestic revenues. All foreign aid receipts were allocated for development budget.

In the third year, a period of transition from the stabilization—rehabilitation to the development period, the balanced budget policy was further modified: a routine budget surplus objective was introduced. In addition to an overall balanced budget, the routine budget was programmed to generate surplus (government savings) to finance a part (initially 25 percent) of the development expenditures. The development budget was programmed within the limits of available foreign aid and government savings.

The balanced budget policies, indicated above, were implemented effectively all along during the stabilization -rehabilitation period, under a strict fiscal discipline. During the first year (1967) the balanced budget objective was nearly achieved, reducing the budget deficit to 5 percent from 56 percent in 1966.

Following the successful implementation of the stabilization policies, in particular in the field of budget policies, during 1967, the Indonesian government entered into the first stand-by agreement with the IMF, in the early 1968. The principal commitment under the stand-by agreement with the IMF was "to pursue the objective of balanced budget." In addition, a tight monetary policy was programmed, in order to lower the inflation rate further, as described below. The balanced budget policy in Indonesia was introduced by Prof. Widjojo as the chief architect of the stabilization-rehabilitation policies, as early as in 1966.

In retrospect, it seems remarkable to consider a balanced budget at a period of fiscal chaos, when controls on government expenditures were lost and budget revenues dried up, not sufficient even to meet half of the expenditures.

Following an ambitious target of an overall budget balance in the first year (1967), another ambitious target of a routine budget balance without foreign aid was introduced in the second year (1968), as indicated earlier. In the third year a routine budget surplus, namely government savings objective, was introduced also by Prof. Widjojo as a major component of the development strategy of the Repelita I. In addition to add foreign aid receipts, Indonesians had to make every effort to meet a minimum portion of development expenditures (initially 25%), namely government savings.

A sensitive area in budgetary policies were budget subsidies, particularly food and oil subsidies. Prof. Widjojo's strong opposition against consumer subsidies received political support from the President to eliminate such subsidies at the early stage of the stabilization period. He was the force behind the dramatic sharp increases in domestic oil prices in early 1967, an increase of 700 percent (from Rp.0.5 to Rp.4 per liter) in gasoline and 500 percent in kerosene prices, respectively. The bold decision, a surprise to the outside world, was welcomed as a sign of determination of the Indonesian authorities to implement a serious stabilization program, as indicated earlier. It also reflected the power and political support given to the economic team.

A similar bold decision triggered by a severe rice crisis was taken in April 1968, the gasoline prices were increased 300 percent further, (from Rp.4 to Rp.16 per liter). The sharp price increase reflected the increase in production cost of oil due to sharp exchange rate depreciations during a 14-month period.

The main force behind the second oil price increase was Prof. Ali Wardhana, assigned by Prof. Widjojo for the job, as a member of the economic team. It was noteworthy that soon after the oil price increase Prof. Ali Wardhana was appointed Finance Minister in a cabinet reshuffle in May 1968, the first minister among the members of the economic team.

Finally, the austerity budgets as prepared according to policy guidelines formulated by Prof. Widjojo were implemented under a strict discipline by ministers Frans Seda and Prof. Ali Wardhana. They were supported by the IMF under stand-by arrangements as from 1968 as indicated earlier.

9. Monetary Policies

Stabilization programs in Indonesia were designed to decelerate monetary expansions as much as necessary in order to reduce high inflation rates swiftly and sharply. Major ingredients were budgetary discipline and credit restraint.

As a huge budget deficit was virtually eliminated, as indicated earlier, the monetary expansion over 700 percent were decelerated successfully to about 120 percent, during the first year of the stabilization period. The rate of increase in money supply was approximately the same as the rate of increase in inflation.

The policy objective of the Indonesian government was to reduce the rate of inflation by at least 50 percent each year. A monetary program for 1968 was prepared, as agreed by the IMF under the first stand-by, to decelerate the monetary expansion by half, on the assumption that there was no change in the ratio between the rate of monetary expansion and the rate of inflation.

The monetary program was conservative and significantly cautious, as favored by the Indonesian authorities. No change in the high velocity of circulation was assumed in view of the circumstances in Indonesia at that period (public confidence to local currency was weak under high inflationary conditions; also, the level of money supply as percent of GNP was low, reflecting low level of monetization). Nevertheless, it was decided that in case of a decline in velocity, indicating an increase in public confidence to hold currency, the monetary program would be modified to allow a larger monetary expansion.

Developments during the second half of 1968 were encouraging. Despite an upsurge in the inflation in the first half, mainly due to non-monetary factors (sharp increases in rice prices owing to crop failures), the inflation rate decelerated during the second half. As the public confidence to local currency (Rupiah) restored as a result of stabilization measures, the velocity of circulation of money decreased significantly, allowing a larger monetary expansion than programmed.

A larger monetary expansion was allowed within the bank credit sector (non-budget sector). The bank credit expansion was directed, on selective basis, to priority areas, in particular to replenish working capital of industries which had been sharply reduced in high inflation years. A significant part of bank credit increase was used to enhance the textile industry production and finance rice procurement operations.

As of January 1969 the annual inflation rate fell to 35 percent, where as the annual increase in money supply was as high as 92 percent. A monetary program for 1969 was introduced, as supported by a second stand-by with the IMF, on the assumption that an already substantially declined velocity of circulation will decelerate further, allowing a considerably higher monetary expansion as compared to the inflation rate target. It is noteworthy that, during the third year of the stabilization—rehabilitation period, representing also the transition to a development period, the annual inflation rate decelerated to 10 percent, while the money supply increase was 60 percent.

A larger expansion of credit not disturbing the price stability facilitated the rehabilitation of the economy and enhanced the production and growth. Thus, Indonesia entered to a growth environment, coinciding with the introduction of the first development plan (Repelita I) in March 1969.

10. Summary and Conclusions

As described above, the stabilization-rehabilitation measures introduced by Indonesia to combat a severe economic crisis were very effective, reducing a hyper-inflation over 600 percent to one-digit level in three years.

An exchange crisis was not only prevented but also a free exchange system and a stable unified exchange rate was introduced at the end of the period.

Under a strict fiscal discipline not only an overall balance objective was achieved, but also in the third year the government budget started to generate significant government savings to finance development expenditures, coinciding with the introduction of the first development plan Repelita I.

Of course the cooperation of creditor/donor countries to extend debt reliefs and progressively increase foreign aid to support Indonesian self-help measures played an important role to help Indonesia recover from the economic crisis.

Also, the IMF played a vital role both in assisting the preparation and the formulation of stabilization policies and support such policies in international fora such as IGGI and debt conferences and in the provision of financial assistance under standby arrangements.

However, the economic team deserves the highest credit for overcoming an exceptional economic crisis in Indonesia with an exceptional success.

Undoubtedly the most important factor responsible for the success of the economic team was the high degree of professional qualifications and leadership skills of Prof. Widjojo. I recall our conversations among the staff of the IMF and the World Bank about the Indonesian experience and Indonesian stabilization policies as a model. But at the end we were admitting that it was difficult to find Widjojos in other parts of the world to carry out such tasks. ◆

23

His Finest Hour:
Indonesia From 1966 To 1969

David C. Cole *

P erhaps the best analogy is a scene from the movies. An airplane
filled with passengers is flying through rough weather. One of
the engines begins sputtering and eventually stops. The plane, losing
power, slants steely downward and soon will crash to the earth in a
mighty explosion. The pilot turns to his chief engineer and urges him
quickly to try to restart the engine. After what seem like endless
minutes the engineer pushes the right buttons and switches and the
lost engine sputters back to life. *The pilot skilfully pulls the plane up
from the crash course into a level path then a steady ascent as it
heads on to its destination.*

The Indonesian economy in the mid–1960s had lost power and
was on a crash course. Food was short, inflation was rising, foreign
reserves gone, poverty pervasive. It was at this point that Professor
Widjojo and his team were asked to help restart the engines, so that
the economy could be pulled back up from its crash trajectory and
gotten back on its proper course.

We all know how the story ends. Perhaps it was not quite so
romantic as in the movies, but for those who were on board that
flight, the results were still dramatic. It may therefore be of interest,
especially for those who came later, if those of us who were there
record our recollection of some things that transpired in the cockpit
during that relatively brief period in which the Indonesian economy

* Dr. David C. Cole (US) was Coordinator of Harvard Institute for International Development (HIID) Program
for Financial Policy Studies and Training in Indonesia.

regained its engines, leveled off, then began to recover and ultimately to ascend into a high growth path.

The Stabilization Program October – 1966

The stabilization program implemented by the Indonesian Government on October 3rd 1966 has never received the recognition it deserves as one of the most successful financial stabilization programs in recent history. Not only did it succeed in bringing the rate of inflation down from over 600% to less than 20% in two years, and less than 10% in four years, but it also set the foundation for rapid recovery of a destitute economy and what has now been three decades of rapid economic growth.

At the time there were no "Standard models" for such stabilization programs. A number of Latin American countries had attempted to deal with their "chronic inflation" problem, but had not been successful. China had solved its hyper-inflation problem in the early 1950s by a draconian revolution that put the economy under state control. Japan had implemented the "Dodge Plan" enforced by the US Military Government at roughly the same time, but its success in achieving economic recovery was due mainly to Japan's becoming a supply base for the Korean war.

The stabilization program for Indonesia worked out by Professor Widjojo and his team in the latter half of 1966, in collaboration with a team from the IMF, led by U Tun Thin, had five main elements: closing down the budget deficit; slowing the growth of central bank credit and money supply; partially freeing up foreign exchange restrictions; renegotiating the existing foreign debt obligation; and opening the doors to foreign investment and foreign assistance. These may not sound very remarkable today, but at that time they represented a complete reversal of the prevailing Soekarno policies, and Soekarno was still nominally the President. Also, at that time Indonesia did not have formal relations with the international financial institutions and bilateral donors, because they had been thrown out by President Soekarno.

The stabilization program was discussed informally by Widjojo and his team with various foreign governments and international organizations, and once it was implemented, these entities began beating a path to Indonesia's door to reopen formal relations. They did so in large part because they quickly came to respect the intelligence and commitment of this group of young professors who had no previous experience in policy-making or management.

Within Indonesia there were many critics of the stabilization program. Some said that severely limiting growth of the money supply would bring the economy to a standstill. Others believed that raising taxes and trying to balance the budget would be impossible in such a poor economy. Still others feared that opening the country to foreign aid and foreign capital would lead to foreign domination. The Widjojo team spent endless hours explaining the program and how they hoped it would eventually lead to stability, recovery and growth. They did this largely out of faith because there were not many comparable experiences that they could draw upon.

I was invited to visit Indonesia immediately after the stabilization program was implemented because Professor Ali Wardhana knew that I had been involved in a somewhat similar, but much less drastic, stabilization effort in Korea in 1964-65. He wanted someone around who could not only explain the logic of the program based on practical experience, but also help anticipate problems and dangers signals that might require corrective measures. As a supplementary activity, in two Saturday morning seminars at Leknas, I tried to explain how restricting growth of the nominal money supply help change popular expectations about inflation and eventually permit an increase in the real money supply.

Poor Rice Crop – 1967

The stabilization program moved along pretty well during the first half of 1967, but then the rains in the middle part of the year were much less than normal. Deterioration of the irrigation systems, and failure to implement major reservoir projects in the waning years of the Soekarno government, meant that the dry season rice crop was basically dependent on rainfall. Shortage of rains quickly led to expectations of future rice shortages and rapid increases in rice prices.

The stabilization program had not provided for this contingency and little could be done to bring in sufficient imports of rice and other grains quickly enough to limit the rise in rice prices. Despite the restrictions on monetary growth, inflation accelerated in the latter half of the year and there were many who were quick to conclude that the stabilization program had failed.

Fortunately, Widjojo and his team neither gave up nor were repudiated by President Soeharto. They apparently concluded and were able to convince the President that the rise in rice prices was a temporary phenomenon resulting mainly from the poor rains, and that, if the stabilization program was continued, it would soon have the desired effects. In the meantime, the various aid donors committed to supply more food grain and build up stocks in Indonesia to offset future shortages. Also, Bulog was given more of a role in accumulating and distributing grain supplies and eventually in stabilizing grain prices.

In 1968 the rains were more normal, the dry-season rice crop was better, and the cost push effect of grain shortages largely disappeared. The rate of inflation declined rapidly after the middle of the year and the free exchange rate stabilized. When the newly reconstituted state banks were instructed to raise their interest rates on one-year time deposits from 30% to 72% in October 1968, this rates was sufficiently above the expected rate of inflation that deposits increased rapidly. As a result, there was a significant inflow of foreign exchange, the free exchange rate actually appreciated, prices leveled off, and the stabilization program was considered to have accomplished its objectives.

The dire prediction that the stabilization program would lead to collapse of the economy, rising unemployment and extreme hardship had been proven unfounded. Restoring public order, stopping roadblocks to collect "contributions", removing trade restrictions and increasing aid funded imports of basic commodities all helped to bring improvements in the economy and restore public confidence. This in turn provided a basis for beginning to look beyond stabilization to recovery and future growth.

Preparing the First Repelita – 1968

Work on the First Repelita did not really get started until the last quarter of 1968. By that time Professor Widjojo had been able to recruit some key staff members for Bappenas such as Emil Salim to head the sectoral division dealing with agriculture, industry and infrastructure, Saleh Affif to head the agriculture section, Adrianus Mooy to head the macro-financial section, plus some temporary assistance form Julius Ismael and others form the Ul Faculty of Economics. Also a large World Bank team, under the leadership of Bernard Bell, and a Harvard University team of four advisors, had recently arrived and were drawn into the process of formulating the Repelita. The World Bank team worked especially on the elaboration of rehabilitation projects to be included in the plan. The Harvard team worked more on sectoral policies in agriculture, industry, foreign trade, and macro-finance. Bernard Bell covered both domains.

Professor Widjojo did a masterful job of weaving these disparate personalities and interests together into a coherent and sensible program for Indonesia's recovery and future development. In the end Professor Widjojo spent three continuous days and nights "finalizing" the document to see that it was not only well crafted, but also conveyed the desired sense of priorities and directions.

Several key issues were addressed in the formulation of Repelita I. The most significant in my recollection were as follows:

Macro phantasies of micro realities: A typical five-year plan of that era normally contained a macroeconomic framework including projections of GDP growth, savings, investment and the balance of payments, often based upon a formal econometrics model. Given Indonesia's recent hyperinflation, chaotic statistics and probable but uncertain decline in real output, there was no realistic basis for specifying Indonesia's macroeconomic parameters as of 1967 or 1968, much less a set of relationships among those parameters that might be expected to prevail in the next few years. Some advisors counseled Professor Widjojo that the plan needed a macroeconomic framework, even if it was admittedly very speculative. A World Bank team even came out from Washington with a fully specified econometrics model for Indonesia that they planned to use to make forecasts and then test the internal consistency of the Indonesian plan (Bernie Bell quickly advised them to forget their model).

Professor Widjojo was never interested in trying to develop a macro framework for the plan, preferring to focus his and Bappenas attention on sectoral issues and the "sore thumbs" of the Indonesian economy—the obvious things that were standing in the way of recovery. As a consequence, Repelita I had no macroeconomic framework and no projections of overall economic growth, savings and investment. It did have a tentative budget, balance of payments and financial program for the first year, with the understanding that these would be reformulated each year as part of an annual-planning process. The most that was said, by Professor Widjojo and others in discussing the plan, was that its various components were believed to be roughly consistent with a 5% rate of overall economic growth.

Priority to agriculture: In terms of sectoral priorities, Professor Widjojo was clear from the outset that the overwhelming emphasis should be on agriculture. The number that came to symbolize this absolute priority for agriculture was a 15.4 million ton rice production target for the end of the plan period. This number originated from some rather simplistic nutrition studies that concluded this amount of rice would be needed in 1973 to feed Indonesia's expected population at an adequate nutritional level. Given that Indonesia's rice production in 1968 was expected to be somewhere in the neighborhood of 9 million tons, various agricultural expert suggested that it was totally unrealistic to think that production might increase by more than 50% in just five years. Still Professor Widjojo stuck to this figure and included it in the plan document. He used it to reorient the thinking of the agriculture sector in general. This absolute priority for agriculture was also useful in fending off overly ambitious proposals for other sectors. The final irony was, however, that this patently unrealistic target was in fact achieved by the end of the plan period. Agricultural development led the way in rehabilitating the Indonesian economy, and the improvement in agricultural productivity set the pattern for equitable development, benefiting both rural and urban inhabitants, that was to be the hallmark of Indonesia's development for the next two decades.

Rehabilitation or new ventures: The third major issue was the relative emphasis to be given to rehabilitation of existing facilities versus initiation of new projects. In responding to requests form Bappenas for proposed activities to be included in the new plan, many agencies found it easier and more compelling to pull out old projects proposals that had been formulated but never approved for funding in previous years. Often these were ambitious, capital-intensive undertakings that had limited economic justification under the prevailing circumstances. Bappenas, under Professor Widjojo's leadership, kept pressing the ministries and departments to focus on less glamorous activities that were likely to yield more immediate benefits at much lower cost. In this regard the outstanding group of World Bank sector specialists were particularly helpful. They travelled widely throughout the country, despite limited trans-portation and accommodation and were very good at identifying rehabilitation activities that could be included in broader sectoral recovery projects. These included irrigation facilities at all levels, plantations, seed and fertilizer distribution facilities, communication and transportation facilities, as well as some industrial facilities, especially those for processing agricultural products.

Linking Planning to Implementation – 1969

Once Repelita I was issued there was an inclination among some of the planners at Bappenas to think that their job was done and that now it was up to the rest of the government to implement the plan. It soon became obvious, however, that the rest of the government was inclined to set the plan aside and go ahead with business as usual, which meant submitting proposals to the Budget Directorate General for funding of new activities regardless of whether they were included in, or consistent with, the plan. Similarly various ministries and departments sought to negotiate directly with foreign governments and international agencies to receive assistance and move ahead with their preferred projects.

Senior officials from Bappenas quickly devised the DIP, or project implementation document, that had to be prepared by the requesting departments and then approved by Bappenas before the project could be included in the development budget on the requests for foreign financing. This provided a mechanism for linking planning, budgeting and foreign assistance requests in a manner that many other countries have never managed to do. It also gave Bappenas and its Chairman, Professor Widjojo, a means for guiding development expenditures, and for assuring that development spending did not become excessive and undermine the overall stability of the economy. It also helped to assure that adequate resources were channeled into reviving the agricultural sector and moving forward to that "impossible" rice production target.

These were some of the great accomplishments that were achieved under Professor Widjojo's skillful leadership between 1966 and 1969. It is not easy for those who came along later to appreciate how bad things really were at that time. Similarly, it is difficult for non-economists to appreciate what a remarkably difficult thing it is to have turned such a large and chaotic economy around from a crash course and get it headed in a positive direction. And it was even more difficult when the human and physical infrastructure of the country was so limited. For these reasons, it is important that we refresh our memories, review these experiences, learn from them, and give appropriate recognition to those who were responsible for them. ◆

Wimberly, Texas
April 27, 1997

24

He Knows How To Persuade
His Colleagues, His Authorities as Well
as Foreign Authorities

*U Tun Thin**

elow, the reader will find how the hyperinflation of over 600%
annually was stabilized successfully. Hyperinflation will begin
in a country when the citizens have lost confidence in their currency
and started buying substitutes such as real estate, gold, foreign
exchange or any other attractive commodities as a hedge against
general inflation rate. So, the solution is to restore the confidence of
the people. It cannot be done easily; it needs a complex series of
economic and socio-political measures. Widjojo's strategic thinking
does not allow him to act alone. To get the support, he would consult
his colleagues, top leaders and administrators. He is very modest
because he has no complex and when he discusses a problem with
you, you would think at the end that it was your idea and you would
naturally go for it. One great thing with him is that he is honest -
incorruptible.

There were many firsts in the standby such as flexible credit
ceilings, approving a standby when there is high inflation and a
flexible exchange rate without a promise when the rate will be fixed,
selling foreign aid to a private market for consumer goods, and very
liberal debt rescheduling, etc.

* Dr. U Tun Thin (Myanmar) was Professor of Economics, University of Yangoon; Commisioner of the Census
and Director, Central Statistical and Economics Department, Yangoon Myanmar; Myanmar Representative
to the Board of Directors of the International Monetary Fund; Assistant Director, Deputy Director and
Director until retirement, Asian Department, International Monetary Fund; United Nations Adviser to the
Government of Myanmar, 1989/1990; Senior Adviser to the Rector, United Nations University, Tokyo, for
several years.

Indonesia withdrew from the Fund in August 1965 and rejoined the Fund in February 1967. Why it took that long was only because of the formalities. The new government did decide from the beginning that they were going to become a member again. And so, until that time, we did have operations in Indonesia, not financial but in the way of advice. Our involvement there was in meetings with the donor countries for rescheduling aid and debt.

I discussed a stabilization program with the authorities in 1966 and a multilateral conference was held in Tokyo in September of the same year. A statement was made on the full economic program. That statement proposed balance in the state budget, a well directed credit policy, proper role for market forces, and establishment of a proper link between the domestic and international economy through a realistic exchange rate.

The meeting was held in Tokyo because of the fact that Japan was quite eager to have influence, and Americans were pushing Japan to take the lead. But later on, the lead was taken on by the Netherlands. The Tokyo conference was successful and people recognized there were problems of all kinds to be tackled. Then they decided to have a debt conference in Paris in late 1966 . We were also there, and at the time, Willem Everts of the Netherlands was putting all the data together about how much Indonesia owed. He was able to get the figures for 1966 and 1967. Thus, the debt conference in Paris rescheduled the debt falling due in 1966 and 1967. After they rejoined the Fund in 1967 the first IGGI (Inter-Governmental Group for Indonesia) meeting was held in Amsterdam.

At the time I had to gain support from the US in the person of Robert Barnett, a Deputy Assistant Secretary of State; he proved very much supportive. He and I had several meetings in Paris and also in the Netherlands, and it was he, Widjojo and I who made up the formula for aid to Indonesia, that one third should come from Japan, one third from the United States, and one third from Europe; and that of the one third from Europe, 50 percent should be from the Netherlands. It was an informal proposal but they accepted this formula.

Mr. Posthumus, a representative from the Netherlands at the IGGI meetings who later became an Executive Director in the Fund published a book on IGGI, in which he said " as it was difficult for most, if not all donor countries to analyze the situation themselves, the IMF team played an important role in the proceedings of the meeting and in the donor countries' decisions thereafter". So the Fund was used in a sense in this conference to give an analysis of the size of the gap, some description of policies and its endorsement.

The BE system was introduced; BE, which means Bonus Export certificates, were issued to the exporters and these certificates could be bought and sold as determined by the market. Depending on the level of exports they could depreciate or appreciate, but usually they depreciated. And so we asked the donor countries to let the Indonesian government issue the BE certificates against foreign aid so that foreign aid funds would go into the market to stabilize the exchange rate. Of course, the donors were initially resistant, but somehow we were able to convince them that this was needed to balance the budget. And so the domestic currency counterpart of the sale of these certificates would go to the government budget.

It should be mentioned that aid through the BE was to expedite the use of foreign assistance quickly; something like Fund money that they could use for whatever they like. It was a bold but successful step. As a matter of fact some Japanese came to complain to us that the Indonesians were now buying cassettte players, radios and music records. "We are helping to stabilize the economy and why should they buy these luxury goods?" So, we had to explain that the best way to mobilize the rupiah was to allow the people to import what they wanted, even luxury goods.

It was a major acomplishment to get the IGGI group to accept that the aid would go through the BE market. In fact, about two thirds of the aid went through the BE market. However, the aid amounts were quite small: $200-$300 millions compared to the present aid of about $3-4 billions.

This type of action had not been attempted before. This was initiated at the time, and I think it was because of the large foreign aid, almost unlimited in promise, that gave confidence to the people and stabilized the exchange rate. And that is why, at present, some countries, especially transitional ones, cannot stabilize because the donor governments are not as rich as before and therefore cannot give substantial aid. Because without sustained foreign aid, it would be very difficult to stabilize these economies and sustain the stabilization process. In Indonesia, the growth was almost negative when we went there. The infrastructure was very poor and factories were not running due to the lack of spare parts. So through the BE system, people could buy spare parts, renovate their plants which caused the growth to resume. The stabilization program in Indonesia, therefore, did not impede growth; on the contrary it promoted growth. This successful move has made Widjojo very popular ever since.

The main point I would like to make is that critical to the success of the early program was the annual rescheduling of debt, all principal and all interest. This annual ritual did not prove sufficient to restore confidence, particularly the confidence of foreign investors. And that is why they decided to completely break with past practices and appoint a German banker, Hermann Abs, to undertake a review of the entire debt problem. He came up with proposals which were accepted in 1970 by the Paris club and which resulted in spreading out the repayment over a 30-year period. His recommendation was that those countries which were not participants in the Paris Club, and they held more than one half of the debt, would be required to provide terms equally generous.

But this whole issue of how debt relief fitted into the stabilization program is important. I would emphasize that along with the willingness of the donors to provide program aid through the BE certificate market, the willingness of the donors and creditors to provide debt relief on exceptional terms, is another major ingredient of the success of the stabilization program. So, debt treatment formed a considerable part of the contribution by Widjojo, his group and the Fund.

We started our stabilization program in February, 1968. At that time, in the Managing Director's office the Legal Department objected why we should have a stand-by agreement with a country that had 50 percent inflation? Those were the days before high inflation in Latin America. But the Managing Director mentioned that the policy is not the concern of the Legal Department. So he went ahead with the stand-by. And since the donor countries were already helping, the stand-by was in a sense a supplementary action. Indonesia had, in any case, already adopted the stabilization program that we negotiated with them.

Inflation continued to rise though the exchange rate was somewhat stable at that time because of the intervention—but the price of rice was rising, due to a rice shortage in Indonesia. Knowing this, the Americans said that they were willing to give Indonesia food under PL 480. We had then a meeting in Jakarta called Food Meeting to which the Ambassadors of the donor countries of the IGGI were invited. We made a presentation showing that to stabilize Indonesia's inflation we needed more food aid, and asked them to give more food aid, additional to the money that was coming through IGGI. They agreed, and when they gave the necessary aid, the price of rice was stabilized. This led to stabilization in the exchange rate, followed by that in the prices of food.

Of course, credit expansion also had to be controlled. These three things had to work together, as just one or even two alone would not work. That is why I think in some countries the Fund was criticized because the Fund said, "you devalue"; and then they devalued, nothing much happened because of the fact that the foreign aid wasn't forthcoming like in Indonesia. That is the problem in many of these transitional economies.

During 1965-1968, the Fund got to accept that a system could be supported though it was not returning to a fixed rate at least not in the immediate future. Without the assurance of the staff that there was going to be an early fixed rate, the Fund was able to generate a stand-by for Indonesia. Of course, we had a certain amount of resistance from the Board but the major innovation of accepting a continued rate of inflation was supported.

There was credit limitation for both the public sector and the private sector. But we put in a clause there—being at the same time an innovative clause—which, to a certain extent, has become the current standard. The credit ceilings that we had agreed upon would be revised depending on the movement of the real cash balances; real cash balances is the rate of expansion in money supply divided by the rate of inflation. When the real cash balances increased, we had to put in a little more money because there would be a squeeze for the businesses. And so a couple of times, we went to the Board to prove that the real cash balance had increased by so much and therefore we needed to stop this cash crunch by giving more money supply and so on.

It worked, and I must say also that thanks to the Managing Director and the Deputy Managing Director, I was given a free hand in the Indonesian matter. I told Kemal Siber, the Fund representative, to call me whenever there was a need to change the money supply ceiling by one billion with the result that I had to be there every three months. I should mention about Kemal Siber from Turkey who did an excellent job supporting the programs

The professors came into power in '66. And they were very, very good. They knew exactly what had to be done. They participated in all the negotiations with us, with their own organizations as well as with foreign governments. I think I should mention that there was one thing they could not do, i.e. firing the corrupt officers, for a simple reason: if they rehired other people, they would also become corrupt in a very high inflationary situation. So we had to devise some means to collect the taxes. This was in fact the only country where we had two resident representatives: one for the Fund and the other for budgetary purposes.

I admit that compared to most other countries, as technicians the professors played a more effective role in Indonesia. They made up a group which generated policies that you could rely on. I think one of the salient features in Indonesia was Soeharto's early decision to put the trust in the technical people and to give them power. We thus found it fairly easy to cooperate with a like-minded group on most issues. So there was a symbiosis there, a connection between the linkage to the outside world, which I was part of, to mobilize the assistance and Wijojo, who was in the right position to be the linkage with the authorities to see that the issues we were worrying about be dealt with.

The professors, such as Widjojo, Ali Wardhana, Mohammad Sadli, Rachmat Saleh, Emil Salim, and Sobroto were in the Central Bank, the Ministry of Finance, Foreign Trade and Planning, all the central economic ministries, as well as line ministries such as Labor, Energy and Mines.

It was a very efficient team which made, in a sense, some of the financial controls that the Fund relies on so that we had a coherent policy. I did not find any occasion where we did not agree. In the IGGI meetings, I did not have to describe all the recent measures that Indonesians have taken; it was enough to say that the Indonesians and the Fund had agreed on the economic policies to be implemented.

They maintained the ceilings under the '68 stand-by, and we went into another one in '69. But we did revise the ceilings because of the increase in economic performance of the economy and the real cash balances.

Of course, revisions to ceilings are possible because in a sense ceilings are not contracts; they are check points and if they are exceeded, we are supposed to establish revised figures under which the growth of the economy, stability of price and the improvement in balance of payments will persist. The reviews went forward smoothly because we could establish that the program was on track—that despite passing particular benchmarks on the credit being given the outcome was not endangering the recovery path. And that was the key consideration presented to the Board and the Board agreed with all the staff proposals.

There is a new division of mathematics, called fuzzy logic. Computers normally solve problems by a series of yes-or-no decisions, represented by ones and zeros. But fuzzy logic allows computers to assign numerical values that fall somewhere between zero and one. Because it does not require all-or-nothing choices, the application of fuzzy logic makes computer-controlled machines run more smoothly and efficiently. For example, a subway system in Japan accelerates and brakes so evenly that a cup of tea will not spill. A camera takes perfect pictures even if the picture taker's hands are unsteady in holding the camera. Fuzzy logic, though introduced by an American, is used mostly by the Japanese manufactures. Western researchers are hesitant to use fuzzy logic because of their adherence to precision in all things which are scientific.

This type of flexibility was applied in the Indonesian programs. We set quarterly monetary ceilings, the objective being to stabilize prices, the exchange rate, and at the same time encourage growth.

The ceilings were precise figures, but the results depended on many things, especially the expectations of people. If the expectations are such that price inflation will not be as high as the rate of expansion of money, then real cash balances would increase. That was a good sign and we would make adjustments allowing more expansion in the money supply so as to induce more growth.

If, however, we gave that leeway from the beginning, then the country would spend that and would never get that real cash balance to increase. And therefore we had to control like this. And so I think it should be popularized more and more in the Fund.

I also mentioned that prices had to be decontrolled in order to abolish preferential treatment to the state enterprises who otherwise buy at controlled prices and then sell at subsidized prices. All these had to be changed including the closing down of some factories. Thus restructuring, which was quite difficult for a country to enthusiastically embrace, had to be done. *The change of the whole structure of the exchange system from control to decontrol, and the freeing of prices, and the freeing of the operations of the enterprises, can be done only by a strong government, i.e. a government that is not afraid politically and whose motto is, if this has to be done let us do it.* Of course there will be the help of donor countries and so it will be a combined effort. The Fund is criticized for shortcomings when one of these elements is missing. But where can you find a country where all the elements are present.

It will be wrong to think that it is easier for an authoritarian or a military regime to act more decisively and achieve results. Legitimacy does matter for policy making. We need, in a sense, a population that accepts our legitimacy and is willing to back us and give us time to achieve results from reforms. In fact, it is difficult for a government that has not done the right things for a long time to get the public to accept that it is now adopting austerity measures or changes which are going to give different results from the programs in the past. Their lack of legitimacy does not inspire confidence and people would think, this is just another step to a further deterioration. So the Fund can be drawn into situations where the politics is not yet jelled to the point where you can get confidence in the measures that are in fact going to stick and to stick absolutely to the right point to deliver the improvement. You need that political strength. You can not do it simply as a technician without a political base.

In short, bringing legitimacy to the country's economic policies was where Widjojo played the key role for success. *It was a great pleasure working with a talented intellectual who knows how to persuade his colleagues, his own authorities as well as the foreign authorities.* Without him, the stabilization program would not have been such a success. ◆

25

His Activities of Helping Other Less Fortunate Developing Countries

Dragoslav Avramovic*

It is a privilege and a pleasure to pay a tribute to Professor Widjojo and wish him many more years of fruitful work in his outstanding career.

On four issues I worked closely with Professor Widjojo: in the 1970s, on the commodity problem of developing countries; in the 1980s, on economic cooperation in the ASEAN; in 1990s on the development of the economic agenda for priority action of the non-aligned countries; and again in the 1990s, on the debt problem of developing countries. In all cases, it was a most productive association, which left me with admiration for Prof. Dr. Widjojo's dedication to development, his outstanding capacity for work, and superb relationship with his colleagues, in and outside the government.

We first met in Geneva in 1974, prior to UNCTAD IV. I was then serving as an advisor to UNCTAD, working on the conceptual framework of the Integrated Programme for Commodities. This is an organization of potentially decisive significance for the improvement of the position of developing countries in international commodity trade through financial action in commodity markets. Professor Widjojo was heading the delegation of Indonesia to the pre-

---

* Dr. Dragoslav Avramovic (Yugoslavia) an Economist, was Governor of the Central Bank of Yugoslavia in 1994-96. In his earlier career he was Director of the Development Economics Department of the World Bank, Senior Advisor to the Secretary General of UNCTAD, and Director of the Secretariat of the Independent Commission on International Development Issues (Brandt Commission). He passed away in 2001.

UNCTAD IV discussions in Geneva and to UNCTAD IV Conference itself in Nairobi, where the main negotiations were held.

His joining these negotiations was decisive for the advance that was achieved in Nairobi. Before his and Indonesia's involvement, the Integrated Programme and the Common Fund had widespread support from many small commodity-exporting countries. But some of the largest commodity producers were still believing, it seemed, that individual commodity arrangements would be as beneficial as an integrated approach buttressed by a Common Fund. Indonesia's belief in a broad action on the commodity front, its very large size as a producer and exporter of a range of major commodities, and Professor Widjojo's personal leadership made an important contribution to the cohesion and bargaining power of the commodity producers from the developing countries at the Nairobi Conference. Prof. Widjojo's involvement made a major difference.

In the early 1980s, when I was working in UNCTAD on economic cooperation among developing countries, Prof. Widjojo invited me to Indonesia to advise on analytical work needed to advance economic cooperation among ASEAN countries. I went to Jakarta. Professor Widjojo had made superb arrangements for my work with ministries and agencies involved in ASEAN matters, and I was in a position to suggest specific actions in the fields of industrial cooperation, trade and commodities cooperation, and financial cooperation, in a fairly short time. Prof. Widjojo's advice and hospitality were most generous.

In 1992, I was asked by Prof. Widjojo to join a small group of developing country economists in advising the Indonesian Government on the priority programme of NAM of which Indonesia had just assumed presidency. *It was an exhilarating experience: one had the backing of a government of a major country for a job one was doing, under excellent leadership and inspiration Professor Widjojo was providing.* This work subsequently evolved in Indonesia's support to the South Centre, a unique organization of developing countries, and it was my pleasure to be invited to contribute to some of the Centre's economic and financial investigations.

In 1993 Professor asked me to join the Experts Group on Debt of NAM, which he was organizing, together with Dr. Gamani Corea as its chairman. I worked with them both on the major study which the Group produced, and I believe some breakthroughs were achieved in the conceptual frame and the precision with which this work was carried out. We argued that for a large number of developing country debtors the scaling down of debt principal was called for, and we used market prices of debt to suggest its possible order of magnitude.

Professor Widjojo and I spent many hours on the telephone between Washington where I was then, and Jakarta, particularly in the early phase of the study and some of the more contestable technical issues involved. I should add that the prestige of the study when published in 1994 (The Continuing Debt Crisis of Developing Countries) and the influence it had imposed, were to some extent due to the fact that *Indonesia was not seeking anything for itself as it was not in debt difficulties; all the efforts that Indonesia had made, in which Professor Widjojo personally took a major part, was to help other, less fortunate developing countries.*

I cannot complete this note without thanking Professor Widjojo and Mrs. Tina Widjojo for the outstanding warmth of their home which I had the privilege of visiting when in Jakarta. ◆

Belgrade, Yugoslavia, 15 July 1997

26

His Role in Restoring
The Creditworthiness of Indonesia

Daniel M. Deguen*

I met Prof. Widjojo Nitisastro in rather tense circumstances: it was thirty years ago and, as Chairman of the Paris Club, I had the privilege—I should say the onus—of presiding over the settlement of the international debt of Indonesia.

Prof. Widjojo Nitisastro was at that time Chairman of Bappenas, the National Development Planning Agency, and mastermind of the exceptional recovery of the Indonesian economy which was to take place during the seventies. In that quality, he had the extremely difficult task to convince the creditor countries that, in their own interest, they should accept to write off the major part of their loans to Indonesia in such a way as to restore the creditworthiness of a major Asian country and to participate in the success of its foreseeable future development.

There is no doubt that the diplomatic implications of a good cooperation between Western Powers and Indonesia, in the then prevalent context of the cold war, had a great weight on the negotiations. The United States was clearly advocating a very generous settlement and its position, during the long process of discussions, was of course influential on most of its partners.

---

* Mr. Daniel M. Deguen (France) was Chairman of the Paris Club (1970) and Deputy Secretary of the French Treasury (1967-1970). Since 1993 he has been member of the "Commission de la Privatisation", an independent authority responsible for the transfer of nationalised enterprises to the private sector. Alongside with his official duties, Mr. Deguen was for ten years a professor in economics at the Institut d'Etudes Politiques de Paris.

Nevertheless, important obstacles had to be overcome to find a consensus.

First of all, the fear to create a precedent in the treatment of international debt problems. The Paris Club, an informal forum which had succeeded to solve smoothly, up to 1967, most of the difficult payment crisis between the developing countries and their creditors, had always adopted a case by case attitude, avoiding all general formulas and any agreement which could disrupt, in the future, a regular flow of public aid and private credits towards the developing countries. Reschedulings of the debt for short periods, partial waivers or renegotiations of interest rates were its principal tools for avoiding continuing defaults or unilateral repudiations of debts, with all the dramatic consequences that such attitudes have always had in the past. It was, however, clear from the beginning, that due to its simple size (US$ 2 billion), the Indonesian debt problem could not be solved by the same methods which had, up to then, been applied to Latin American countries or to India.

A second difficulty resulted from the fact that Indonesia was, at that time, indebted not only vis-a-vis Western countries but also vis-a-vis the Eastern Block for an even more important amount. No solution could be found if a similar treatment for both categories of debts was not negotiated by Indonesia. At the time, it was certainly not possible to invite USSR and its satellites to join the Paris Club, so separate rounds of discussions had to be conducted in parallel.

The third difficulty was to ascertain the economic viability of a settlement, taking into account the alleviation of the external debt burden accepted by creditor countries, the amount and conditions of the foreseeable flow of aid and capital available and the potential economic growth of Indonesia and its consequences on the balance of payments.

The first difficulty took several provisional reschedulings and three years of hard negotiations to overcome. Finally, Western countries accepted, in April 1970, a thirty-year period of re-imbursement for principal and interest payments due on government and government guaranteed credits. No further interests were to accumulate on the amounts thus deferred. Repayment was to be made in 15 annual instalments, beginning in 1985.

The second obstacle was also surmounted when the USSR signed, in August 1970, a similar arrangement for a long term settlement.

The third, on which the whole process had been dependent, was to demonstrate the credibility of the Indonesian stabilization and economic recovery program. It was obtained thanks to a very important technical assistance from IMF and The World Bank, to the authority of Dr Hermann Abs, Chairman of The Deutsche Bank, who was called in the negotiation as a mediator and proposed, to all countries concerned, the draft of a settlement and, finally, to the impressive efficiency of Prof. Widjojo himself who convinced all the negotiators that the final agreement was, at the same time, neccessary and sufficient to give Indonesia a sound basis of sustainable development. The progress made by Indonesia during the years 1967-69 was his best argument.

May I conclude these brief remarks by a personal reference: at the last phase of the negotiations it was still difficult to reduce the gap between Indonesia, who wanted a longer period of reimbursement, and some creditor countries, who thought 30 years excessive. As Chairman, I proposed to grant Indonesia the option to defer until the last eight years of the agreement part of the payments due during the first eight years and to open, furthermore, the possibility of a revision of the agreement after 1980 in order to either accelerate the payment, if justified by the economic situation of Indonesia, or accept further reductions of the contractual interests already rescheduled.

It is my great satisfaction, and it must also be Prof. Widjojo Nitisastro's, that this clause, apparently decisive in 1970, was never implemented. So fast was the creditworthiness of Indonesia restored and so fruitful, for all its partners, were the trade and financial links developed since 1970.

A few years ago, Prof. Widjojo Nitisastro expressed the view that the 1970 Indonesian debt agreement should be considered as an example for the treatment of debts of other developing countries. As a former President of the Paris Club, I would not adhere to such a generalization, except if the developing countries concerned entrusted the conduct of their economy to Prof. Widjojo Nitisastro. ◆

June 1997

27

His Role in Sensitizing the International Community To the High Debt Burden in Many Poorest Countries was Critical to Success

Mark Baird*

I first met Professor Widjojo in 1985, when I was a "young" economist working for the World Bank on Indonesia. He had asked to see me about some work I had done on Indonesia's public investment program and I was obviously flattered to have the opportunity to present my findings. As always with Professor Widjojo, he showed great interest in whatever was said. However, he was especially enthusiastic about a simple framework I had prepared for tracking project costs and sources of funding over time. He asked me to work with Bappenas staff to apply this to the planned projects for Repelita IV and offered me a nearby office to facilitate this work. This was a fantastic experience. But what I subsequently found out was that Professor Widjojo had in fact proposed such a framework himself many years earlier and I was now simply helping him implement *his* proposal! This was a pattern that was to repeat itself many times.

I was fortunate to move to the Jakarta office of the World Bank in 1986 and to work closely with Professor Widjojo over the next three years. He would actively seek inputs from many sources, including the World Bank, but always arrive at his own solution to problems. I remember one particular example in 1986, when Indonesia was considering devaluation of the rupiah. Professor Widjojo asked: what

* Dr. Mark Baird (New Zealand) was Vice President, Strategy and Resource Management at the World Bank (1997-1999); World Bank Country Director for Indonesia (1999-2001). He worked with Professor Widjojo during 1985-1989 as country economist on Indonesia, including a three-year assignment as chief economist in the World Bank Resident Mission in Jakarta.

should we do about prices? And we scrambled to give him the appropriate answers from World Bank experience. Again, he studied these with great interest. But then he said that Indonesia had experimented with different approaches to price changes after past devaluations. They had concluded that it was best to leave private prices free (because they could not be effectively controlled anyway) but to phase in public price adjustments (to cushion the pass-through effect). This is indeed what they did and it worked very well. Another lesson in development economics from the master!

Professor Widjojo is *the ultimate master of strategic thinking and planning. He would never see one piece of the puzzle in isolation or forget about the follow-up actions needed to make a whole.* This was evident after (and even before) the 1986 devaluation, when he immediately seized the opportunity to push ahead with trade deregulation. He argued that the devaluation provided added protection to import-competing industries and therefore there was added scope to reduce tariff and quota barriers. But he also realized that the short-term balance of payments (and budgetary) impact of trade reform could well be negative, compounding the problems caused by the drop in oil prices and exchange rate changes. He therefore insisted on a package deal, whereby the donor community—including the World Bank and Japan—would provide special assistance to close the gap and reassure international financial markets. Professor Widjojo orchestrated the mobilization of this funding with masterful skill. I do not believe anyone—least of all me—was sure it could really be done, certainly not at the levels being proposed. But, as always, Professor Widjojo's confidence was unswerving, and soon everyone was rallying around the cause. The positive donor response was a critical element in Indonesia's successful adjustment program.

The last time I met Professor Widjojo was at the Annual Meetings of the World Bank in Madrid in 1994. He was presenting a paper on Indonesia's experience with poverty reduction. As always, people listened attentively to what he had to say. But the real message was hidden at the end, when he talked about the burden of external debt. He concluded: "If you ask people working in a country to take care of poverty problems while worrying about the payment of debt the next year, I think that is too much to ask." Afterwards, I questioned him on this statement.—*He explained his concern about the high debt burden in many of the poorest developing countries and the need for the World Bank to take the lead in finding a solution.* In those days, this was almost heresy—at least in the World Bank—and so I respectfully disagreed. However, now, less than three years later, the HIPIC debt facility is a reality. *The role played by Professor Widjojo in sensitizing the international community to the problem—and providing constructive support behind the scenes to finding a solution—was again critical to success.*

I have had the privilege of working with two of the world's very best development economists over the past decade: Professor Widjojo and the late Michael Bruno. Both had that infectious curiosity in finding new ideas *and* doing something with them to better the lives of people. They motivated people by their commitment and their integrity, and their personal interest in individuals: for what they can contribute, rather than who they are. They measured their success by what was achieved, never by who got the credit. Indonesia and the World is very much richer by the contribution of Professor Widjojo. And I am one of many who feel very much richer for having spent some time in his presence. We have all taken—and learnt—a lot from Professor Widjojo. This personal tribute is a small token of appreciation in return. *Terima kasih banyak!* ◆

28

His Influence on Economic Policy Issues Extend Far Beyond Indonesia

Hubert Neiss *

It is a great privilege and honor to contribute to this volume commemorating Professor Widjojo's 70th anniversary. We at the IMF have long admired Indonesia's economic achievements and derived lessons from the sound developments' strategy and the consistent implementation of market-oriented policies under the stewardship of Professor Widjojo and his colleagues from the University of Indonesia. As a prominent member of Indonesia's "Economic Team" since the mid-1960's in various functions, Professor Widjojo was instrumental in bringing fiscal and monetary discipline to Indonesia's economic policy, removing exchange controls, and liberalizing foreign trade. While these policies are widely accepted today as the key prerequisites for sustained economic growth, this was not always the case in Indonesia and other developing countries during the 1960s and 1970s.

In the first half of the 1980's, in the wake of a large increase in resources from oil exports, Professor Widjojo played a major role in reorienting the development strategy of Indonesia to create a more dynamic and diversified private sector, and to eventually reduce the economy's reliance on oil and gas resources. At the same time, he was a highly effective proponent responsible for fiscal management to safeguard domestic stability during a period of accelerated growth.

* Dr. Hubert Neiss (Austria) was Director, Asia and Pacific Department, International Monetary Fund (1997-2000).

His strategic approach spurred rapid growth, which has continued in the nineties. It was my very good fortune to be assigned to the IMF Resident Representative Office in Jakarta during 1973–1975, which provided a special opportunity to observe the wisdom and insight of Professor Widjojo at close quarters in this crucial period. The experience has had a lasting impact on my own thinking and on my work throughout the Asian region.

The Indonesian Government and officials in many different agencies continue to benefit from Professor Widjojo's invaluable advice as Economic Advisor to the Government. Furthermore, *his influence on economic policy issues extends far beyond Indonesia*. He has been at the forefront of leaders from developing countries, including his colleagues from Indonesia, who have shared the lessons from their own experience, especially in the areas of fiscal management and on how best to limit the distortionary impact of state intervention policies. We are immensely grateful for this contribution, which has strongly reinforced our own efforts in promoting macroeconomic stability and structural reforms in member countries. ◆

29

Nikkei Asia Prize Winner

*Takuhiko Tsuruta**

In May 1996, on behalf of Nihon Keizai Shimbun, Inc. (Nikkei), Japan's leading publisher of economic news, I had the privilege of awarding Dr. Widjojo a Nikkei Asia Prize in honor of his work as a policy planner. His work has contributed greatly to economic growth in Indonesia.

Nikkei Asia Prizes are designed to recognize outstanding achievements that improve the quality of life in Asia and contribute to regional stability. *Nikkei established the Prizes in 1996 in commemoration of the company's 120th anniversary. Dr. Widjojo was the first award winner of the Prize in the regional growth category.*

I am convinced that very few would meet the criteria of the Prize better than Dr. Widjojo. He was selected by a distinguished committee chaired by a respected business leader, Mr. Gaishi Hiraiwa, former chairman of Keidanren (Japan Federation of Economic Organizations), the nation's most influential business organization.

Mr. Hiraiwa informed me that the selection committee chose Dr. Widjojo for two basic reasons. First, Dr. Widjojo played such an important role in helping Indonesia achieve economic growth through market mechanism. Second, the Indonesian growth model

---

* Mr. Takuhiko Tsuruta (Japan) is President & CEO Nihon Keizai Shimbun, Inc. (Nikkei).

to which he has been so instrumental has provided valuable lessons to other Asian nations.

As Dr. Widjojo mentioned in his speech in Tokyo in 1996 upon accepting the Nikkei Asia Prize, the fundamental economic transformation of a nation requires national resolve, determined leadership and clear directions together with mutually advantageous economic cooperation with other nations.

When we observe the current growth strategies of such countries as Vietnam, Myanmar, and India, I am sure the leaders of those countries must have learned and are still able to learn a lot from the experience of Indonesia of the last 30 years.

Dr. Widjojo's speech in accepting the Nikkei Asia Prize also reminded me of Japan's current position in Asia. While Japanese private sector is continuing to increase its direct investments in Asia, the Japanese government because of its budget deficit is now starting to curb the amount of official development assistance.

I believe that Japan in a spirit of cooperation should take more initiatives in the economic area to enhance relations with neighboring nations, as outlined in 1977 by Takeo Fukuda, then the Prime Minister, what has become known as the Fukuda Doctrine.

I believe that it is good for Japanese political and business leaders to be reminded once again of the spirit of that doctrine, as Dr. Widjojo reminded us of it in his acceptance speech for the Nikkei Asia Prizes. This spirit of cooperation will enable Japan to continually build and improve healthy and lasting relationships with other Asian countries.

It is well known that Dr. Widjojo worked with Prime Minister Fukuda in the late 1970s to enhance cooperation between Indonesia and Japan. Through his work, Dr. Widjojo also has close personal ties with other Japanese leaders. Among them is former Prime Minister Kiichi Miyazawa.

When my staff asked Dr. Widjojo whom he wished to meet at the awards ceremony of the Nikkei Asia Prizes, one of those he named was Mr. Miyazawa. When told of this, Mr. Miyazawa immediately agreed not only to attend but also to offer a toast at the welcoming reception for the winners.

In presenting the Nikkei Asia Prizes, our company wishes to better inform the world of important initiatives by Asians that will benefit people in the region now and in the 21st century. Prizes are awarded annually in each of three areas of achievement: regional growth, technological innovation and culture.

Dr. Widjojo is a most worthy winner, a man of achievement who has contributed enormously to growth in Indonesia and other parts of the Asian region. I sincerely wish that Dr. Widjojo will be blessed with good health for many more birthday celebrations. He surely will continue contributing to Indonesia and other Asian nations all his life. We honor him. ◆

30

Remembered as One of The University of California's Most Prominent and Successful Alumni

*David Pierpont Gardner**

I am honored to be included among those who enjoyed the pleasure and privilege of meeting Professor Widjojo Nitisastro and to be invited to submit my recollections in commemoration of his seventieth birthday on September 23, 1997.

It was my honor as president of the University of California and on behalf of the University to confer upon Dr. Nitisastro the 1984 Elise and Walter A. Haas Award. This Award is presented to a former foreign student of the University of California's Berkeley campus who contributed in special and unique ways to the development and improvement of his or her native country. The Award is made annually and is presented at the University's Charter Day banquet, which is the occasion recognizing the founding of the University of California in 1868. The Award was presented to Dr. Nitisastro in 1984 in San Francisco in the presence of nearly 1,000 alumni of the University and distinguished Californians.

I enclose as a reference the citation read and presented on that very special evening as the most succinct way of sharing the basis upon which this award was made to Professor Nitisastro. His record of outstanding contributions to his country and the important role he played internationally are all embodied within the text of this citation.

Beyond the formal acknowledgment I also recall his gracious and memorable acceptance of this Award crediting the friendships made

---

* Professor David Pierpont Gardner (US) was President of the University of California (1983-1992)

and the experience gained during his four years of graduate study at the University of California as having played a key role in forming his views, broadening his base of knowledge, and internationalizing his outlook on issues and problems confronting his country. We were all proud of his accomplishments.

He is remembered here as a man of great accomplishment, of high intelligence, of dedication to the long-term well-being of his country and of its further development and as one of the University of California's most prominent and successful alumni.

My warmest personal good wishes to him on this auspicious and, I am sure, most pleasant occasion when his colleagues, friends, and family commemorate the seventieth anniversary of his birth. ◆

The Elise and Walter A. Haas International Award
of the University of California

Presented annually to a former foreign student of the University who has made an outstanding contribution to his or her native land

Awarded to

Widjojo Nitisastro

Ph.D. 1961

For more than two decades, recognized as one of Indonesia's leading economists, you have contributed significantly to your country's stability and vitality. Your perceptive policies and skilled counsel were key to reversing a deteriorating economy and to giving new and promising direction to national planning which has improved the lives of your countrymen. After receiving a doctorate in economics from the University of California's Berkeley campus, you returned to the University of Indonesia in 1961 as Director of the Institute of Economics, and your reputation as a scholar was fully established. Then you were called to national service by President Soeharto to help him prescribe and administer reforms that brought such dramatic recovery to Indonesia's economy and recognition to the government of which you had become an important member. At the president's request, you also headed the National Planning Board from 1968, and continued in this post after becoming Coordinating Minister for Economic, Financial and Industrial Affairs. Despite your heavy cabinet duties, you represented your country at many international conferences in which you played a wholesome and moderating role. Your highly regarded book, "Population Trends in Indonesia", has been hailed as "a milestone in the attempt to understand and resolve some of the problems inherent in the complex demographic situation in Indonesia." It is well known that after you asked to be relieved of the official responsibilities you carried for over fifteen years, you remain an active advisor to your president and his cabinet. In November, 1983, you received the highest decoration of the Japanese government, the First Class of the Order of the Sacred Treasure. We are proud that the University of California, your Alma Mater, also recognizes your achievements. You are known throughout the world as a man of keen and clear judgment, and in addition, as the leader of the University of California alumni in Indonesia, many of whom are active in government at the highest level. For your many distinguished accomplishments, and for the invaluable service you have rendered to your country, the University of California is pleased and proud to honor you here today. ◆

Seal of the
University
California Berkeley, California
United States of America
March 23, 1984

David P. Gardner *President*

Ira Michael Heymen *Chancellor*

31

His Remarkable Accomplishments Serve as an Inspiration to Many to Make Future Contributions to the Global Economic Arena

*Chang-Lin Tien**

O n behalf of the University of California, Berkeley, I wish you a very Happy Birthday. It is fitting and appropriate that your alma mater and colleagues in higher education wish to honor you on your special day. *Your remarkable accomplishments serve as an inspiration to many and have paved the way for Indonesian students to make future contributions to the global economic arena.* As it is well known, your life has been marked by the following notable achievements:

- Contributing significantly to your country's stability and vitality by establishing policies and providing skilled counsel in economics.
- Giving new direction to national planning and improving the lives of your countrymen.
- Earning a doctorate in economics from the University of California, Berkeley in 1961.
- Returning to the University of Indonesia to serve as the Director of the Institute of Economic and Social Research and ultimately becoming Professor and Dean of Economics of the Faculty of Economics.

* Dr. Chang-Lin Tien (US): Chancellor of the University of California at Berkeley, CA. (1990-1997) – the first Asian-American to head a major research university in the US He was also A. Martin Berlin Chair in Mechanical Engineering. In 1997 he holds the professorial title of NEC Distinguished Professor of Engineering.

- Answering your country's call to service by prescribing and administering reforms for Indonesian President Soeharto and bringing about economic recovery.
- In 1968, playing an active role in the National Development Planning Agency at the President's request while serving simultaneously as the Coordinating Minister for Economic, Financial and Industrial Affairs.
- Writing the highly regarded book *Population Trends in Indonesia,* a "milestone" in resolving economic problems inherent to Indonesia.
- In 1983, receiving the highest decoration of the Japanese government, the First Class of the Order of the Sacred Treasure.
- In March 1984, earning the Elise and Walter A. Haas International Award of the University of California, Berkeley.

Throughout the years, you have earned titles and awards in Indonesia and in the United States at large. *The University of California, Berkeley, your alma mater, is proud to pay tribute to your life's work and to recognize you as a leader among alumni in Indonesia.* I would also like to take the auspicious occasion of your 70th birthday to applaud you for the many historic contributions you have made, and to offer my warmest thanks for the invaluable service you have rendered to your country and to UC Berkeley. ◆

32

An Economist For Whom I Have the Deepest Respect

Mitsuhide Yamaguchi*

I feel it a great honor to be allowed to contribute to the essays commemorating the 70th birthday of Professor Dr. Widjojo Nitisastro, *an economist for whom I have the deepest respect*. After retiring from many years of service in the Japanese Ministry of Finance, I became President of the Overseas Economic Cooperation Fund, Japan (OECF). I then served as the Governor of the Export-Import Bank of Japan (JEXIM), after which I accepted my current position as the President of the Tokyo Stock Exchange (TSE). These positions have afforded me many chances to travel in Asia, as well as a number of opportunities to enjoy the company of Professor Dr. Widjojo. *His excellent, broad academic activities and achievements have commanded widespread admiration, and I was always deeply impressed when I listened to his views concerning economic issues of the developing countries.* Backed by the studies of Professor Dr. Widjojo and others, Indonesia's central government has achieved rapid economic growth for the country through its economic policy and management. As a matter of fact, Indonesia's annual growth has been recorded as high as around 8% in recent years, supported by buoyant exports and consumption. The dramatic economic changes in Indonesia are now attracting increased attention from the people of the world.

---

* Mr. Mitsuhide Yamaguchi (Japan) is President & CEO, Tokyo Stock Exchange; after retiring from many years of service in the Japanese Ministry of Finance, he became President of the Overseas Economic Corporation Fund (OECF) and then Governor of the Export-Import Bank of Japan (JEXIM).

In this context, I believe that Japan should, as an Asian country, make an effort to contribute to further economic development and prosperity in the region, while maintaining the good relationships currently existing among Asian nations. In this paper, I would like to express my own views on the issue of economic progress of developing countries, which Professor Dr. Widjojo has made the subject of his life's work. *I will discuss the subject matter from the viewpoint of supply of needed funds from Japan for economic growth in these countries, on the basis of discussions I have made with him.*

In short, I think that there are three major funding channels, depending on the stage of economic development of a given country, which Japan can employ in order to play a role in the economic development of Asia. The first channel is the so-called ODA loan, a type of loan provided by the Japanese government through the OECF as part of Japan's official development assistance to developing countries. In addition, Japan has supplied funds via the World Bank and the Asian Development Bank.

These funds, including ODA loans, can be used to facilitate the establishment of an economic or social infrastructures in countries where an industrial foundation has yet to be built, and accumulation of capital is still limited such as electric power, transportation, agriculture and education. Since many of the projects necessary for establishing an infrastructure entail high commercial risk, it is extremely difficult to raise funds in the private sector for these projects. This is particularly true in the case of a country suffering fund shortages. Thus, the supply of funds with long repayment periods at low interest rates like ODA loans are critically needed. If the development of a country's industrial foundation is accelerated through cooperative measures such as ODA loans, foreign investment in the country will increase, and the country can build a base for further economic growth.

With the establishment of an industrial foundation, a nation's economic activity accelerates, and the per capita income level gradually rises. This economic base allows the nation to launch such projects as telecommunications which entail high risk but are expected to yield profits. These projects require additional funding, and here, the second channel becomes necessary, if Japan is to achieve its economic role. This second channel is the provision of funds through JEXIM loans along with ODA loans. JEXIM has provided vast amounts of funds to many countries, not only in response to the capital needs of nations witnessing rapid economic growth, but also as a means of recycling Japan's trade surplus.

These funds include untied loans, investment loans which support overseas direct investment activities by Japanese corporations, export loans, and resource-related development loans. Business activities supported by these funds contribute to an increase in job opportunities and vitalization of the economy of the country, which in turn leads to faster growth of the nation's government-related and private enterprises. Growth of the nation's economy helps increase national income, household savings, and the accumulation of capital. In addition, the country's money and capital markets rapidly develop and expand, as shown in many countries in Asia in recent years.

As the economy advances to this stage, the role of the capital market becomes more important. There is no denying that foreign investments, including joint ventures, contributes to the economic growth of a country through an increase in job opportunities and transfer of technology. Nonetheless, equally vital is the role of domestic enterprises, if the nation wishes to see firm and stable economic growth. The reason for this is that just as people generally have deeper attachments to the country where they were born and raised, a stronger desire to place roots in that country, and a stronger will to sail in the same boat with the home country, domestic corporations tend to be far more sedentary than foreign corporations.

In order for corporations to experience sustained growth, they need to acquire a more stable source of funding than debt financing, namely, equity financing. Some countries may also endeavor to vitalize the economy by privatizing government-owned enterprises. To meet such capital needs, the country must foster a sound securities markets. Both the government and private sectors of Asian countries recognized the economic importance of securities markets from an early stage, as evidenced by Indonesia and many other countries in Asia where securities markets have developed and expanded rapidly.

I wish to pay my profound respect to those who had the foresight to set such a plan in motion. When I had the honor of meeting with him in 1995, President Soeharto underscored the importance of the development of the Indonesian capital market, and in particular the Jakarta Stock Exchange, to further growth of the Indonesian economy. He informed me that the government had made various policies and taken actions toward this end. At the same time. President Soeharto asked us to extend further assistance to Indonesia for the development of its securities markets. The TSE has cooperated in Indonesia's efforts by dispatching TSE experts to provide technical assistance.

Some countries may find that the financing needs for corporate growth or privatization are too heavy to be met only with domestic savings invested in the securities markets. To help countries cope with this situation, I believe that Japan should supply the necessary funds through the third channel, i.e., stock investment, in addition to ODA loans and JEXIM loans. In other words, the time has now come for Japan to play its economic role in Asia by optimizing the use of these three channels.

At this point, Japan has sufficient ability to meet the capital needs of enterprises in Asia through stock investment. Japanese personal sector now possess ample financial assets which amount to as much as 1,200 trillion yen.

In conclusion, I think that the promotion of mutual understanding and cooperation in the context of fair, healthy competition is vital to the continued growth of the Asian region's economy. The younger generation will lead us in the 21st century. I hope that the rising generations in Japan and Indonesia will closely cooperate with each other to make Asia the most flourishing region in the world. I believe that Professor Dr. Widjojo is also earnestly hoping to see a thriving Asia in the 21st century. ◆

33

Is Equality Important?

H.W. Arndt *

I t is an honour and a privilege to be allowed to contribute to this celebration of the 70th birthday of Professor Widjojo Nitisastro, the wise leader of the team of technocrats whose harmonious, efficient and successful economic management of Indonesia over a quarter of a century is probably without parallel in the world.

In an interview on the occasion of the 30th anniversary of the New Order, Emil Salim commented on 'the criticism levelled against the Widjojo group—that their policy has created a wide economic gap between the country's haves and have-nots' (*Jakarta Post* 10/3/ 96). The criticism is perennial and it is as old as the New Order itself. In 1974 a distinguished political scientist of the Cornell School, denouncing what he saw as the Widjojo group's strategy of imitation of the developed industrial countries and integration into the capitalist world economy, was quite categorical: 'Evidence has mounted fast throughout the Third World that these theories and strategies can do little to alleviate poverty, that they tend to turn poverty into misery for the rural masses, aggravate the misery of the urban masses and raise underemployment to even greater levels of extremity' (Herbert Feith,'*Bulletin of Indonesian Economic Studies (BIES)*, April 1974:115).

* Prof. H.W. Arnd (Australia) was Professor Emeritus of Economics at Australian National University. Founder of ANU Indonesia Project and Editor, *Bulletin of Indonesian Economic Studies,* 1964-1983. Prof. H.W. Arndt passed away in 2002.

I would like to take this opportunity to discuss this criticism of the Widjojo group. Has inequality increased in Indonesia in the past thirty years? And how important is equality? I shall suggest that there are different kinds of inequality and that we need to distinguish the economic and political consequences. But before I turn to these issues, allow me to reminisce a little about my personal associations with Professor Widjojo.

I met Professor Widjojo thirty-three years ago, on 8 October 1964, my second day in Indonesia. Dr Panglaykim to whom I had been introduced by the Australian Ambassador, took me to the University of Indonesia, then still all in Jl. Salemba Raya, to call on Dr. Ali Wardhana. At his office we were soon joined by him and Widjojo. I recorded in my diary that 'both make an excellent impression'! Widjojo, recently appointed head of Leknas, the Government Economic Research Institute, suggested names of other economists whom I should see and arranged for me to give a seminar two weeks later, after my planned visit to Bogor, Bandung and Yogyakarta. On my return from Yogya, at Kemayoran airport, I found a jeep and driver waiting for me, kindly sent by Widjojo to take me to Kebayoran where Professor and Mrs. Sadli had invited me to stay with them.

On 23 October, at 12.15 pm all the talents assembled at Leknas, in Jl. Gondangdia Lama: Ali Wardhana, Sarbini, Sadli, Panglaykim, Emil Salim (recently returned from Berkeley), Benny Moeljana, Kartono Gunawan, Wanda Mulia, and two foreigners, Don Blake and George Hicks. Widjojo, unfortunately, was at the last minute called away by his Minister. I talked about the inflationary process, arguing (quite wrongly, as it turned out) that the hyperinflation then under way could not be slowed down and would have to be allowed to run its course until a new currency could be introduced.

Widjojo did attend my next seminar at Leknas, on my second visit in June 1966. The two-hour discussion on 'prices and interest rate, the budget deficit, free exchange rates and much else, with Widjojo in the chair, was led by Ali Wardhana. Others present included Subroto, Kartono, Emil Salim and Hariri Hadi.

In the following years, when I visited Jakarta four or five times a year, staying first with the Sadlis in Kebayoran and later with the young Australian diplomat (later my PhD student and now Deputy Governor of the Australian Reserve Bank), Stephen Grenville, at his house at Jl. Tosari 90, opposite Emil Salim's house—both houses have since been demolished—I would run into Widjojo occasionally. In Kebayoran, his house was next to Sadli's, and we would look in on him, or he on us, on one occasion in 1967 to discuss a possible visit by him to Canberra to attend a demographic conference. In Jl. Tosari, Emil Salim would sometimes ask Stephen and me over to talk about the economic situation; once, in 1968, I noted in my diary that we were 'lucky to find Widjojo and Guy Pauker' with Emil.

Two years later, in May 1970, I was invited to attend the formal defence of a PhD thesis, by a demographer, Nathanael Iskandar. The ceremony was held in the Auditorium at the University of Indonesia, before a large mixed audience of family, friends and colleagues. I found myself sitting next to Suhadi and Brooks Ryder. At the appointed hour, the solemn academic procession of the Rector and some dozen others entered, all in cap and gown with magnificent gold and silver chains. The Board of Examiners included half a dozen Cabinet Ministers—certainly Professors Soemantri Brodjonegoro (Rector and Minister of Mining), Sumitro, Widjojo, Ali Wardhana, Sadli. The formal 'Disputation' was led, appropriately on a thesis in demography, by Widjojo. When the prescribed hour was up, the Marshall broke into it, banging on the floor with his huge staff. The Board retired behind a screen for fifteen minutes, then returned to announce the decision—the candidate had passed—*summa cum laude.*

In 1971, I was invited to another great occasion. Professor Widjojo had been appointed to a United Nations panel of experts on economic development issues. In his honour, Professor Sumitro organized a very large party at the 'Oasis' restaurant, perhaps a hundred guests, including almost all the top Indonesian economists with wives and quite a few foreigners. There were speeches by Sumitro and Widjojo, I recorded in my diary that I had talked with Widjojo, Ali Wardhana, Rachmat Saleh, Radius Prawiro, Suhadi, Ismael, Subroto, Sumarlin, Moh. Sisman, and many others, including Mochtar Lubis.

In 1972 I was appointed to the Governing Council of the United Nations Asian Institute for Economic Development and Planning in Bangkok, established some years before to train officials of ECAFE countries. Widjojo was already a member. On my way to Bangkok, Widjojo joined my plane at Singapore airport—it gave me the opportunity to ask him to look at Professor Benjamin Higgins's 'Survey of Recent Developments' for the March 1972 issue of BIES. In the taxi to the Bangkok hotel, he gave me many useful comments on points of fact but agreed to differ about some of Ben's opinions. The next morning, the Council met to discuss the delicate question of the Deputy Directorship, Widjojo starting off. But this was his last meeting of the Council. He was succeeded by Dr. Sumarlin whom I had known since his return from the States and with whom I cooperated closely on the Council for some years.

In the following years I saw little of Widjojo who was constantly preoccupied with his key role as Minister and then Coordinating Minister for Economic Affairs. I would frequently be at Bappenas to see Sumarlin or Saleh Affif or Adrianus Mooy, or the foreign economists, from Bernie Bell, Mort Grossman, and Bill Hollinger to Tony Churchill or Dave Cole. I would sometimes seek an appointment with Widjojo, but he was carefully guarded by his secretary. I recall only two occasions in those years when I managed to call on him in his office, latterly just to the right of the main entrance.

In 1990, BIES celebrated its twenty-fifth anniversary. Encountering Widjojo at a reception in Jakarta in June of that year, I took my courage in my hands and asked him whether he would write a Preface to the anniversary issue. He agreed but said I would need to help him, which I promised to do. A few days later I delivered a draft of a few paragraphs indicating (with becoming modesty) how useful the journal had been to Indonesians and others. Widjojo added a congratulatory sentence, and in this form '25 years of BIES: an Indonesian perspective' appeared in the August issue.

My most recent encounter with Widjojo was last year, on the occasion of the conference in honour of Frans Seda. On the morning after my arrival in Jakarta, I phoned Sadli as usual and incidentally asked him for Widjojo's telephone number. Ten minutes later,

Widjojo phoned to say he would send a car for me. Punctually, at 10.30, his secretary collected me, and an elderly, efficient driver took me to the *Departemen Keuangan* building on Taman Lapangan Banteng Barat. At Widjojo's suite, he greeted me warmly, and we then talked for almost an hour. I showed him my most recent book (*50 years of Development Studies*), the latest issue of my Journal (*Asia-Pacific Economic Literature*) and gave him a copy of my little book of memoirs. I also showed him an article on the Balibo tragedy (of the five Australian journalists killed in cross-fire in East Timor in 1975) which I had just written for an Australian newspaper; he got photocopies made for himself and me.

I asked, without too much confidence—having been warned by Sadli and others that it was a long shot—whether he might be willing to be interviewed for the BIES 'Recollections' series, perhaps on the understanding that it would not be published until he ceased to be an adviser to the President. Widjojo was non-Committal; he agreed to inform Thee Kian Wie if, on reflection, he could make himself available. He told me he had read my paper for the Frans Seda conference and liked it. I had ended it by quoting from article by Sadli in which he had expressed his confidence that Indonesia would continue to do well 'unless the political leadership really commits a series of grave political stupidities', adding my own "Amen" or *Insya Allah*.

Later that day, as we all assembled at Atma Jaya University, I had the pleasure of sitting in the ante-room opposite Mubyarto, Widjojo, Sumitro, Sadli, and Subroto. *Kompas* the next day published a photo of the remarkable group.

Many others, even non-Indonesians, have been much closer to Widjojo than I have been. But I treasure the relatively trivial memories I have recounted here because *among the innumerable people I have met in my eighty years there is no one more distinguished and likeable than Professor Widjojo Nitisastro.*

Let me now turn to the issue of equality. The first point to make is that the policies of the Widjojo group have certainly not 'turned poverty into misery for the rural masses' or aggravated the misery of the urban masses'. On the contrary, sustained economic growth at an average rate of 6% a year over a quarter of a century has dramatically reduced the incidence of poverty in Indonesia. Between 1976 and 1993, the proportion below the poverty line declined by two-thirds, from 40% to 14%, and the decline was even greater for the rural than the urban population (Table 1). Nor has the distribution of income become more unequal, as measured by the usual indicator, the Gini ratio. This has remained fairly constant in urban areas and has actually improved somewhat in rural areas (Table 2). Of the East Asian countries for which estimates are available (the four NIES and the other four ASEAN countries), only Taiwan had more equal distribution than Indonesia in the early 1990s (Table 3).

Even if these figures can be taken at face value—and they have been questioned on the grounds that the poverty line is debatable and the Gini ratios are based on household expenditure surveys which do not adequately capture the very rich and the very poor— they do not justify complacency. There are still millions of very poor people in Indonesia, and some are a lot better off than others. But the evidence resoundingly confirms that the remedy for poverty is growth, not redistribution, of income. Even if it were possible to distribute Indonesia's national absolutely equally among all the people, this would not benefit the poorest fifth as much as a dozen years of growth of 6% a year. And complete equality is obviously impossible and undesirable. Even Karl Marx who thought an ideal communist society would operate on the principle of "from each according to his capacity, to each according to his need", conceded that in the meantime, under 'socialism', incomes must bear some relation to contributions. Society cannot work without material incentives. The objective at best must be equality of opportunity, not equality of outcomes.

In the rhetoric of the New Order in Indonesia, the development 'trilogy' has been prominent. In the early days, it was interpreted as 'stabilisation, rehabilitation, development'. Later it became 'stabilisation, growth and equality' or sometimes 'redistribution', Professor Widjojo has been said to believe firmly that growth must precede redistribution (Emil Salim, quoted by *Jakarta Post*, 10.3.96). Indeed, for measures to redistribute income or wealth, to promote greater equality? Is equality important?

The most obvious objection to inequality, of incomes or wealth, is that it is unfair to the poor. The poor could be made less poor if they were given a larger share of income or wealth. But if the objective is reduction of poverty, the most effective way, as we have seen, is to increase the size of the cake, economic growth. Of course, economic growth is not a sufficient cure for poverty. Large pockets of poverty are left behind and need special attention. That is the case for welfare services in the developed countries, though there are now second thoughts about their financial cost and the social consequences of welfare dependency. It is also the case for poverty programs in Indonesia of kind my old friend Mubyarto has long passionately advocated and now administers. It is also the case for government provision of public goods of special benefit to the poor, such as *Inpres* programs for housing, schools, roads and family planning facilities to which the Indonesian Government devoted much of its oil bonanza revenues in the 1970s and early 1980s. But the target here was and is poverty, not equality.

Most of us, moderately well-to-do middle-class people, find gross inequality distasteful, offensive. We support moderately progressive taxation on the principle of 'capacity to pay' (but would generally draw the line at the argument for subsidizing low-income consumers in the market on the claim that"the price mechanism is unfair to the poor'). But here again, our concern is with those less well off, not with inequality as such. Even Rawls defines justice in term protection of the poor, not equality. When some of us in Australia thirty-five years ago tied ourselves in knots trying to devise a really equitable tax system, my colleague Dick Downing finally said: "Let us look after the poor and leave the rich to God."

But it would be wrong to conclude that equality is unimportant. Economically, equality matters less than poverty. Any widening of the gap between rich and poor that economic growth may bring with it may be a price worth paying for the benefit of higher incomes and a better life for the poor. But socially and politically, inequality is divisive and potentially dangerous.

Envy is not pleasant, but is a fact of life. In Indonesia, as we have seen, there is no evidence that the overall distribution of income has become more unequal under the New Order. But there has been enormous and conspicuous increase in the wealth and economic power of a small number of individuals and groups, many of them well-connected politically. The role of these tycoons and conglomerates, many known or suspected of having acquired their wealth through 'cronyism', favouritism often bordering on corruption, has bred increasing resentment among the general public in Indonesia. While most of the recent incidents of rioting and violence appear to have owed more to ethnic and religious tensions, they are widely believed to be not unrelated to this resentment. In the longer term, it carries the risk, as the President has warned, of undermining Indonesia's social and political stability.

We have to remind ourself that the emergence of tycoons is an invariable feature of vigorous capitalism. American capitalism, in its late 19th and early 20th century heyday, had its Carnegies, Morgans, Mellors and Fords. The risk taking entrepreneur is the central figure in Schumpeter's theory of capitalist development. What motivates these people? Greed, the mere accumulation of wealth, is a simplistic answer. They want to flatter their self-esteem through achievement and acquisition of power. What ever the motive, entrepreneurship has been the engine of economic progress under capitalism. The lack of it has been the death of communism. Whether history will give credit to the present generation of Indonesia tycoons for Indonesia's economic progress into the 21st century remains to be seen, though it can plausibly be argued that, by introducing private-sector competition into an economy hitherto dominated by state-enterprise monopolies and by giving *pribumi* for the first time a substantial role in Indonesia's private sector, cronyism is performing a valuable function.

Is there then a case for greater emphasis on equality in Indonesian economic policy? The economic case may not be strong, but it would be in everyone's interest, not least in that of the economic and political elite, if the Government were to impose some restraints, especially by more effective enforcement of taxation and greater transparency in the granting of government contracts, and if the tycoons followed the example of their American predecessors by donating a large part of their wealth, now or in their wills, to public purposes through the establishment of foundations.

To this extent, equality is important. ◆

Table I
Trends in poverty incidence, 1976-93

Year	Numbers in poverty		(million)	%		of population
	Urban	Rural	Total	Urban	Rural	Total
1976	10.0	44.2	54.2	38.8	40.4	40.1
1978	8.3	38.9	47.2	30.8	33.4	33.3
1980	9.5	32.8	42.3	29.0	28.4	28.6
1981	9.3	31.3	40.6	28.1	26.5	26.9
1984	9.3	25.7	35.0	23.1	21.2	21.6
1987	9.7	20.3	30.0	20.1	16.4	17.4
1990	9.4	17.8	27.2	16.8	14.3	15.1
1993	9.1	16.4	25.5	14.2	13.1	13.5

Source: Hal Hill, 1996.*The Indonesian Economy since* 1966, New York:Cambridge University Press.

Table 2
Trends in the Gini Ratio, 1964 – 65 to 1993*

Year	Urban	Rural	Total
1964–65	0.34	0.35	0.35
1969–70	0.33	0.34	0.34
1976	0.35	0.31	0.34
1978	0.38	0.34	0.38
1980	0.36	0.31	0.34
1981	0.33	0.29	0.33
1984	0.32	0.28	0.33
1987	0.32	0.26	0.32
1990	0.34	0.25	0.32
1993	0.34	0.26	0.34

* Based on household expenditure data
Source: Hal Hill, 1996.*The Indonesian Economy since* 1966, New York:Cambridge University Press.

Table 3
Gini ratios in East Asian economies

Country	Gini Ratio
Hong Kong (1991)	0.45
Indonesia (1993)	0.34
Korea (1988)	0.40
Malaysia (1988)	0.46
Philipines (1989)	0.45
Singapore (1989)	0.49
Taiwan (1990)	0.31
Thailand (1990)	0.50

Source: Medli Krongkaew, 1994.'Income Distribution in East Asian Developing Contries', *Asian Pacific Economic Literature*, November, 8(2).

34

An Example for North and South

L.H.J.B. van Gorkom *

E arlier this year, we celebrated in the Netherlands the 50th anniversary of the Marshall Plan to rehabilitate Europe after World War II. The story was retold of how Averell Harriman, the special emissary of Truman, visited the Hague to find out whether our country was eligible for American assistance. Since it was a Saturday, the Prime Minister, Dr. Drees, received him in his modest house on the Beeklaan and Mrs. Drees served tea with a "Maria biscuitje". In the car back to the airport Harriman was overheard saying that the US could safely invest its aid funds in a country presided over by a man of such modesty and wisdom.

Much the same story could be told about Prof. Widjojo Nitisastro and the rehabilitation of the Indonesian economy after 1966. Whoever entered Prof. Widjojo's modest and somewhat cavernous office at Bappenas and listened to his views on the Indonesian economy, came away with the conviction that this man could be trusted and that it was safe to invest in Indonesia's future.

There are other similarities between the Marshall Plan and Indonesia's economic rehabilitation and the Intergovernmental Group on Indonesia (IGGI). In both cases, the essential conditions for success were:

---

* Mr. L.H.J.B. van Gorkom (Netherlands) was the Ambassador of Netherlands to Indonesia (1980-1984); He was the Director General for International Cooperation in the Netherlands Foreign Ministry. He represented the Netherlands Chairman of the IGGI. He works in the National Advisory Council on Development Cooperation and the Advisory Commission on Human Rights (since 1990).

1. the capability and the firm commitment of the country and the people themselves to rebuild their economy;
2. the political will of the other side to commit their long-term support for the process of rehabilitation;
3. equality of the partners;
4. respect of the supporting countries for the policies of the assisted country in the context of its own culture and tradition.

In the IGGI, all these conditions were met. The Indonesian commitment to economic and social recovery came first in the far-reaching policy decisions of President Soeharto and his economic team under the leadership of Prof. Widjojo, who initiated the economic measures known as "October Package" for the sta-bilisation of the economy and the reorganisation of the economic system. On this sound basis, the political will to assist was affirmed by the participants in the first meeting of the IGGI, convened by the Netherlands in February 1967. That political will was reconfirmed ever since, because of the consistent soundness and prudence of Indonesia's economic policies. The decision to convene the IGGI was one of the more fortunate initiatives of my country in its long and often painful relationship with Indonesia. It was due to the foresight of the Minister for Development Cooperation, Mr. Udink and Foreign Minister Luns and of their collaborators Meijer and Everts and young economists like Posthumus and De Wit. They all immensely respected and trusted Prof. Widjojo. [1]

It has been argued that the Marshall Plan was unique and cannot be repeated. Prime Minister Wim Kok, however, has proposed a Marshall Plan for Eastern Europe. The example of Indonesia and the IGGI shows that it can be done, provided that the essential conditions for success are met: political will and long-term commitment on both sides, mutual trust, equality and respect for the culture of the receiving partner. This last condition was always essential for Prof. Widjojo, but it has too often been disregarded in international development co-operation. In the case of Indonesia, no effort was made to impose Western style market capitalism, which

---

1 For the origin and first years of the IGGI, see G.A. Posthumus, *The Intergovernmental Group on Indonesia*, Rotterdam University Press, 1971.

would have been alien to Indonesian culture. Indonesia's insistence on adequate planning through its own institutions and in its own tradition and a realistic combination of public and private investment was always respected. In the case of Eastern Europe and in particular Russia, and of Africa for that matter, any effort to impose market capitalism by way of some kind of a "new secular religion" will surely fail.[2]

Easy accessibility was not one of Prof. Widjojo's top qualities. It took me more than two months after I presented my credentials, before I could call on him. I was unhappy about that delay, but other ambassadors had to wait more than two years. Prof. Widjojo was simply too busy for diplomatic chit-chat.

When I finally was requested to call on him on 19 November 1980, he opened up an entirely new perspective for the bilateral economic relations with the Netherlands and other industrialised countries in the IGGI. He pointed out that since 1966 Indonesia had made great economic and social progress and that, although external assistance would for some time be needed, the principle of self-reliance and enhanced national self-conscience demanded that the donor-recipient relationship be changed into a relationship of equality and mutual interest. He suggested a much broader and deeper model of co-operation between Indonesia and the Netherlands, covering an integrated manner. Besides aid and technical assistance, it should also cover such areas as investment, trade and access to markets, industrial restructuring and science and technology. If such a new, more integrated model of cooperation with the Netherlands could prove successful, it could be applied to other countries and to the IGGI as a whole.[3]

I was thrilled by Prof. Widjojo's suggestions, not only because they represented a tremendous new opportunity for mutually beneficial co-operation with my country but also because his views were similar to the new policy options on development and more integrated co-operation which in the months before my departure for

---

2 Cf. Pfaff, William, "Genuflecting on the Altar of market economics" *International Herald Tribune,* 14 July 1997.
3 Cf. Prof. Widjojo's address to the Davos Management Forum 1982, "In the Mutual Interest of Rich and Poor Nations".

Jakarta we had drafted in the Directorate for International Co-operation. We felt that development co-operation should be based on equality and mutual interest and should be integrated with co-operation in investment, trade and science and technology. These new policy options were first tested out with India in a successful high-level mission under the leadership of H.R.H. Prince Claus of the Netherlands, Special Advisor to the Minister for Development Co-operation.[4]

I cabled the report on my conversation with Prof. Widjojo to the Minister for Development Co-operation, the late Mr. Jan de Koning and urged him to make Prof. Widjojo's suggestion the central theme of discussion in his forthcoming visit to Indonesia as chairman of the IGGI. I forgot, however, to copy my cable to the Ministry of Economic Affairs, which obviously would have a major say in the matter, and this led to an interdepartmental controversy.

In our own Ministry, Prof. Widjojo's suggestion met with hesitations, presumably because they would affect the bureaucratic powers of the aid-sections. Meanwhile, the elaboration of our new "India policies" had led to controversy as to who should be responsible for them. In the end, I never received a reaction on Prof. Widjojo's proposals and when Minister de Koning visited Jakarta in the spring of 1981, he was not ready to respond to them. He promised a reaction within six months, but by that time he had been replaced by Mr. C. van Dijk who became absorbed by budgetary problems and a request from Parliament for a re-examination of our overall aid-policies.

Our failure to respond to Prof. Widjojo's suggestions was impolite to him; it was a missed opportunity for our bilateral economic relations, one of many missed opportunities in our relations with Indonesia.

In the IGGI, some gradual broadening of its scope was achieved, so as to include special topics like transmigration, energy and human resources development. Bilaterally, we gave more prominence to the IGGI-meetings. The Indonesian delegation was received by the

---

4   Our $ 200 million aid program which was almost totally unrelated to other economic relations.

Queen and the Prime Minister and in 1982 a "third day" (IGGI meetings never lasted more than 2 days) was added for Prof. Widjojo to meet other government ministers and private enterprises.

The story of Indonesia's remarkable and unique economic recovery and rehabilitation is well documented in the reports of the World Bank and the IMF, the press-releases and other documents of the IGGI and in economic literature. I refer in particular to William C. Hollinger's *Economic Policy under President Soeharto: Indonesia's Twenty-five year Record*, Background Paper no. 2, The United States-Indonesia Society, 1996.

From my own experience in Jakarta and with special reference to Prof. Widjojo's role in Indonesia's success story, I should like to emphasize some striking features of that story.

One of my most vivid recollections is the impressive quality of Indonesian Ministers and top-officials. I refer in particular to Prof. Widjojo and his longtime associates in the "economic team": Rachmat Saleh, Ali Wardhana, Moh. Sadli, Emil Salim, Subroto, Radius Prawiro, Sumarlin, Saleh Afiff, and others and their predecessors like Prof. Sumitro. I also recall with deep respect Prof. Mochtar Kusumaatmadja, Prof. Habibie, and Ali Alatas as well as military leaders like Nasution, Ali Sadikin, Yusuf, Panggabean, Sudomo, Simatupang, Sutopo Yuwono, and Supardjo Rustam. The economic leaders are often referred to as the "Berkeley Mafia". May I respectfully recall the "Rotterdammers": Sumitro, Radius Prawiro, Arifin Siregar and others and that lonely "Tilburger" Frans Seda? I often said to myself how I wished that my own country had so many outstanding ministers!

What I considered as unique was the leadership and the wisdom of President Soeharto and his remarkable talent to consistently appoint the right people at the right time to the right function. All the way from 1966, he thus ensured the indispensable continuity of successfully sound and prudent economic and social policies which, in turn, ensured the confidence of the international financial world and business-community.

President Soeharto's leadership also ensured a clear, workable and effective division of responsibilities between the *dwi-fungsi* of the Armed Forces and the Economic Team and the confidence and mutual trust between the two. Hollinger had pointed out the budgetary stinginess with which the armed forces were and still are treated. As an economist, Prof. Widjojo is a stingy man. In 1981, ABRI-Day was organised by the Indonesian Navy somewhere in West Java. Their corvettes, newly acquired from the Netherlands, used live shells and rockets to fire at a distant island. With each salvo Prof. Widjojo shrunk in his chair and muttered:

" There goes another $ 10.000."

An important condition for the Indonesian success story and a key element in Prof. Widjojo's thinking was the policy of careful planning and a just measure of regulation, combined with all due recognition of the role of the market and the private sector as well as the link between public and private investment. In fact, this applies to most Asian countries and represents economic thinking in conformity with Asian culture and tradition. Indonesia and other Asian countries have successfully resisted calls for the embrace of full-fledged market-capitalism and a Western inclination "to make market economics a new secular religion". They should continue to do so. Prof. Widjojo's wisdom should be heeded by the next generation in his own country and by Western economists as well.

Another policy element which comes to my mind is human resources development (health, education and population control) as a key to growth. Both President Soeharto and Prof. Widjojo are compassionate men: the welfare of the people comes first in their mind. I cannot recall meeting with the President or Prof. Widjojo without the conversation at one point turning to the Javanese farmer or the urban poor and the need for grass-root development. Hence the importance of the so-called *Keppres-projects* for the people, by the people which we encountered everywhere in the country and the successful role of regional planning in the Bappeda.

Besides the emphasis on agriculture and infrastructure, I, finally, recall the effectiveness of the Government's structure, with strong co-ordinating ministers and in particular the key role of the Co-ordinating Minister for Economic, Financial and Industrial Affairs, the function exercised by Prof. Widjojo for so many years.

Prof. Widjojo's strength and effectiveness was built on his capacity to conceive his economic and social vision squarely on the basis of Indonesia's culture and history and his capability to formulate and carry out his policies in the context of the actual political realities of the country. He did not interfere with essentially political and security matters and those responsible for stability and security did not interfere with his economic policies. As a consequence. Prof. Widjojo always strongly resisted any attempt to introduce matters of human rights into the IGGI, as demanded in some participating countries. Informally, however, he was always ready to listen to expressions of concern on human rights issues which were of great concern to him too.

I was never denied an opportunity to discuss questions of human rights, formally or informally, but I always felt uneasy to do so. The Netherlands government, parliament and press, are last and least entitled to lecture Indonesia on human rights. We denied Indonesia one of the most elementary human rights, the right to self determination, we deported and imprisoned their leaders, we fought a colonial war to preserve our power and we left no viable economic, administrative and legal infrastructure when we departed in 1949.

Human rights are no longer matters of internal jurisdiction. The Charter of the United Nations and the Human Rights Conventions have made them matters of legitimate international concern. The Vienna Human Rights Conference has reaffirmed the universality of human rights and, today, the Security Council can be seized with human rights violations. *Western human rights critics however, all too often disregard two basic factors, one of which is the time-factor, related to culture and history: before 1954 many black American citizens were not allowed to vote; barely two generations ago, the Netherlands fought a colonial war which, today, would be unthinkable!*

The realisation of human rights took and takes its time in all countries; not all human rights can be realised at the same time. *The other factor often disregarded is the equality and the balance between political and economic and social rights laid down in the two United Nations Conventions. Too many Western critics persistently downgrade economic and social rights below political rights.* In 1965 Indonesia was bankrupt, its people in desperate poverty. What President Soeharto and Prof. Widjojo and his team *achieved in one generation, stands out as an unprecedented realisation of economic and social rights.* In time, the full link with political rights is bound to be realised and implemented by the Indonesian people themselves.

It was a great honour for me, 13 years after I left Jakarta, to be invited to contribute to the volume in Commemoration of the 70th birthday of Prof. Widjojo. I was asked to share some of my impressions about him and my work with him in particular with the younger generation in Indonesia.

What I tried to write down is based on my experience from 1980 to 1984. Since then, Indonesia's economic growth and social progress have continued almost uninterrupted. Yet, the country still faces problems of poverty, environmental degradation, inequality and unequal distribution of economic power and the tension between economic and social progress and political freedom. At the time of this writing, South East Asia is hit by financial and monetary turmoil and the prospect of slower growth, "corresponding uncomfortably with an era of political transition with familiar leaders probably passing from the scene." (Philip Bowring in the International Herald Tribune of 19/20 July).

Thanks, again, to its prudent fiscal and monetary policies, Indonesia is, so far, not directly affected and, knowing Prof. Widjojo, I do not believe that he will pass from the scene so quickly, but precisely in this time of uncertainty and transition, it is timely and fitting to remind not only the younger generation in Indonesia but also leaders and policy makers elsewhere in the world of his outstanding qualities in guiding Indonesia from poverty to prosperity: professional competence, complete trustworthiness, prudence and courage, loyalty and deep faith in the culture and history of his country. ◆

35

A Pioneer of ASEAN Economic Cooperation

Gerardo P. Sicat*

Professor Widjojo is known for his enormous contributions to Indonesian growth and development in the course of his fruitful years of service in the government. *It is not as well-known that he also played a major role during the formative stage of ASEAN regional economic cooperation. He will therefore be remembered as one of the pioneers of ASEAN economic cooperation.*

The first time I met Professor Widjojo was when he paid me a visit in Manila in early 1975. Accompanied by the Indonesian Minister of Trade, Radius Prawiro, he suggested that Indonesia host a meeting of economic ministers of the ASEAN countries to strengthen cooperation projects. He gave an example of one promising area of cooperation which was designed to create a safety net for the supply of energy and food. This timely proposal was in line with reducing the adverse impact of the energy crisis and with improving food security in ASEAN countries.

The response to these ideas was very positive not only in Manila but in all the other ASEAN capitals that he also visited. By November of that same year, the first meeting of the economic

* Prof. Gerardo P. Sicat (Philippines) was Minister of Economic Planning and Director-General of the National Economic and Development Authority when he headed the Philippine delegations to the ASEAN Economic Ministers Meeting from 1975 to 1981. He joined the World Bank in 1985 where he has worked in various capacities: as chief of public economics in the Development Research Department, as economic adviser in the Economic Advisory Staff of the Senior Vice President for Operations, and as principal economic evaluation officer in the Operations Evaluation Department. He retired from the World Bank in November, 1997, thereafter his address is: School of Economics, University of the Philippines, Diliman, Quezon City; at present he is Professor Emeritus, School of Economics, University of the Philippines.

ministers of ASEAN took place in Jakarta as he had proposed. Discussions of economic cooperation among ASEAN became a hot topic of regional interest especially since it started in 1967. But there was disappointment on the scope of cooperation achieved at that time. One problem was structural. ASEAN meetings were considered the business of the foreign ministers. Since their periodic meetings often mainly dealt with issues related to political affairs, economic cooperation issues did not get their direct attention. Besides, the foreign ministers were not equipped to deal with complex economic issues. It was therefore essential that the economic ministries be more directly involved in the decision-making process towards promoting economic cooperation.

The first ASEAN meeting of economic ministers in Jakarta was conducted with great informality. After the opening plenary session in which President Soeharto gave an encouraging speech on future economic cooperation, Professor Widjojo as chairman of the Indonesian delegation invited all the economic ministers to talk among themselves. The small conference room accommodated only the ministers in attendance, and their executive session lasted for a whole day. Working in shirtsleeves in this informal and friendly atmosphere, the economic ministers literally learned from each other the various possibilities and the limits that prevented any quick advances in cooperation. They realized that a long drawn out process lined the road ahead. There were many possibilities, but they realized that many obstacles lay ahead as cooperation ventures were discussed. Visionary proposals of a common market or free trade would have to wait in the future. But they would have to set up a machinery for discussing and carefully scrutinizing proposals and work from there to determine by consensus which projects could be feasible. Thus, step by step efforts in cooperation would have to be made, and this would have to be undertaken in various sectors where those possibilities existed. More importantly, they had to get a mandate from the leaders of the ASEAN directly.

The reality was that the economies of the ASEAN countries were more oriented towards the rest of the world than towardseach other, despite their shared geography. Moreover, years of separate development policies in each country had built barriers to trade and cooperation. These obstacles to intra-ASEAN commerce were many. They were built in the course of years of developments as each country sought its own industrial growth policies after independence.

By 1975, the degree of industrial protection varied widely among the ASEAN countries. With the exception of Singapore, which had only a small market and which developed as a city state geared to open trading with the world economy (it was the entreport center for trade in the region), each ASEAN member country was bent on developing its own domestic market for its own industries. The result was that the industries of the larger economies of ASEAN— Indonesia, the Philippines and Thailand—developed under relatively high tariff and non tariff protection barriers. And Malaysia was on its own course to develop large scale industries. There were, however, advantages in devising industrial policies with regional market sharing in mind. This was the rationale advanced in favor of cooperation in new investment projects, especially those producing basic products used in industry—mineral processing industries, fertilizers, petrochemicals, etc. In the case of industrial finished products, there was also much scope for industrial complementation: the manufacture of component parts in several regional locations, creating specialization in the production of components so that, as demand within ASEAN rose for these products, intra-ASEAN commerce in components would correspondingly rise. Such cooperation would involve allotting investment projects by countries and aligning special incentives, including tariff and tax concessions. On a general level, the problem of tariff harmonization of existing high tariffs would take a long time to get off the ground, but the harmonization of tariff and investment incentives for new investments and industries would be a simpler matter, for this could be planned as industrial projects were agreed upon.

The reforms regarding the reduction of overall tariff levels would have to be approached differently. Changing the rates of protection of existing industries would likely meet strong domestic resistance. The business interests affected in the countries would exert pressure on their governments to make the adoption of tariff reductions impossible. For this reason, discussions of common markets and free trade regimes would be impractical. The approach would be to use the existing tariff regimes and to introduce margins of preference for trading among ASEAN partners. These principles of regional trading preferences were within the rules of international trading under GATT. In the meantime, they would be efficacious in approaching highly protectionist tariff regimes. The method sidetracks the need to change the tariff levels for existing industries, but would provide a margin of trading advantage to members of ASEAN. Even in this case, it would be important to introduce only those commodities that members of the group would be willing to offer within the framework of a preferential trading system.

There were also other practical projects for economic cooperation that did not raise a lot of controversial problems and which, therefore, would make a list of good projects to start with. One of these would be to work together on international issues where ASEAN interests were often already in agreement. ASEAN member countries have always been involved in the international discussion of commodity issues, as they are among the most important exporters of primary commodities—rubber, coffee, cocoa, vegetable oils, sugar, minerals such as tin and copper. A coordinated approach by ASEAN in the discussion of these international economic issues would strengthen regional solidarity. Improving cooperation in energy and food would be timely and would improve the safety net for supplies of these important commodities. The monetary authorities of the ASEAN could facilitate commerce and create greater liquidity by strengthening payments arrangements among them. These could include schemes to create faster currency swaps to facilitate exchange. Many projects in infrastructure, transport and communications could be accelerated and new projects could be planned with regional development goals taken into account. Thus, the pipeline of regional investment projects could be extended.

Other cases of cooperation would improve efficiency and coordination of existing practices in government regulations affecting travel and trade. Improving customs and immigration entry forms were obvious to travelers within the region who had to fill up forms which were not only complicated but which differed from country to country. These forms could be regularized and simplified, thereby easing business travel and promoting tourism in the region.

To realize these potentials, a machinery for economic cooperation had to be set up. As long as the proposals for cooperation lacked any channels where they could be discussed by the members, little action on them could be expected. The ministers therefore would propose a machinery for economic cooperation to the Summit Meeting of ASEAN leaders.

The Bali Summit of the five leaders of Indonesia, Malaysia, the Philippines, Singapore, and Thailand, which was held on February 23-25, 1976, issued the Declaration of ASEAN Concord. Two thirds of the substantive content of this declaration outlined future areas of economic cooperation in ASEAN, stressing four aspects: (1) cooperation on basic commodities, particularly food and energy; (2) industrial cooperation; (3) cooperation in trade; and (4) joint approach to international commodity problems and world economic problems. To achieve all of these, (5) a machinery for economic cooperation was to be entrusted to ministerial meetings on economic matters.

The economic ministers were asked to: (a) formulate recommendations for the strengthening of ASEAN economic cooperation; (b) review the coordination and implementation of agreed ASEAN programs and projects on economic cooperation; (c) exchange views and consult on national development plans and policies as a step towards harmonizing regional development; and (d) perform other functions as agreed upon.

The economic ministers created five standing committees to deal with cooperation matters in various sectors. Having in mind some division of labor and in view of the lack of regional secretariat resources (the ASEAN Secretariat in Jakarta was a very small body), the economic ministers divided the substantive work for economic cooperation by the work to technical committees to be housed in a country secretariat where a lead economic official could take charge of organizing agenda. The working organs of ASEAN economic cooperation were: the Committee on Finance and Banking; the Committee on Food, Agriculture and Forestry; the Committee on

Industry, Minerals and Energy; the Committee on Transportation and Communications; and the Committee on Trade and Tourism.

During the first five years of the ASEAN economic ministers meetings, these committees worked to develop their agenda of cooperation. The activities of the working committees built up quickly. A lot of the initial work was exploratory, but many tangible projects were put into action. During their second meeting of the economic ministers in Kuala Lumpur one month after the Summit meeting, they were already busy with discussing actual schemes for preferential trading arrangements. A list of industrial projects was prepared for the purpose of examining their feasibility by experts, and a mechanism for dialogues with other economic groupings to discuss joint approaches was proposed. By the third meeting of the ministers in Manila (January, 1977), the economic ministers approved the basic draft for the establishment of the ASEAN Preferential Trading Arrangement (PTA), together with the rules of origin and the certification procedures for implementing the agreement. By the fourth meeting (Singapore, June, 1977), initial trade concessions on a list of products was ready for implementation under the PTA. Working groups were established to study shipping issues within ASEAN. An action program on cooperation in transportation and communications was put in place, which included early implementation of various segments of the ASEAN submarine cable systems and establishment of working groups to improve the utilization of existing satellite communications facilities for regional and domestic use. And it noted the participation of ASEAN central banks in a US$ 100 million swap arrangement to help bridge temporary liquidity problems in ASEAN.

By the eighth meeting in Manila (in September, 1979, this meeting being the second round of meetings to take place in this city), the Preferential Trading Agreement (PTA) had achieved bringing the number of items under its regime to 2,327 products, and it was further agreed that every round of negotiations on trade preferences would increase the number of items offered under the system from 100 to 150 products for each country. An agreement was also reached on the ASEAN Food Security Reserve, which had already been initialled by the Agricultural Ministers of ASEAN. This meeting also approved the package settlement of a controversy that arose between ASEAN on the one hand and Australia on the issue of airline competition plying the European-Australia routes, which used ASEAN countries as a stopover.

This last issue was the first test of a direct confrontation with a third country. The Australian government issued an International Civil Aviation Policy (ICAP) which reserved for Australian carriers the benefits of long-distance air travel between Europe and Sidney. The ICAP was designed to give direct advantages to Australian carriers by regulating quotas on passenger traffic carried by non-Australian carriers and setting regulations which affected stopover traffic in intermediate travel points. This adversely affected ASEAN airlines, especially Singapore Airlines, which had the largest exposure to the air traffic from London to Sidney. By bringing this issue to the ASEAN economic ministers, Singapore was able to bring the combined strength of ASEAN to bear on this issue. The ASEAN economic ministers conference was able to pressure the Government of Australia to negotiate the issue and bring it to a mutually satisfactory closure.

The tenth meeting in Bangkok (October, 1980) especially noted the issue of oil supplies in ASEAN countries. In view of the disruptions of oil supplies arising from the war betwen Iran and Iraq, Indonesia was asked to undertake consultations with OPEC member countries in the Gulf area for additional supplies for ASEAN countries. In addition to noting the efforts of the ASEAN ministers working to strengthen cooperation and energy security, the meeting thanked the governments of Indonesia and Malaysia for the assistance extended to some ASEAN member countries to supply a part of their need for oil supply during this critical period. This meeting also noted the need to explore new approaches to expand trade under the PTA beyond negotiations involving mutual offers of tariff concessions by countries, and it approved a deeper tariff cut of 20 and 25 percent margin of preferences for items already under the PTA and to study the implications of raising the coverage of the PTA to trade items whose import values in 1978 were in the range of US$100,000 cif to US$500,000 cif, with an exclusion list for sensitive items.

By the time of the eleventh ministers' meeting (Jakarta, May, 1981), the first set of ASEAN industrial projects had already been on stream and advanced plans for a succeeding set of projects were under discussion. A basic agreement on an ASEAN Industrial Complementation (AIC) scheme was concluded, with projects in this area being planned for an automobile industry complementation scheme, with the range of projects being allocated among different participants. In terms of PTA, the total number of products included under the agreement was 6,581 items. The decision taken in the previous meeting (the 10th meeting) to include under the PTA all imports with a trade value of less than US$50,000 cif, as recorded in the trade statistics for 1978—a total of 4,508 items—with a tariff preference of 20 percent was considered inadequate. But the trade negotiators were beginning to run out of ideas using the incremental approach, and they were themselves becoming impatient. They were ready to recommend a major enlargement in the coverage of products, using trade volume as the basis. The economic ministers therefore decided to increase the cutoff level for imports further under the PTA. Specifically, they took these measures to further increase intra-ASEAN trade: (l)to raise the import values up to US$500,000 cif, based on 1978, with an exclusion list of sensitive items at the preferential rate of 20 to 25 percent; (2) to study further the implications of raising the concession level to US$1 million cif; (3) to study deeper cuts in food trade; and (4) to raise the voluntary offers per country to 400 items during tariff negotiations. Within the space of five years, much of the original room for step by step increases in the coverage of preferential trade was almost exhausted, and the time for examining a change in framework was evident. But it would take another decade before the big step towards a free trade area concept would be taken.

Professor Widjojo headed the Indonesian delegation continuously for a period longer than any economic minister during the early years of the meetings of the ASEAN economic ministers. I attended eleven of the economic ministers as head of the Philippine delegation until mid-1981, a total period of five years. There was a quicker turnover in the other country delegations, reflecting governmental changes in ministerial portfolios. For instance, during the period when I participated in the economic ministers meetings, Hon Sui Sen, Singapore's minister of finance, was succeeded by Goh Chok Tong; Datuk Hamzah, the primary industry minister, by then Deputy Prime Minister Mohammad bin Mahathir of Malaysia; and several heads of delegations of Thailand including Amnuay Virawan. *Professor Widjojo, backed up by Radius Prawiro, the Trade Minister, would continue to head the Indonesian delegation for a few more years. This helped to provide some degree of continuity to the course of developments in ASEAN economic cooperation.*

Forging tight ASEAN economic cooperation on a number of trade issues was not one that we had expected to yield major benefits quickly. As stated earlier, major difficulties were encountered once actual projects began to be discussed. Some of these were inevitably the result of discussion on project benefits and costs of sharing. This was best illustrated in the discussions of ASEAN industrial projects, which were possibly the greatest source of potential friction. Aside from discussing what types of industrial projects would be qualified, there was the issue of determining which country would undertake the project. The project would have to pass certain tests of project feasibility, and this to some extent depended on critical arrangements related to principles involving the pricing and supply arrangements. Details of project arrangements would also include the capital structure and other issues. In short, the project required a lot of micro-decisions on which government bureaucracies are unfit to act on quickly. In time, it would be realized that the ASEAN industrial projects were consuming too much time and were too difficult to structure because the business world moved much faster than governments. This is one reason why large scale industrial projects under the private sector and within a given country boundary were implemented much faster.

The ASEAN Preferential Trading Agreement (or PTA) had a relatively easy sailing compared to the industrial projects during the early years of the economic ministers meeting because it began to affect only the marginally traded commodities among the countries in a setting where the major countries involved had fairly high protection rates. Once those products became exhausted, the main issue was how to advance the trade preferences further to more sensitive sectors. Perhaps all that time was needed to prepare the ASEAN governments for the advantages of finally enlarging the coverage of their preferential trading arrangement. Once the trading arrangement reached these highly protected industries, the negotiations were likely to slow down or force a radically different approach. As the search for improved and deepened trade preferences became evident, the idea that a free trade area would make more sense gained greater support even among those who had thought that the setup was premature. As a result of the early frustrations of an incremental trading preference agreement, the ASEAN Free Trade Agreement (AFTA) came into being to replace the PTA, but this would take another decade of further efforts. When it finally took place, it marked, in my view, the second major leap towards regional economic integration. The first major leap was marked by the historic ASEAN summit meeting in Bali which outlined the need for the economic ministers to work on economic cooperation.

The benefits of closer ASEAN economic cooperation were almost immediately observed as soon as the economic ministers established the machinery for economic cooperation. The first impact was the change in the expectations of the private sector. The private sectors of each country responded eagerly. On their own, business groups across ASEAN countries began to get in touch with their counterparts in the other member countries. In turn, this stimulated foreign investment flows into the region. Private sector interest from other countries became more evident from the various meetings organized to enlarge the contacts of private sector groups in other countries with ASEAN country businessmen. Meetings of ASEAN businessmen with private sector groups from the European Common Market, Japan, Australia, other parts of Asia (including South Korea, Taiwan, and Hongkong) and the United States began to enlarge. The large flows of capital into the ASEAN region during the 1980s were the results of these increased business interest. Some of these foreign investment flows came in because of the high growth rates achieved in the ASEAN countries. But few of these were isolated from the perception that the ASEAN market was enlarging and that business opportunities were expanding fast.

A second, but more immediate, impact was the interest shown in ASEAN by policy makers in the major trading partners. During each of the succeeding meetings, the economic ministers noted the increased contacts with other economic groups to discuss issues involving trade, investment, commodities and industrial cooperation in ASEAN. By the time of the ASEAN Summit Meeting in 1978 held in Kuala Lumpur, the summit took on an "ASEAN + One" summit meeting with each of the leaders of Japan, the United States, and Australia. Although there was a political agenda included in all these ASEAN + One meetings, economic relations did not take a backseat either. A series of dialogues of the economic ministers with their counterparts in Japan and the United States also took place. The European Common Market (now the European Union) sent its officials to maintain a dialogue with business leaders and officials gathered in different capitals. The strengthening of ASEAN as a grouping also encouraged the faster move on the part of the larger group of Pacific countries—Japan, United States, Canada, Australia, New Zealand, and South Korea—to push forward the concept of the Asia and Pacific Economic Cooperation (APEC) to serve as a forum for common issues affecting economic relations among countries in this region. ASEAN member countries are members of this regional forum.

During the early years of the ASEAN economic ministers meetings, the idea of an ASEAN economic community was only in its formative stage. The germ of a large economic community could only be said to take a tighter form after it was realized that the small steps taken earlier were too small to move the organization forward more fully. More efficient arrangements were discovered only after experiencing difficulties with the existing projects. The beginning of wisdom was when the members themselves discovered that their own frameworks for cooperation were flawed and that they had to replace them. They had to learn from the lessons of difficult and slow arrangements.

If Professor Widjojo had not gone around the ASEAN capitals to propose the formation of the economic ministers meeting, the road travelled towards cooperation would have been postponed perhaps many more years. These early years were very significant in making feasible grander ideas of regional community that are now being discussed within ASEAN. These early meetings brought ASEAN economic leaders to come to grips with the issues of cooperation directly, to get to know each other at the working levels, and to cement personal and business working relations across ASEAN.

At the country level, these meetings created a deepening of understanding of the areas of possible regional cooperation. In terms of my personal experience in this process, working on ASEAN economic cooperation led me to work closely with my colleagues in the Philippine government also on regional economic cooperation. Among the officials directly affected by this involvement included the ministers of Finance, Industry, Trade, Tourism, Natural Resources, Agriculture and Transportation and Communications.

It has been more than twenty years since the first economic ministers meeting took place in 1975. Looking back today, it would be fair to say that had we not begun in that year, the shape of ASEAN economic cooperation would not be as extensive as it is today. We can possibly question whether we have achieved our goals about ASEAN. But goals are defined by their relative position in time and in terms of feasibility. The road travelled in ASEAN is more substantial than I could have predicted at the beginning. The "least common denominator" among the ASEAN partners has become much broader than when we first began. The framework for consensus is much more promising today over a wider range of issues than existed at the beginning. Now, a free trade area has replaced the preferential trade agreement as the cooperative vehicle, and there has been much greater harmonization of tariffs as a result of internal measures taken by each government trying to adopt economic liberalization measures to conform with what was best for their national interest. Also, as a result of the many achievements in economic cooperation in ASEAN, the common policies surrounding these economic cooperation ventures have bound all the countries to pursue common structural economic policies that are compatible with their own national goals.

ASEAN has become a much stronger organization especially after 1975 when economic cooperation activities began to help cement regional ties. In the 1980s, the five ASEAN members became six, with the admission of Brunei. Just recently, Vietnam, Laos and Burma have been added to this group of countries. One major cost of admission into ASEAN now is that any new member will have to accept the series of economic cooperation agreements built over the years. But these costs are probably little compared to the benefits of membership in an enlarging economic community. ◆

36

His Remarkable Stamina For Consensus Building In ASEAN Trade Expansion

Vicente B. Valdepenas, Jr. *

The First Summit Meeting of ASEAN Heads of Government in Bali, Denpasar on 23-25 February 1976 was a watershed in economic cooperation among the Member States of ASEAN. This Summit turned out the 24 February 1976 Declaration of ASEAN Accord on Economic Cooperation, which set the guiding principles of cooperation as well as identified the areas in which economic cooperation would be pursued.

A very key element in the guiding principles is the process of consensus building as the methodology of reaching policy decisions and bringing forward the mission of ASEAN economic cooperation. In the nearly 10 years of working with Professor Widjojo on ASEAN economic cooperation, the lasting impression I have of him is that of a professional economist with a remarkable stamina for the process of building up consensus towards a policy decision. As anyone who has ever worked in inter-governmental bodies including the United Nations system, the General Agreement on Tariffs and Trade/World Trade Organization, International Monetary Fund, the World Bank and the Asian Development Bank, getting a policy decision by a process of consensus is a slow and sometimes frustrating way of getting anything done. It is not the way to do things in Wall Street or in private corporations generally.

* Dr. Vicente B. Valdepenas, Jr. (Philippines): Chairman of Helenica Capital, Inc.; Former Minister for Economic Planning, 1983-1986; Former Deputy Minister of Trade, 1976-1983, Government of the Philippines.

Surprisingly, though, consensus building does get things done in ASEAN. While it involves plenty of time and effort, once achieved the consensus quickly translates into a program of action which eventually evolves into a much larger engagement and development than initially expected. This has been my experience on a number of ASEAN programs. My first exposure to the ASEAN process of consensus decision making was the negotiation in mid-1976 of the ASEAN Preferential Trading Arrangements (ASEAN/PTA), which went on for almost a full year. At the time, the ASEAN Committee on Trade and Tourism (COTT) was chaired by the Government of Singapore. Once a quarter, all the other ASEAN negotiators would converge in Singapore, crafting out over 3-day periods every paragraph of what eventually became the ASEAN/PTA. It was a time-consuming process. However, it was necessary as it defined the basic framework for the preferential trading arrangements which were to be subsequently negotiated among the ASEAN Member Countries. A complicating circumstance was the fact that several of the ASEAN Member States had by this time already signed up with the GATT and several others were contemplating signing up with it. Thus, the ASEAN/PTA negotiators had to carefully steer their efforts towards a framework agreement which would stand the scrutiny of a GATT working party that would have to determine whether it complied within the terms of the most favored nation clause (Article 1) of the GATT.

The following year, the handiwork of the ASEAN trade negotiators was adopted by the ASEAN Foreign Ministers as the implementing agreement on trade cooperation among the ASEAN countries. Over the next six years, rounds of item-by-item negotiations were mounted accrediting an increasingly large number of products for an ASEAN preferential trading club. Preferences were exchanged between ASEAN countries mainly on the basis of margins of preference on the existing tariff for a given product. Occasionally, there were commitments to simply bind the tariff at the current level. In the absence of a positive tariff, preferences took the form of commitments to bind it at zero. In the course of these negotiations, market access also widened as a result of a subsequent liberalization of non-tariff barriers to trade. Customs clearances for the eligible ASEAN tradables were also simplified.

Such a program of trade cooperation, while helpful at the beginning, did not go far enough. At the same time, new initiatives were being exercised within the GATT Council for a new round of multilateral trade negotiations as the Tokyo Round concluded its work. Thus, as early as 1981, the ASEAN/COTT began considering a more comprehensive program of trade cooperation. In one of these initial discussions, the present writer on behalf of the Philippine Government at the time tabled a working paper outlining a larger trade cooperation among the ASEAN countries. Essentially, it proposed the idea of a 10-year across-the-board reduction of ASEAN tariffs at the rate of 10% per annum. This implied that by year 11 ASEAN countries would bind their respective tariffs at zero as their contribution to a preferential market access for tradables originating from any ASEAN country. Several of the other ASEAN negotiators found this idea too difficult to sell to their individual authorities back at their capitals. It was accordingly set aside for the moment. In the meantime, everybody went back to the old track of item-by-item and margin-of-preference on the existing tariff modality of negotiating incremental market access into the individual ASEAN countries.

Meanwhile, the GATT Council was getting across its message for a new round of multilateral trade negotiations in efforts to rekindle a world trading system which has been withering in the aftermath of the 1982 international debt crisis. The GATT Ministerial Meeting in Geneva that year sounded a call for a new round of trade negotiations. However, this call went largely unheeded over the next three years. It took the GATT Ministerial Meeting at Punta del Este in 1986 to launch the Uruguay Round of Multilateral Trade Negotiations (MTNs). This Round went on for nearly six years, negotiating sector by sector a larger market access for everyone in the international marketplace and covering almost anything which was traded across national borders including financial services. Clearly, the scope and vision of the Uruguay Round would quickly dwarf the ASEAN preferential trading arrangements. Rather than getting lost in the shadow of the Uruguay Round, the ASEAN

Governments swiftly moved towards a comprehensive sector-by-sector program of trade cooperation and expansion. This time, they were inspired to embrace a program of trade liberalization within the ASEAN countries that would substantially bring down their respective tariffs on manufactures to between 5% and 0% by year 2008. Thus, the ASEAN Common Effective Preferential Tariff (ASEAN/CEPT) program was born. It also called for the elimination of non-tariff barriers to trade in 15 years from 1 January 1993. While it took a while to sell and excluded from its coverage some key sectors like raw agricultural products, the ASEAN/CEPT program represents a substantive improvement over the 1977 ASEAN/PTA program.

Some indications of this improvement in ASEAN trade cooperation and expansion are suggested by recent data on Philippine import and export trade with the other ASEAN countries, as the following charts show. In the period 1985-1995, for example, while overall imports of the Philippines rose 18.4% annually, its imports from the other ASEAN countries rose every year by 17.6%. The annual volume of imports from the other ASEAN countries averaged $837.2 million during 1986-1990, and $1,985.4 million in 1991-1995. This is a remarkable rate of growth of imports from ASEAN suppliers considering the fact that some 90% of the overall imports of the Philippines consist of capital goods, intermediate goods for further processing and mineral oil and lubricants. Over this same period, the share of ASEAN suppliers in the overall imports of the Philippines increased by 1 percentage point from 9.8% during 1986-1990 to 10.8% in 1991-1995. This suggests that the incremental market access provided by the Philippines to its ASEAN trade partners has progressively widened.

This is quite evident from the individual charts tracking the imports of the Philippines from Brunei, Indonesia, Malaysia, Singapore and Thailand for the period 1985-1995. A logarithmic trendline has been fitted to the annual importations which the Philippines has undertaken from each of these other ASEAN countries. Smoothing out the yearly fluctuations over the 11-year period, all the trendlines are persistently upward. Except for Philippine importations from Brunei which are limited to a narrow range of products, there has been a visible acceleration in the rate of Philippine importations from Indonesia, Malaysia, Singapore and Thailand in the last five years to 1995. This suggests that tradeables from these particular ASEAN countries are becoming increasingly competitive in the Philippine import market.

On the export trade, overall exports of the Philippines to the world market rose 14.4% annually in 1985-1995, while its exports to the other ASEAN countries went up by 20.5% every year. The annual volume of Philippine exports to the other ASEAN markets averaged $493.3 million in 1986-1990, and $1,088.3 million by 1991-1995. Over this 10-year period, the share of Philippine exports to the other ASEAN countries increased 1.59 percentage points from 7.33% of its overall exports during 1986-1990 to 8.92% of the overall exports of the Philippines in 1991-1995. One could infer from this development that Philippine suppliers are increasingly getting wider market access to the other ASEAN import markets. What is perhaps more notable is the fact that some 85% of all the exports of the Philippines are manufactures generally. This implies that Filipino manufacturers have become increasingly competitive in the import markets of the other ASEAN countries.

This is somehow confirmed by the country charts showing the pace of Philippine exportation to the other ASEAN import markets during the 11-year period from 1985 through 1995. To the annual exports shipped by the Philippines to these other ASEAN countries, a logarithmic trendline has been fitted. In every case, it is upward. In addition, as the individual charts show, there was a sharp increase in the rate of Philippine exportation to Malaysia, Singapore and Thailand in the last five years to 1995. This suggests that the market access of Philippine tradables in these other ASEAN import markets has become wider. The annual volatility of Philippine export shipments to Brunei and Indonesia during the same period apparently masks a similar market access liberalization in these two other ASEAN import markets made possible under the growing scope of the ASEAN preferential trading arrangements. However, taking the whole stretch of the 11-year period 1985-1995, the individual charts for Brunei and Indonesia unmistakably show that Philippine exportation to these countries is on the upward trend.

In conclusion, what began as a modest initiative in economic cooperation in Bali has become over the last 21 years of progressive consensus building among ASEAN Member States a growing program in trade cooperation and expansion. The lesson in all this is that there is virtue in slow but sure process of consensus at creating and growing regional economic cooperation. It ensures that every partner to the enterprise of regional interdependence gets something out of the partnership, and that nobody feels shortchanged in the process. This seems like the way to go about integrating everyone in the regional economy of ASEAN. It is a process which owes a lot to the quiet and confident ways of Professor Widjojo. ◆

37

The Rapid Reduction of Oil Export Prices in the 1980's Became an Opportunity to Increase Non-Oil Production and Exports by Way of Devaluation and Deregulation

Sumio Edamura*

1. Introduction

I feel very honoured to be counted as one of those lucky people who have had close association with Prof. Widjojo in the course of his fruitful and brilliant career. It is a real pleasure to talk of the rewarding experiences which I shared with Prof. Widjojo.

2. Effective and Sustained Cooperation

The Republic of Indonesia has achieved remarkable success in economic and social development in the past three decades under President Soeharto's distinguished leadership. Everybody is well aware of the crucial role Prof. Widjojo played in designing and implementing the development strategy of the country.

Indeed, in May 1996, Prof. Widjojo so deservedly received one of the first Nikkei Asia Prizes from the prestigious Japanese economic journal. It was given in recognition of his prominent role in guiding the Indonesian economy along the path of steady growth and development. In the short speech of thanks he gave for this distinction, he mentioned two occasions in which Japanese co-operation was particularly effective.

The first was when Indonesia was faced with a crisis of foreign debts accumulated from the era of the previous government. The

---

* Mr. Sumio Edamura (Japan) was the Japanese Ambassador to Indonesia from 1987 to 1990. Then, he served as Ambassador to the Soviet Union and the Russian Federation. After his retirement from the Foreign Service in 1994, he works as advisor to Daiwa Institute of Research, Sumitomo Corporation and East Japan Railway. He is also a Vice-Chairman of the Japan Indonesia Association (JAPINDA).

Japanese Government took the initiative of convening a conference of debtor countries in Tokyo in 1966. Eventually agreement was reached among the debtors. Then, the Japanese Government took extraordinary steps of amending relevant legislation with the sole purpose of removing legal barriers to the implementation of the agreed debt restructuring in favour of Indonesia.

The second occasion referred to by the Professor was when in the last half of the 1980's the price of oil plummeted drastically and the value of Japanese yen rose to a record high. This situation put severe pressure on the foreign exchange position of Indonesia. The Japanese Government helped Indonesia overcome the crisis by providing an ample amount of new money in the form of soft loans. In fact, the amount of financial assistance provided by Japan in 1988 was double that of the year before.

On this second occasion I was the Japanese Ambassador in Jakarta. I was in constant contact with Prof. Widjojo, trying together to find out an effective and viable formula for Japanese assistance. When I received the final instruction from Tokyo containing an aid package worked out with utmost consideration to the needs of Indonesia, I found out that Prof. Widjojo was attending a national day reception at the Embassy of Turkey. I could not wait for Prof. Widjojo to return home. I hurried to the Turkish Ambassador's residence. There, at the side of the porch of the residence, we reached agreement on the outline of Japanese assistance for the next year. It was in the evening, starting to get dark. But I can still recall quite vividly how a smile of satisfaction started to take shape in Prof. Widjojo's intelligent face as he listened to my explanation.

In his speech at the prize awarding ceremony, Prof. Widjojo, by quoting these two examples, explained how effective Japanese official development assistance to Indonesia has been to meet the real needs of Indonesia at various contingencies.

I first met Prof. Widjojo in 1969, when I was a counsellor at our Embassy in Jakarta. It was the first year of the first Repelita. Since then Japan has increased its assistance in a consistent and continuous manner as Indonesia's development needs have continued to grow. I feel that the Japanese Government and people may be allowed to take a just pride in having been consistent and continuous in its efforts to assist in the development of Indonesia over those decades.

3. Consistent and Continuous Indonesian Efforts

Consistent and continuous efforts have also been the economic policy of Indonesia throughout these years. Its sound fiscal policy has been consistent. Its efforts for the promotion of exports through liberalization and deregulation have been continuous.

As I mentioned earlier, *in the final years of 1980's a big drop in oil price had created severe difficulty for the Indonesian economy. But the Indonesian Government saw it as a "blessing in disguise". In its view, the drop in oil price provided a golden opportunity to correct Indonesia's excessive dependence on income from oil and gas sales, and started to promote vigourously the exports of non-migas (non-oil and gas) products.*

This was a brave strategy. I was greatly impressed with it. I was even more impressed when in fact the exports of non-migas products exceeded migas exports only in a matter of a year or two. Today, Indonesia's non-oil/gas exports are almost four times greater than those of oil and gas. What made this achievement even more admirable is the fact that it was achieved through the policy of liberalization and deregulation.

This policy enabled Indonesian industries to import capital goods and intermediate materials at low prices. This policy also encouraged foreign investment in Indonesia, bringing in needed capital and technologies. As a result, the ability of Indonesian textile and other products to compete in world markets has been greatly strengthened.

When I called on Prof. Widjojo on my last trip to Indonesia, he gave me a paper submitted at the Consultative Group meeting held in Paris on June 19-20, 1996. It was a paper on June 1996 deregulation, setting forth an impressive package of measures for deregulation on various aspects of the Indonesian economy. I was pleased to know that the commitment of Prof. Widjojo and his associates to the policy of liberalization and deregulation remained unchanged, despite some recent developments which had cast a slight shadow of apprehension in my mind.

4. Good Wishes For Prof. Widjojo's Continued Good Health

Thanks to the confidence in the economic policy of Indonesia created by its continuity and consistency, private investments from Japan have continued to grow. The accumulated total of Japanese investments in Indonesia occupies the number one position among foreign investors with the figure of almost 35 billion US dollars as of the end of 1996.

Indeed, Japan-Indonesia cooperation both in the official and private sectors has been a pillar and axis of the vast and profound economic interdependence in East Asia which now exists to the benefit of all the countries and areas in the region.

On the basis of these achievements, some people both in Indonesia and Japan have gone so far as to say that *the Japan-Indonesia relationship in recent years may be regarded as a model of the relations between two countries at different stages of development.*

If indeed this is true, we are greatly indebted to Prof. Widjojo's wisdom and intelligence for this happy state of affairs.

I would like to express my heart-felt appreciation for the great contributions he rendered to his country and his people and also for the consolidation of friendly ties between our two nations. On this happy occasion of celebrating the 70th anniversary of Prof. Widjojo's birth I would like to join his numerous Indonesian and foreign admirers in wishing for his continued good health. ◆

38

It is Encouraging to See Younger Officials and Scholars Whom He Had Educated Now Treasuring His Legacy and Meeting New Challenges

*Michihiko Kunihiro**

I was pleased more than anybody else in the selection committee when it agreed on awarding Prof. Dr. Widjojo Nitisastro the Nikkei Asia Prize for Regional Growth last year.

Bapak Widjojo—chosen from among about a dozen candidates— was the first to receive the Award. He amply deserves it since he is indeed the pioneer of strategy for economic development in South East Asia.

It was almost thirty years ago (1969) when I met *Bapak* Widjojo for the first time. He was chairman of the Bappenas then and came to Japan rather frequently to negotiate Japanese aid to Indonesia. Since I was a junior official (deputy director of the office in charge of Yen loans in the Ministry of Foreign Affairs), I did not have much time to talk personally with him. But *Bapak* Widjojo, flanked by Dr. Rachmat Saleh, Deputy President of the Bank of Indonesia and Prof. Emil Salim, Deputy Chairman of Bappenas, developed a way of *musyawarah* with Japanese political leaders as well as government officials by judiciously talking with them. He must have been shouldering a daunting task at that time; he had to get the rescheduling of the debt, a staggering amount by the standard then,

---

* Mr. Michihiko Kunihiro (Japan) was Minister at the Embassy of Japan in Indonesia (1975-1978) and later in 1990 he was Japanese Ambassador to the Republic of Indonesia until 1992. He retired from the foreign service in 1995 after serving as Japanese Ambassador in China and is currently advisor to the Chairman of Keizai Doyukai (Japanese Association of Corporate Executives), NTT Data Corporation and other private companies.

inherited from the previous regime and, at the same time, to get a commitment for new loans.

Japan's resources for foreign aid was still very much limited and Japan had legal problems to deal with such a rescue project. But he patiently and forcefully explained Indonesia's difficult situations and policy to reconstruct its economy. He did not mind repeating the same explanations to different people and different organizations. He talked to administrative officials as earnestly as to political leaders. I am sure he did the same with the World Bank officials, Americans and Europeans. I saw many Japanese so much impressed by *Bapak* Widjojo's reasoning presented with clarity and enthusiasm that they became converts nursing sense of trust in his development policy.

Back in his own country, he must have been confronted with pressures: demand for easy money for rebuilding particular sectors of Indonesian industry, demand for raising the salary of government officials, need to spend scarce foreign exchange for the imports of food, etc. But we knew he stood firm in the management of an austere fiscal policy with the support of President Soeharto. He could have occasional set backs, but he sustained the confidence of donor countries by sticking to what we call today a sound macro-economic control.

Japan began Yen-loan aid to India. But it was through the experiences with Indonesia that Japan developed its aids policy which served as a model in extending economic cooperation to developing countries. The rapport between the Japanese officials and Indonesian counterparts was almost exemplary, and as I look back today, even romantic. Those Japanese and Indonesian officials and engineers engaged in the 3-K project (Brantas), for example, were united in not only the implementation of the project but also raising skilled public works engineers in Indonesia.

For two and a half years from 1975, I was stationed in Jakarta as the deputy head of the Embassy. During that period, I had many opportunities to talk and work with *Bapak* Widjojo, Chairman of Bappenas and Coordinating Minister for Economic, Financial and Industrial Affairs. On the strength of our personal acquaintance, I was accorded opportunities for personally meeting him on various subjects. As it was after the Malari incident and oil boom, the general mood in Indonesia was different from the one I used to know, but the attitude *of Bapak* Widjojo was the same. He was just as sincere and gentle as before. His policy stance was as firm as before although evidently he had to deal with anti IMF-World Bank sentiment from both the political field and the private industry. Accordingly, the confidence of Japanese Government in him remained the same.

When I returned to Jakarta as Ambassador in 1990, *Bapak* Widjojo was the advisor to the President. But I had no doubt that he had strong influence in the decision making of fundamental economic policies. He was up-to-date with any major problems the Indonesian economy was confronted with. Also, he continued to play a crucial role as interlocutor between Japan and Indonesia. As a matter of fact, I took the liberty of looking to him as an invaluable advisor to me.

He even acted internationally as interlocutor for Japan. I heard that when an American criticized Japan—at an international symposium—for using ODA for commercial purposes, he stood up to remind that America's knowledge was out of date; the fact being that since many years before, Japan had stopped tying its yen loans to its exports. I had the pleasure of representing my government at two IGGI meetings, where *Bapak* Widjojo played a key role in seeing to it that the donor countries, the World Bank and Indonesia speak a common language.

A big change was emerging in the Indonesian economy, then. That was a change for liberalizing and opening the Indonesian economy to the world. Indonesia was able to bring about the necessary change successfully, thanks to the tradition of the sound macro economic policy and the improved infrastructure albeit the need for further improvement. *I was encouraged to see those younger officials and scholars whom Bapak Widjojo had educated now treasuring his legacy and meeting new challenges.*

The new challenges cannot be underestimated. It ranges from the issue of social inequity within the country to the reversion to protectionism under the justification of industrial policy. The followers of Professor Widjojo must join their efforts to promote the country's economic policy on the right track.

The good news is that *Bapak* Widjojo is only 70 years old. When I met him for the first time 30 years ago, he already carried with him an air of a venerable *guru*. But, in today's idea of life-span, we can count on his service to Indonesia as well as other Asian countries for many more years to come in the progress of the global market economy, in which I understand he has been placing his belief all through his life. ◆

39

A Lighthouse Continuously Showing The Way to Stability and Prosperity

Derek Davies*

For well over three decades Dr. Widjojo Nitisastro has occupied a major position on the Indonesian economic landscape. It has been as if he were a lighthouse somewhere in the complicated islands and waters to the north of Tanjung Priok, consistently showing the way to Jakarta's haven of stability and prosperity. At times, the lighthouse has been located too far away from either the economy's main shipping lines or the centre of political power, and his guiding light has been obscured by political storms or ignored by ships under military or piratical command. But it has always been there, showing the way to those sensible enough to follow its signals.

I must, in my own defence, stress that this is very much a tribute to Dr. Widjojo's career by an outsider. The Indonesian economy was only one of thirty Asian economies covered by the *Far Eastern Economic Review* during the nearly thirty years I worked for the magazine. Nevertheless, I took a special interest in its dramatic fortunes from my first visit in 1964 (Presiden Soekarno's Year of Living Dangerously) until the early 1990s, visiting Jakarta as often as I could, interviewing Dr. Widjojo and others of the gifted team of "technocrats" he gathered round him whenever possible.

---

* Mr.Derek Davies (U.K.) was born in London in 1931, obtained a Master of Arts degree from Cambridge University, British Foreign Service 1956-1962, serving in Hanoi (then North) Vietnam and Vienna. Worked for Reuters *Financial Times* and the *Far Eastern Economic Review* of which he was Editor from 1964 to 1989, during which time he frequently visited Indonesia. Retired, he free-lanced from London and France. He passed away in 2002.

I could not keep away. Indonesia exerted a special fascination. Other nations of the region were trying to find a way towards stability and prosperity between the political extremes of the Cold War, and between the forces of nationalism released by the post-colonial era on the one hand and more sober pressures to achieve self-sufficiency in food, less dependency on imports, growing indigeneous industries and exporting potential on the other. But the clash between these forces was nowhere played out with the dramatic intensity as it was against the Indonesian backdrop. When I first began to get to know the country, politics were in command. President Soekarno was preaching his vague doctrine of Marhaenism, which purported to enshrine a socialist egalitarism. In fact the Bung regarded the economic welfare of the country as secondary to its political progress—and said so in so many terms. In the end, his charisma crumbled before harsh economic facts. By 1966 the rate of inflation had ballooned to over 600% and the people knew they could not fill their bellies with rhetoric. Soekarno's fall was of heroic proportions, like an episode from the Ramayana acted out on the terraces of Borobudur.

During these years, we outsiders only gradually became conscious in the mid-1960s that a new, steadier hand was on the tiller. We learned of a shadowy figure who had been charged by the new President Soeharto with the task of stabilising the economy. But he was not an ivory tower academic. He had fought with the Students' Army in the 1940s, and gone from the University of Indonesia to further studies in the US. Many of the disciplines necessary to restore economic stability were unpopular but, in addition, Dr. Widjojo had to be content with the powerful remnants of a national paranoia about the West, a natural post-colonial inheritance fanned into flames by Soekarnoist nationalism. He and his colleagues, many of whom had been trained in the West, were dismissed as part of a Machiavellian plot (which had its parallel conspiracy among the military); as a team of economists deliberately trained at US universities to subvert Indonesian economic independence. In short, the "Berkeley Mafia."

Such accusations, a wide-spread calumny that he was working against the country's strategic interests, must have been wounding.

They seemed to me to have been influential in persuading Dr. Widjojo and many of his closest colleagues to maintain low profiles, to eschew publicity and to seek the status of non-political technocrats. One can speculate that the experience gave Dr. Widjojo his evident distaste for politics. Other East Asian "technocrats" have been less careful. In the Philippines, for example, several men saw in the power that President Marcos seized when he declared a State of Emergency an opportunity for imposing a much-needed discipline on a free-booting society which had suffered a surfeit of politics. They stuck with or became part of the Marcos team in the hope that necessary measures, even including land reform, might be implemented under his regime. Their hopes were illusionary and during the long years of the corrupt Marcos dictatorship the Filipino people received no economic advantages to compensate them for their lack of freedoms. Much the same happened in South Korea, Taiwan and Thailand.

Dr. Widjojo must have been tempted to exercise direct power. By the early 1980s he had become the highly respected economic overlord: Minister-Coordinator for Economy, Finance and Industry and Chairman of Bappenas, the National Development Planning Agency. At the time, many put his name forward as a running mate for President Soeharto in the 1983 elections for the Presidency and Vice-Presidency. But the economic technocrat refused to be sucked into politics. He told me that mention of his name in that context "should be completely discounted." He said he had made very clear that "I do not consider myself suitable for that responsibility," adding for good measure, "And I mean it".

During the same interview he was careful to make it clear that his great prestige was in no sense to be seen as a challenge to President Soeharto's supremacy or overall responsibility. He told me: "Major decisions are presidential decisions because he is after all the one who is responsible. He is elected and the rest are appointed. So he makes the decisions." But it was never quite clear to outside observers just how the decisions were made, particularly those decisions which promised to be unpopular. But it is evident that the advice of Dr. Widjojo carried great weight, for unpopular decisions were made even when elections loomed (as when in the early 1980s, domestic oil subsidies were slashed and a ban imposed on log exports) which a political leader must have wished to evade or postpone. Nevertheless, Dr. Widjojo insisted that he and his professional team of officials stuck to an advisory role: "We simply operate in a way in which the facts are brought to the attention of the government."

Much always remains under the surface in Indonesia. Its culture favours indirect references and oblique comments. This had not seemed to be much of a problem during the presidency of Soekarno for his political style was direct to the point of conflict. But after some early unhappy brushes with the press, President Soeharto rarely confided with the media or used the press, domestic or foreign, to justify or explain his decisions and policies. A more typically Indonesian mist enveloped Jakarta's governing style—which made life more challenging for those of us trying to gain insights into the economic, political and social problems facing the country and how they were being tackled. Even well-informed Indonesians, never mind we foreigners, could only guess as much of what went along the corridors of power in Jakarta. The dramas were no longer being played out against a heroic landscape, but in the form of flickering silhouettes like those seen on the screen of a *wayang* shadow play; we could see the outlines, hear the clash of the accompanying music, listen to the public dialogue and guess at the internal drama, but we could rarely get a glimpse of the puppeteers who were manipulating the shadows.

But Indonesia still provides its dramas. Sometimes they have been the result of political in-fighting or intrigues and clashes within the military power structure, as with the *Malari* affair. Sometimes they have taken the form of violent protest against official policies or corruption. Sometimes they have had a more direct impact on the economy and the responsibilities of Dr. Widjojo, as with the dramatic rise and fall of Ibnu Sutowo. For the outsider, they too often call in question the "double function" of the armed forces in Indonesian society, which gives the military too much autonomy in many areas which fall outside the control of those trying to coordinate economic policies. The special status for the military is in turn a function of the feudal tradition within which authority is devolved and exercised—

all of which makes life extremely difficult for the economic planner. It is remarkable how often the talents of Dr. Widjojo and his team have had to be called in to clear up economic and financial disasters perpetrated by people operating outside any planning or budgetary restraints. Dr. Widjojo started by clearing up President Soekarno's legacy. He has cleared up many others since, cutting his own plans back to pay for the prodigal spending of others, absorbing the debts, building up depleted reserves, reassuring international bankers and the international community. Dr. Widjojo may have wisely eschewed any ambitions to wield political power himself, but one has often wished that the President had given him both the trust and the powers necessary for Bappenas to act as a true economic watchdog.

Despite such anomalies, prosperity has come to large sections of the Indonesian community, and one can see the material rewards for all the hard work Dr. Widjojo has put into his vision of an Indonesia less dependent on its natural resources and able to banish poverty from its shores. Some of the core problems remain. One only has to wander around the night clubs and discotheques of Jakarta in the early hours, to see the carparks full of BMW's and their VIP passengers high on *ekstasi, elsid, sabu sabu* or *putau* to know that too much wealth is concentrated in too few hands.

Both Jakarta and the rest of the country reveal how much more work remains to be done. But Dr. Widjojo and his fellow "technocrats" have laid the foundation despite all the obstacles placed in their path, and his vision of the final goal remains alive. Many of those who admire his life's work are carrying on in his tradition within the most senior levels of the government and the bureaucracy. On the international scene, he still works in the field of South-South co-operation, particularly searching for a solution to Third World debt. He is one of the main supporters of Professor Bintoro Tjokroamidjojo, the architect of President Soeharto's Declaration to the 1994 Summit of the Asia-Pacific Economic Cooperation, which committed that five-year-old grouping to a timetable of trade liberalisation by the year 2020.

Dr. Widjojo Nitisastro was truly "Bapak Bappenas", the father of Indonesian planning. His legacy of moderation and common sense

will benefit his country for many years to come. The lighthouse will
go on shining. ◆

40

I Always Admire His Sincerity, Openness, Fairness and, Above All, His Willingness to Listen to Others' Argument

Toyoo Gyohten*

Thirty years ago I met Prof. Widjojo for the first time at his residence in Jakarta. I was Special Assistant to the then President of the Asian Development Bank, Mr. Takeshi Watanabe. At that time, the ADB was a newly born institution. It was the first multilateral institution in which the regional members of Asia controlled the majority share. Mr. Watanabe was the first president of ADB—a bank with two principles. The first was that the ADB was a bank and not an aid-giving agency. Therefore, the financial soundness must come first. The second was that the ADB should play the role of a family doctor for Asian members. The doctor may not own sophisticated medical equipment, nor prescribe expensive medicines. He knows, however, the health record of each family member best, he hurries to the patient whenever called, and he is the doctor who is trusted most.

When Mr. Watanabe presented his vision of the ADB, Prof. Widjojo encouraged him and said " Asians must learn how to help themselves." By that time I had known many Asian economic leaders who were eager to secure loans from the ADB for financing various projects in their own countries. Prof. Widjojo's remark was refreshing and impressive because it clearly demonstrated his broad perspective as a statesman.

* Mr Toyoo Gyohten (Japan) is President of the Institute for International Monetary Affairs and Senior Adviser of the Bank of Tokyo-Mitsubishi.

Since then I had the pleasure of meeting with Prof. Widjojo many times, in Jakarta, Tokyo, and elsewhere as representatives of the economic authorities of Indonesia and Japan. Many of the meetings were simply pleasant. I always enjoyed talking to the remarkable wise man whose immense wisdom and irresistible personal charm never failed to fascinate me. However, there were occasions when we had to negotiate seriously. How much the Japanese ODA (Official Development Assistance) to Indonesia should be, how to deal with the adverse impact of the wild fluctuation of exchange rates, how to organize the international support to cope with the Indonesian economic difficulty caused by national disaster, were among the things that we negotiated.

I will not claim that we have come out of these negotiations with 100% satisfaction. Nevertheless, I am pleased to tell you that the outcome of the negotiation has never affected my respect and affection to Prof. Widjojo. *I have always admired Prof. Widjojo's sincerity, openness, fairness and, above all, his willingness to try to understand others' position.* There is no question that Prof. Widjojo is an undaunted patriot. He loves Indonesia more than anything else. However, because he loves his country he has known others love their own countries as well. *He possesses remarkable amount of patience to listen to others' argument.* He never loses his temper. He always tries to convince others that the best solution will benefit not only Indonesia but also they themselves. Such intellectual maturity as such made Prof. Widjojo the most successful negotiator.

Although Prof. Widjojo is only four years older than I am, I cannot but feel that he is twice as matured as I am.

Prof. Widjojo, I send you my very best wishes. ◆

41

A Personality with an Intelligent and Decisive Perspective on the Development of His Country

Masao Sawaki*

S ince I spent the longest time of my diplomatic life in the field of economic cooperation, Indonesia is naturally a country with which I had contact for a long time.

I dealt with the reparation payment to Indonesia when I was Director of the Economic Cooperation Section, Economic Co-operation Bureau of the Foreign Office. As Indonesia requested early payment of the reparations, we invented a system whereby we extended loans to Indonesia with the guarantee of future reparations payment as collateral. This was, in effect, to move up the yearly reparations payment. Nusantara Building and several hotel projects were constructed under this system.

When Mr. Soeharto became President and most of the accumulated debt during Soekarno's time was rearranged, the IGGI (Inter-Governmental Group on Indonesia) was established in 1966. I participated in the IGGI meeting in its early stage, representing Japan, where I met Professor Widjojo Nitisastro, representing Indonesia.

At the time I was the Deputy Director-General of the Economic Cooperation Bureau, the Japanese assistance was developing rapidly in accordance with increasing Japanese economic power. *I was deeply impressed by the excellent presentation of the Indonesian economy by Prof. Widjojo, which was backed up by solid and sound*

---

* Mr. Masao Sawaki (Japan) was Former Japanese Ambassador to Indonesia during 1981 to 1983. He passed away 1999.

spirit of economic liberalism represented by the so-called "Berkeley Mafia". As his presentation style was not fanatical nor haranguing, but a quiet pleading and steady type traversed with solid ideas, I developed a personal confidence and friendship with him. As I was promoted to Director-General of the Bureau, I contributed considerably to increasing our assistance to Indonesia, which became one of the biggest recipients of bilateral Japanese foreign assistance.

When I was transferred to be the Japanese Consul-General in New York in 1972, Prof. Widjojo telephoned me there, asking for emergency assistance of the Japanese Government to provide rice to Indonesia. I told him that I was not in charge of international assistance anymore. But as he had asked for my personal intervention as his friend, I personally sent a cable to Tokyo and it was achieved somehow, which he personally appreciated.

Since we developed such personal confidence between us, when I was assigned to New York and later to Geneva, he was always kind to send a cable, in advance of my arrival to the Indonesian Consul-General in New York (Mr. Bustanil Arifin, who later served Bulog) and to the Indonesian Ambassador in Geneva (Mr. Ali Alatas, now Foreign Minister), both with whom I developed an intimate friendship. In both cases, the Indonesian mission were the first foreign mission to invite me for a diplomatic dinner which considerably facilitated my work in both posts.

When I was transferred to the Philippines, Prof. Widjojo was very kind to invite both my wife and myself for an extensive trip inside Indonesia, which contributed in a large way to understand the reality of Indonesian progress.

When I arrived in Indonesia as Japanese Ambassador in 1981, I proposed concentrating the Japanese assistance in education, population and family planning, and the increased production of rice. As we could not reach agreement in the education field, I concentrated in family planning and increased production of rice. There was a considerable difference between my proposal and their counter-proposal, so I went to Mr. Widjojo who immediately understood the significance of such an aid program and took me to President Soeharto for final clearance.

In those years, Indonesian production of rice was always short and every year Indonesia was importing about 2 million tons of rice, making Indonesia the biggest importer of rice in the world, which affected their balance of payment and budget deficit. Moreover, part of the salary of government employees was paid in rice. About 60% of their population were farmers. Therefore, a shortage of rice immediately became a political and social problem affecting their national and political stability. Although many leaders of developing nations were advocating faster industrialization, the Indonesian government believed that unless the social stability was maintained, industrialization would not succeed. At the same time, unless Indonesia succeeded in controlling the rapid increase of its population, the increase of rice production would not have its desired effect. President Soeharto agreed with my proposal and such assistance was put into action.

In the field of rice production, it covered the whole process of rice from production to consumption. It was my experience that piecemeal assistance in various steps of rice production did not ultimately produce the desired effect because improvement in one sector of production is usually effaced by failure or defects of other sectors and does not lead effectively to an increase of production. For instance, at that time, post harvest loss amounted to nearly 20%. Therefore assistance has to cover the whole course of pre-harvest and post-harvest of rice. My proposal also included a new attempt to provide assistance in the form of monetary aid including yen-credit for irrigation and stoppage of land erosion, provision of grant aid for fertilizers and farm implements, technical assistance in the form of research for the most fitting variety of seeds and training programs for various fields. Since they were given simultaneously, co-ordination between various types of aid was one of the biggest problems.

We started up a development of a seed variety most-suited for the area, seed stocking, seed distribution system, irrigation and stoppage of land erosion in rice fields, early warning system for insect damage, and provision of farm implements, including dryers, threshing machines, milling machines and rat damage-proof warehouses. We conducted the project in two provinces and the rest of provinces were to follow the model. Indonesia achieved self-sufficiency in rice in 1983, which constituted the social and political foundation for later fast industrialization.

In the population field, we constructed a condom factory under yen-credit, established an information center for production of information, education and communication materials, provided various contraceptive devices, and conducted training of field workers. It was a collaboration between Japanese aid in the form of yen-credit and technical assistance, bilateral USAID and multilateral aid of UNICEF. Although Indonesia had started a population program earlier, this collaborative program expanded their efforts in technology and raised their program to a new height.

During my stay in Indonesia, I succeeded in a breakthrough in increasing the Japanese aid program to new heights. All this was made possible because I developed a good relationship with Mr. Widjojo who was very kind to put me in full confidence of my proposal. His door was always open to me, and I enjoyed working with him, as he had such *a good personality with an intelligent and decisive perspective on the development of Indonesia.*

He is one of the people who will long remain in my memory through more than 40 years of my diplomatic career. ◆

42

In Terms of the Practice of Political Economy, He Has no Peer in the Period since the Second World War

Nicholas C. Hope*

1. Introduction

In something over 50 years, the World Bank Group has completed successfully many hundreds of projects. One can question, however, if any of those projects returned benefits of the order that the Ford Foundation provided Indonesia when it invested, during the 1960s, in US graduate educations for some highly talented Indonesian economists. It was this investment, especially in the smaller group that did its graduate work at Berkeley, that trained the core of Indonesia's "technocrats". Under the leadership of Professor Widjojo Nitisastro, either from within the Cabinet or from his current position of Senior Advisor to President Soeharto, this justly famous group of economists has served its President and country superbly. Under the technocrats' nurturing for a virtually unprecedented period, Indonesia's economy has flourished; its performance ranks very high amongst all developing economies in the past quarter century.

Indonesia has many people to thank for the impressive accomplishments of the new order government, and among them are

* Mr. Nicholas C. Hope (Australia) joined the World Bank as an Economist in the Programming and Budgeting Department in 1977. He was a member of the Core Team of the *World Development Report 1980*. In July 1980, he was promoted to the position of Division Chief, External Debt Division, in the Economic Analysis and Projections Department. He became Chief of the Industrial Development and Finance Division in the East Asia and Pacific Projects Department in October 1986. In July 1987, Mr. Hope was selected as Division Chief, Industry and Energy Division in Country Department V of the Asia Region. He was appointed Director of the Resident Staff in Indonesia in August 1990. On April 4, 1994, he became Country Director, China and Mongolia, in the East Asia and Pacific Region. At present he is Deputy Director Stanford Center for International Development.

225

the pre-eminent economists who have served President Soeharto as ministers and advisors for 30 years. Amongst those who practice political economy, however, none would disagree with the assessment of Professor Sumitro Djojohadikusumo, himself the doyen of Indonesian economists, that Professor Widjojo's hand has been the one on the tillers of the economy.

2. Professor Widjojo and the Bank's Resident Staff in Indonesia (RSI)

I had met neither Professor Widjojo nor Ali Wardhana before taking up the post of Director, RSI, in August 1990. Both men had near legendary status amongst the Bank Indonesia hands. Widjojo for his comprehensive grasp of economic matters and his extraordinary strategic sense; Wardhana for his shrewd understanding of practical macroeconomic management and his ability to push through the tough decisions necessary to keep the Indonesian economy on track. I was an Indonesian hand, but my emphasis during the previous four years had been on projects in finance, energy and industry, not the major priorities for Indonesia's top decisionmakers at a time when the Indonesian economy had lost its ability to rely on oil earnings and urgently needed structural change.

The deregulation program that the Government pursued determinedly after the second oil shock in 1986 was still underway when I arrived in Jakarta, and the situation was quickly complicated by the promise of renewed oil earnings as a result of the Gulf War. The economic situation was delicately poised.[1] The economy was enjoying fast growth under the stimulus of buoyant domestic and foreign investment, expanding non-oil exports, and government expenditures that matched revenues under Indonesia's interpretation of its balanced budget requirement.[2] The Bank was concerned that Government spending could convey unwanted impetus to an already booming situation if additional oil revenues were spent.

---

1   As it always was during my association with Indonesia. Perhaps more than any other country, Indonesia has seemed to get the most out of its economy: fast growth, but with constant challenges for policymakers trying to maintain internal and external economic balance.

2   Two early initiatives of Professor Widjojo and his colleagues were the balanced budget regulation (1968) and convertibility of the currency (1970). Both measures were used by the technocrats to impose discipline on an economy in which, at least initially, the tools of macroeconomic management were far from adequate for their needs.

For an evaluation of the Jakarta office commissioned by the Bank in 1988, Ali Wardhana characterized the RSI as a "sparring partner" for the Government's economic team. At the time, that seemed to me a very appropriate term for what gave every appearance of being a dialogue between equals, based to a great extent on the respect that each side had for the views of the other. Once in Jakarta, Professor Widjojo changed my perspective. To a very large extent, the chief architect of Indonesia's economic policy making saw the RSI as a secretariat.[3]

He expected the work program of the Economic Unit at RSI to be shaped by the emerging priorities of the Indonesian economy, and by his own need for advice on how to respond to those priorities. Of course, we had our own work priorities, too, and concerns for the economy that were both macroeconomic and structural. Visiting Directors and Vice Presidents provided the opportunity to elevate discussion of the Bank's own agenda, when the "sparring partner" mode would predominate. But I became accustomed to, and indeed eagerly awaited, the telephone calls from Professor Widjojo—often on Saturday morning, and usually beginning with courteous apologies for the delay since our last conversation—that ended almost invariably with the request to come and see him. The perennial "When, Professor Widjojo?", usually answered by "Now, in my office".

And it was then, in his office, that I and the economic team from RSI, on the frequent occasions when its members accompanied me, learned of his current concerns. The Professor was interested in everything.[4] For his work with the Bank, however, his preoccupations were the stability of the macroeconomy; the still inappropriate incentive system; and balance in the external sector.

One of Professor Widjojo's jokes, often expressed in the presence of his colleagues, was that every time the technocrats solved a

---

3 This was not a unique situation to the Bank. Widjojo and his colleagues used the ably led team from the Harvard Institute for International Development (HIID) similarly, and the same could be said for the IMF, ADB, the Boston Group, the "three houses" advisory team, and numerous other quasi-official and unofficial sources of economic advice.

4 So much so that on one occasion when I was seeking to narrow priorities and asked what was important to emphasize, his answer was: "Everything. Because you can't possibly predict on which issue the President will be able to move first."

problem in Indonesia's economy a more complex problem emerged. This fact reflected the changing roles of the public and private sectors in Indonesia's economy, and clearly added zest to the work of a team that had long functioned smoothly together. As structural change increasingly created incentives for profitable private involvement in the economy, and as rising demands for investment in human and physical infrastructure stretched the Government's capacity to supply these services, the Government found itself unable to continue its heavy, direct involvement in agriculture and industry. In the event, this was also unnecessary as, with the right incentives and institutional support, the private sector was eager to do the job. For the economic managers that meant the need both to encourage and to accommodate the private sector.

In the early 1990s, that accommodation meant adjusting public expenditure to dampen demand because private expenditure levels were high enough to maintain a desirable pace of economic activity. Many of the Professor's requests were for analysis of the macro-economy and advice on where to trim expenditures.[5] He was frustrated during this period by emerging resistance to what he knew was essential structural change. The deregulation process had slowed rather than stalled, but successive reform packages became less potent in both their scope and their impact on incentives. Increasingly, he looked to the external sector and the competition it could bring as a means to spur deregulation and put in place the incentive framework needed to ensure the productivity and efficiency of private investment. Of this, more below.

3. Managing the External Sector

For all of Professor Widjojo's emphasis on export performance and the climate for foreign investment in Indonesia, his two abiding external concerns, during my time in Jakarta—and probably for the 25 years prior to it—were Indonesia's external debt, and the level of formal donor assistance for Indonesian development. These issues

---

5   In the conventional sense, Indonesia's "balanced budget" led to an average fiscal deficit of about 0.8 percent a year, during my time in Jakarta. By 1996, Widjojo and his team had converted this into a surplus of almost 1 percent of GDP, with beneficial effects on macroeconomic performance, especially on inflation.

are obviously related, and both gave me opportunities to see how effectively Widjojo worked in Indonesia's interests.

In the early years of the Soeharto Government, Indonesia wrestled with a debt problem so intractable that extraordinary measures were required to tackle it. When I headed the World Bank's External Debt Division, the solution was called "Indonesian terms" because of the unusual concessionality and the length of the period over which Indonesian debts were rescheduled. The experience of orchestrating (with his colleagues) the debt restructuring agreement made a profound impression on Professor Widjojo, and left him with a deep determination to see that Indonesia never again was put in the position of having to approach creditors for debt relief.[6] In his words: "Ali Wardhana had to write far too many letters that began Dear Mr. Schweitzer![6]" It made him, as well, an impassioned advocate for similarly realistic terms of debt restructuring for highly indebted poor countries in the 1980s and 1990s, with Indonesia's early experience as a model.

To render the fear of poor management of foreign borrowing all the more indelible, Professor Widjojo had seen the consequences of Pertamina's ill-advised borrowing, based on the transitory creditworthiness conveyed by oil revenues after 1973/4. The mess that ensued was still providing employment to foreign auditors in 1981, when I paid my first visit to Indonesia - to look at foreign borrowing policies.

Partly for reasons of history, Professor Widjojo moved fast in 1983 (after the first big oil price fall) to curtail foreign borrowing and postpone or cancel large projects that required massive imports of foreign capital goods. The Professor credits Ali Wardhana for his resolve in explaining to President Soeharto why those measures were essential.

A similar situation emerged in 1991. With an economy that was clearly overheating and with debt that had risen dramatically to finance Indonesia's adjustment program after the second oil price fall in 1986, Professor Widjojo knew that the economy was very

---

6 It left him, as well, with a deep appreciation for the work of Dr. Abs, who devised the agreed terms on behalf of the creditors and Indonesia, and hammered out the broad framework of the agreement.

badly positioned to absorb a hugely ambitious program of massive, mainly petrochemical, investments, despite the strong support they enjoyed from domestic and foreign sponsors. The World Bank shared his concerns, and so did almost all of the other foreign advisors to the Government.

It was a time of hectic activity for RSI, responding to the Professor's need for analysis of foreign indebtedness, the emerging current account position, and the implications for foreign debt and imports of some of the largest of the proposed new projects. The decision to postpone projects undoubtedly was a difficult one; but, after the economic team presented Professor Widjojo's analysis to President Soeharto, the President, as in so many other situations, took the decision that served Indonesia best.

At the end of 1991, the tragedy in Dili caused the Dutch Foreign Aid Minister to suspend development assistance from the Netherlands to Indonesia. The lack of prior consultation upset the Indonesian Government, and Professor Widjojo and his colleagues questioned the continuing value of the aid relationship, and, especially, the role of the Netherlands as chair of the Inter-governmental Group for Indonesia (IGGI).

No one had a keener appreciation for the contributions of the IGGI to Indonesia over many years than Professor Widjojo. The World Bank staff believed that he had attended every IGGI meeting, vivid evidence of the importance he gave to a secure external assistance framework for Indonesia. Even at the end of 1991, when Indonesian economic performance and creditworthiness were both internationally recognized, and the bulk of the assistance was provided by only three donors—Japan, the Asian Development Bank, and the World Bank—Professor Widjojo still felt strongly that the aid group framework was needed by Indonesia. He and his colleagues began to consult with the World Bank on the possibility finally of converting the IGGI into the conventional consultative group format, i.e., a meeting in Paris, rather than the Hague, and chaired by the World Bank.

After the Government's independent review of the incident in Dili, and with considerable consultation both in Jakarta and in Washington, agreement was reached that a consultative group for

Indonesia would be formed. Two of the major contributors behind the scenes were the Japanese Government and the Dutch Government; the latter agreed strongly with Widjojo that the time had arrived for the baton to be passed, and that the Bank should continue to support Indonesia in the role that the Netherlands had discharged so effectively for so long.

As usual, in advance of the meeting, Professor Widjojo, assisted, in particular, by his associates in Bappenas, assessed the support needed by Indonesia and canvassed the donors to determine if the financing available would be adequate for Indonesia's needs. Also as usual Professor Widjojo visited Tokyo himself to discuss the envelope of Japanese support. But an unusual development was the visits of selected cabinet ministers to the capitals of all the members of the IGGI to explain the change. In the event, the CGI meeting in Paris in 1992 was a very successful one, a tribute to the effectiveness of Indonesian preparation, as well as to the combined, coordinated support of the whole of the donor community. Five years later, in 1997, the venue for the CGI meeting would be in Tokyo, and observers now can legitimately question how much longer the CGI needs to function before Indonesia graduates.

4. Indonesia in International Associations

The early 1990s saw Indonesia's emergence on the international scene as a growing economic power with an enhanced leadership role in the Association of South East Asian Nations (ASEAN); and with important opportunities to revitalize the flagging Non-Aligned Movement (NAM), then under Indonesian chairmanship; and to help shape the agenda of the nations forming the Asia Pacific Economic Cooperation Group (APEC). The engagement of President Soeharto himself and the high quality of the preparatory work by Indonesia led to internationally important developments at the meeting of Non-Aligned Nations in Jakarta in August 1992, and at the Bogor meeting of APEC Economic Leaders in November 1994.

The significance of these events to Indonesia and the President demanded the engagement of the best minds Indonesia could muster. Beyond Ministers Moerdiono and Alatas, the President mobilized many of the senior economic advisors who had served him as

Ministers in previous cabinets, again with a major coordinating role assigned to Professor Widjojo. The description here makes no attempt to do justice to the multi-faceted agendas prepared for both of these highly successful international conferences. But there were two main thematic areas where the Bank was both consulted and involved.

Within APEC, and also in ASEAN, economic concerns began to acquire greater importance relative to politics. In both cases, there was emphasis on the need to reduce tariffs on trade between member nations. This created the opportunity that Professor Widjojo sought to link deregulation to international developments in a way that ensured growing competitiveness in the Indonesian economy. The Professor supported non-discriminatory reduction of tariffs within both groups of nations so as to maximize the benefits to all countries from the implementation of the Uruguay Round. At the same time, we at the Bank could recognize that what both sets of commitments required of Indonesia was the adoption of a pre-announced program of deregulation measures that could not be abandoned without detriment to international relations. This was the discipline that Professor Widjojo felt would complete the structural changes needed to equip Indonesia with a price structure that aligned incentives to investors, producers, traders, and consumers with economic costs. Although much needs to be accomplished before the trade regime is as free as would be desired, the necessary blueprint is in place.

For the NAM meeting, Professor Widjojo asked the Bank for its help in supplying voluminous information, including data and analytical reports, on the plight of the poorest highly indebted countries. From this was to come Indonesia's championing of radical rescheduling of debts for those countries, built on Professor Widjojo's conviction that only restructuring of external liabilities on "Indonesian terms" or better could afford them any hope of managing their external financial situation. This initiative, which was echoed by similar proposals, for example, by former British Chancellor of the Exchequer, Kenneth Clark, is still to win uniform acceptance, though the principles have been accepted and championed by current World Bank President, James D. Wolfensohn. That must have been a great satisfaction to Professor

Widjojo, who was disappointed by the World Bank's inability to respond positively to President Soeharto's request in March 1994 for the Bank to spearhead a major initiative to relieve the debt burden of the poorest countries.

5. A Final Assessment

These scattered reminiscences are fragmentary. They refer primarily to the three plus years of my tenure as the Bank's Director, at RSI, a scant one-tenth of the time that Professor Widjojo, either directly or indirectly, has exercised his oversight of the Indonesian economy. His success in this endeavor has been extraordinary; the impact on his country has been enormous. Many of my colleagues have observed that I was singularly fortunate to be in Indonesia during such an interesting period. My reply has always been that my predecessors and my successor undoubtedly also deem themselves extremely fortunate to have served the Bank in Indonesia during a time of intense interest.

The main source of that interest—for me, and probably for most of my colleagues as well—was the chance to interact with and to observe one of the most extraordinary economic minds of the century. *Indeed, in terms of the practice of political economy, I believe that Professor Widjojo has no peer in the period since the Second World War.* That is why whenever I am asked to comment on Indonesia's transition, I always need to pause to determine whether the question refers to the successor to President Soeharto or the successor to Professor Widjojo. *Indonesia is fortunate indeed to have been served by two such men; and blessed to have been served by them concurrently.* ◆

43

"Never, Never, Never, Never, Never Give Up". The Economic Team Never Did

Stokes Tolbert*

"**D**r. Widjojo, you could be elected to office in my state if you ran on that platform!" Representative Clement Zablocki of Wisconsin, then chairman of the Subcommittee on Asian and Pacific Affairs of the US Congress, was congratulating Widjojo on his presentation of the Indonesian stabilization and recovery program. It was late in 1967, after the second IGGI meeting; the State Department and AID had invited Widjojo to Washington, and were seeing to it that he met legislators and officials concerned with aid to Indonesia. John Bullitt, AID Assistant Administrator for Southeast Asia, and I took Widjojo to meet Rep. Zablocki and also Rep. William Broomfield of Michigan, a member of the same subcommittee.

Representative Zablocki had earlier urged upon AID a go-slow approach to resuming aid to Indonesia and rebuilding the US presence there. Rep. Broomfield in 1963 had persuaded the House of Foreign Affairs Committee to endorse an amendment prohibiting further US aid to Indonesia unless the president made a determination that continued aid was in the national interest. The congressmen were clearly impressed by Widjojo's intellect and sincerity, quite apart from his account of progress under the economic program. Both later strongly supported continued and expanded aid to Indonesia.

* Dr. Stokes Tolbert (US) was Director of USAID Mission Jakarta (1967-1969); Division Chief for Indonesia, the World Bank (1969-1972).

One meeting could not of course change long-held views of people who had endured the virulently anti-US in the later years of the Soekarno era. But at least they were now seeing Indonesia's new face and I believe this had some lasting impact. This and many other meetings were triumphs for Widjojo; he proved a virtuoso performer, as we had expected. His account of measures taken to balance the budget, restrain inflation, dismantle controls, attract investment, wowed Democrats and Republicans alike on Capitol Hill. In those days we were not only seeking to help Indonesia establish its credibility with other donors, but also to make known within the US the facts of the startling turn-around in Indonesia. Widjojo was our exhibit No.1.

One highlight of that visit was a meeting in the White House with Walt Rostow, then President Johnson's chief economic advisor. We went over in the evening, the only time Rostow's schedule permitted. He and Widjojo were obviously delighted to have the opportunity to meet, and they talked long past the scheduled time, despite attempted interruptions from Rostow's staff. It was love-in, and it ended with Rostow's assurance of his and President Johnson's strong support for generous assistance to Indonesia's efforts.

I first met the Economic Team in early 1967. They—Widjojo, Emil Salim, Ali Wardhana, and Subroto; Sadli was elsewhere—were sitting on the floor of Harrison Parker's living room in Jakarta. Parker, then AID program officer, had been a member of the Ford Foundation staff in Jakarta in the mid 1950's, when, as he proudly put it, he had " packed the Mafia's bags and put them on the plane to Berkeley"—alluding to that far-sighted and uniquely productive initiative of Professor Sumitro Djojohadikusumo and the Ford Foundation. He had kindly invited the team over that evening so I could meet them. Sprawled on the floor, eating popcorn as I remember, unassuming, relaxed and joking, they resembled students more than anything else. They certainly did not look like the revolutionaries who were about to reverse the course of Indonesian history, taking as their manifesto classic the textbook economics.

At that time the Team had great responsibility coupled with little authority; some had been asked to join President Soeharto's personal Staff, and Widjojo had become chairman of Bappenas. By the time I left Indonesia most were at ministerial level, holding key economic posts in President Soeharto's "Development Cabinet".

Their prowess and their achievements over the next decades are amply recorded elsewhere (most recently in 1996 in William Hollinger's valuable and admirably compressed background Paper Number 2 for the US Indonesia Society, *Economic Policy Under President Soeharto: Indonesia's Twenty-five Year Record*) while my contribution here is a highly personal view of the team's inimitable leader, back in the early days of the New Order.

When I arrived in Jakarta in February of 1967, I found I had jumped onto a moving train. The first IGGI meeting was held in the Netherlands later that month, followed by preparations for another in November, and, in between, the Paris debt rescheduling meetings. In these meetings, Widjojo constantly pushed his colleagues forward to present Indonesia's case, but it was his own personality—his modest demeanor, sunny disposition, formidable skill and tenacity in pushing Indonesia's requests for aid and debt relief—that set the tone from the beginning.

In Jakarta, each week brought announcement of a new measure to rehabilitate and liberalize the economy and integrate it into the world market. It was an altogether exciting time to be there. The Economic Team was attacking on a dozen fronts at once. Widjojo, at the center of the tumult, always appeared calm and relaxed despite seemingly intolerable demands on his time. The local representative of the growing number of aid donors all wanted to see him, to get his blessing for their actions, to find out what was going on, "to touch his garment", as one observer put it. Widjojo found time and energy to meet with, to coordinate, to inform, to unify and inspire this disparate group.

At first the principal US aid weapon was agricultural commodities provided under Public Law 480. Fortunately, these fit Indonesia's need beautifully. The economy was in shambles and needed a transfusion of resources that could be quickly absorbed. The commodities helped cushion the impact of the austerity regime, and generated rupiah resources for the development budget. Project aid would come later.

We were providing mainly wheat, plus smaller quantities of rice. The drought-caused rice crisis in the fall of 1967 was one of the first challenges to the stabilization program. Widjojo made clear the gravity of the situation: the "rice mystique" in Indonesia was such that a prolonged shortage of rice could threaten the stability of the government—this at a time when the fledgling New Order was imposing an unpopular retrenchment program. In fact the rice shortage did lead to attacks on the program, even by the students who had hitherto been reliable New Order backers.

The crisis sent USAID scurrying for more rice. In Washington, John Bullit and the AID desk officer for Indonesia—the redoubtable Alex Shakow (once Peace Corps Director in Indonesia, fluent in the language, and a great and good friend of the country)—went into action. They persuaded the US agency involved to procure more of the expensive California and Louisiana rice; they sought to buy rice where available in Thailand or Korea; and they urged Japan to provide more.

One scheme was totally unsuccessful: Bullitt came up with the idea of obtaining rice from India in exchange for twice the amount of wheat. On the way to Jakarta from Washington Bullit and I presented what we considered a thoroughly vetted proposal to the Indian Minister of Agriculture, who quickly dismissed the idea, though he got a good laugh out of it. India, he averted, was not giving up any rice. We did manage, to Widjojo's relief, to increase substantially our rice shipments, mainly through Bullitt's and Shakow's success in grabbing a greater share of PL 480 rice for Indonesia, at the expense of other aid-receiving countries.

In many aid programs there is frequently disagreement over the adoption of needed reforms, with aid often provided to enable—or to bribe—the aid recipient to do "the right thing", as defined by the aid donor. Not so in the case of Indonesia. There would later come occasional disagreements between the Economic Team and its foreign advisers over the pace of reform, but *in those early days the Indonesian economists were moving faster and further than any of us expected. It was all we could do to keep up*. So the politics of this particular aid game were simple: support the economists. This often found expression in a query I became accustomed to hearing from

Washington when we sent in various proposals: "Is this what Widjojo wants?".

The US Government had decided to follow a multilateral approach to aid to Indonesia and to adopt a "one-third" formula (the US would provide a third of justified aid requirements, with the hope that Japan would give one-third and other donors the remainder). When we announced this, some of the Indonesian leaderships were disappointed, having envisaged a more generous and leading role for the US Widjojo however with his customary quick perception, accepted the formula easily, seeing its potential for leverage with other donors. Robert Barnett (Deputy Assistant Secretary of State) who, if anyone, was the father of the one-third formula, and Rutherford Poats (Deputy Administrator of USAID) who became its US executor, worked tirelessly and effectively to convince other donors to sign on. Widjojo later confided that he had not been confident the formula would produce enough aid in later years, when needs were sure to rise. But, aided by his strong efforts, the formula did work, and it led several donors to aid Indonesia in larger measure than we had hoped.

From those tumultuous times, some snapshots remain in my mind:

- Sometime in mid-1967, I went to Widjojo's home to discuss some aspects of the AID program. As we talked, I heard a chirping sound from the corner. The family was raising chickens to supplement their diet. On the table was the modest ration of rice to which he was entitled as civil servant. Here was a man who, like any of the Economic Team, could have become rich by simply stretching out his hand and accepting a payoff from one of the many opportunists seeking concessions from his government.

- Once, at my request, Widjojo came to my house to review a weighty memorandum I was drafting. He showed up very late, after a six-hour meeting somewhere, and charged into the memo. He was a great simplifier. When we finished, well after midnight, the draft was half as long and its argument clearer, with all economic jargon replaced by simple language. It was still my memo, but it was also a good example of Widjojo's ability to communicate. He went out, woke up his driver, waved goodbye and roared off, still seemingly fresh. But I knew he was working eighteen-hour days, and I feared for his health.

- Once Widjojo, other delegation members, and I flew on the same plane from Jakarta to an IGGI meeting in Amsterdam. I woke up more than once during the night. Each time all was dark, everyone was asleep; just one reading light was still on. There was Widjojo, going over his documents. Indonesia, I thought again for the hundredth time, was fortunate to have such a patriot.

Over the years, I had the opportunity to observe economic planners and decision-makers in some twelve developing countries. I considered Indonesia's by far the best. Some factors in their success were fortuitous, and could not be recreated unless indeed the gods were smiling. Among the most important were the President's sustained backing and Widjojo's long-term leadership role in maintaining the cohesion of the team. It also helped to have the enthusiastic support of the foreign aid community in the days before aid fatigue set in. Another critical ingredient, it seems clear, was the precept embodied in the seven word speech variously attributed to Churchill and others: "Never, never, never, never, never, give up". The Economic Team never did; even today, they are still working to remove remaining restrictions and to tune the economy for greater efficiency.

I am writing this while on vacation in southern Italy. Without notes or records, I have probably gotten some dates, titles, or facts wrong, for which I apologize. I have not mentioned the World Bank's Bernie Bell, whose wise counsel was so valuable to the Economic Team, or similarly Kemal Siber of the IMF. I did not even find place to mention the astute leadership of US Ambassador Marshall Green, under whose sage direction the entire program of US political and economic support of Indonesia revived and grew. I have said little about the other gifted members of the Economic Team. I could, for example, happily write another chapter on the mercurial, brilliant and brave Emil Salim, with whom I worked most closely. But this is for a book about Widjojo, and it is a source of great pleasure to know that he will receive these plaudits while still enjoying life, whereas most great men have to die before a commemorative volume is published.

I did not expect that we would be able to look back after twenty-five years on an Indonesian economy with an average GDP growth rate of more than 6 per cent a year and with the proportion of its people living in absolute poverty reduced from 60 to 14 per cent. It is an astounding performance, though it is likely that Widjojo, with his unquenchable optimism, is not at all surprised at this outcome. ◆

44

My Recollections of His Contributions to Indonesia's Development

Marshall Green *

I n my book, Indonesia's Crisis and Transformation (1990, Compass Press), I mention (page 114-115) Professor Widjojo as the most influential of a talented team of Indonesian economists committed to economic stabilization in the critical 1966-1971 period and to Indonesia's subsequent rapid economic development. I also mention his special rapport with President Soeharto.

The Soeharto-Widjojo relationship proved most fortunate for Indonesia and its friends. As I once said, it was President Soeharto and the army who kept Indonesia united and stable, while it was Professors Widjojo, Sumitro, Sadli, Wardhana and other far-sighted economists who moved Indonesia forward economically.

Professor Widjojo played a major role in the critically important rescheduling of debts incurred during the Soekarno years. Under the leadership of a prominent German banker, Dr. Herman Abs, and with the working-level directing and genius of Mr. Robert Barnett of the State Department, this "Ugly Debt" problem was resolved in a definitive and non-discriminatory manner, *thus eliminating a serious drawback to Indonesia's international creditworthiness and opening the way for Indonesia's successful economic programs.*

Mr. Barnett has just completed a 600-page study on the Soekarno Debt Settlement, complete with relevant papers.

---

* Mr. Marshall Green (US) was Ambassador of the United States to Indonesia, 1965-1969. He passed away in 1998.

I only wish to add a final note about how officers in the US Embassy as well as in Washington greatly admired Professor Widjojo not only for his outstanding professional achievements, but also for his admirable qualities as a friend and dedicated public-servant. ◆

45

His Role, The World Bank and Indonesia's Development: a Study in Partnership

*Gautam Kaji**

1. Introduction

As I sat down to write this piece, I tried to imagine Indonesia's past three decades without Professor Widjojo Nitisastro. I could not. The contributions of 'The Professor" to Indonesia's extraordinary development successes within the New Order Government are so manifest, so central, that it is simply not possible to think of one without the other. The same holds true when I try to think of the World Bank in Indonesia: the Bank's contributions to Indonesia's development, whatever they might be, are intimately linked to the Professor. His quiet orchestration of Indonesia's economic policies, his supreme ability to build teams, to forge consensus, to navigate political waters, has extended just as much to the World Bank as to his colleagues in the Government.

One could write volumes on Widjojo's contributions to Indonesia's development, and, indeed, I am sure others will. However, since many of my World Bank colleagues are also writing for this volume, I will keep my own remarks short.

The World Bank's relationship with Professor Widjojo remains one of the most remarkable partnerships in the annals of the Bank's

* Mr.Gautam Kaji (India) was recruited to the World Bank under the Young Professionals Program in 1968. Initially attached to the Western Africa Department, the International Finance Corporation, and then the Eastern Africa Department at the World Bank, Mr. Kaji has since spent time in various capacities in several countries; and most recently, as a regional Director with oversight of development work in several East Asian Countries. As Regional Vice President, Mr. Kaji managed a.o. the Bank's lending program to some 20 countries in East Asia and the Pacific. He was appointed Managing Director on December 1, 1994, with broad responsibilities for the Bank's lending and economic activities.

history. It began, quite literally, at the beginning, during the very early days of the New Order Government. Before I talk about the Bank and Professor Widjojo, let me put that relationship in context.

2. The Context

Indonesia's development record is well known among students of economic development, but not nearly so well known among the public at large. *Even the great majority of the Indonesians sometimes seem to take Indonesia's successes for granted.*

Indonesia's record over the past 25 years has earned it a place among the elite "Asian Miracle" countries. To understand why Indonesia may deserve such recognition, we need to step back to the mid 1960s and to the start of what was to become known as the New Order Government.

In 1966 Indonesia was dirt poor (per capita income was less than $50, about a third of India's at that time). The Government was bankrupt and in disarray. The economy was out of control, trapped in a vicious inflation spiral (inflation hit 635 percent that year). Most of Indonesia's 100 million people were desperately poor (7 of every 10 Indonesians were in severe poverty), hungry (average consumption 1,650 calories from mainly cassava and maize) and population was expanding rapidly (2.5 percent a year). The social fabric had been ripped apart by one of the worst episodes of domestic violence in modern history (it is said that more than 400,000 people died in the aftermath of the abortive 1965 coup). Economic and political conditions were grim, and future prospects appeared far worse.

As the New Order Government took over, Indonesia hardly qualified as a country: 13,000 islands (7,000 inhabited) stretching over 3000 miles, in excess of 300 diverse ethnic, linguistic and religious groups drawn together more by historical accident than by natural grouping. Few observers at that moment in history would have bet on Indonesia's survival as a nation, let alone on its ascension into the ranks of Asian success stories.

The progress in the past three decades has been enormous on almost any criterion. In 1996 the country's 200 million people passed the US$1000 per capita threshold (almost triple India's per capita income). With a per capita average daily consumption of 2,750 calories, hunger is at worst a dim memory for most Indonesians. Fewer than 1 in 7 Indonesians fall below the poverty line. Education is up; health statistics have improved.

Indonesia's transition over the past three decades has been described as a modern-day development miracle. In important ways, that success was no miracle at all. *Indonesia's rise from among the world's poorest countries to the ranks of the lower middle income countries came about by its Government's systematic application of fundamental principles of economic policy.* To grow well, a country needs a stable macroeconomic environment; high saving rates; heavy investment in human capital; a desire to work with the country's natural comparative advantages; and, above all, a reasonably stable investment climate.

How was Indonesia able to apply this policy recipe when most other developing countries could not and, indeed, cannot? An important part of the answer lies in a unique 30-year partnership between President Soeharto and a small group, known variously as the Technocrats or the Berkeley Mafia, who shaped economic policy. They brought the right answers to President Soeharto at the times when the President needed them most. It was their capacity to deliver that gave them their authority, an authority that was greatest when times were worst.

Membership in the group of Technocrats has changed over the years. But the core, which represents the heart as well as much of the brain of this loosely-defined team, remains in place today, led by the extraordinary man this volume is honoring, Widjojo Nitisastro.

3. Widjojo and the World Bank

There is a consistent pattern to Indonesia's recipe for its success. In the face of some economic problem (of internal or external origin), the Technocrats would seek advice, often solicited personally by the Professor, and generally from several sources. They would listen, often with great patience, to the "foreign experts," asking just a few questions along the way. The Bank, its Washington staff, but especially its field-based staff was privileged to be among those on whom the team relied. *Then - and this is the key - the team would decide among themselves what could be done in the Indonesian context, often operating within very tough political constraints. With options and a preferred course of action in mind, one of the team members would take the proposals to the President, and a decision would emerge. When the options were particularly difficult, it often fell to Professor Widjojo to carry them. His ability to present clearly the pros and cons of different courses, to inform the President of his options, and the trust the President had in Widjojo, are essential ingredients to Indonesia's recipe for success.*

I like to think that the Bank's role in Indonesia has been an important one, but it was certainly not one of leadership. What success the Bank has had in helping Indonesia to develop has stemmed from a support rather than starring role. To believe otherwise confuses acquiescence with the intelligence and patience of key figures such as Professor Widjojo. *The Indonesians run their country. They take all the decisions. But they have done so with an unusual willingness to listen to advice and to learn from the experience of other countries. Policy-making in Indonesia is uniquely Indonesian.*

Professor Widjojo's leadership and the role of Indonesia's economic team carry important lessons for the World Bank's relationship with other countries: the payoff to government ownership of policy reforms cannot be oversold. *We hear much talk these days of concepts such as accountability, ownership, and effectiveness of policies. These concepts came naturally to Widjojo and his team.*

The Bank first came to Widjojo in the person of Bernie Bell, then-President McNamara's hand-picked first director of the World Bank's resident mission in Jakarta. It is a shame that Bernie is not here today to relate first-hand those early days of collaboration. Folklore has it that meetings between Widjojo and Bell regularly ran into the small hours of the morning, in the rush to make up for years of macroeconomic neglect. It must have been an extraordinary relationship, highly personal, built on strong mutual respect and great trust. Those who have followed Bernie as directors of the Bank's resident mission, and, indeed, all of us who have had the privilege to work with the Indonesian authorities, have benefitted from the foundation of cooperation and trust that Widjojo and Bell built together.

4. The Personality and the Accomplishments

The first time I met The Professor, I confess that I was surprised. Could this frail-looking, gentle man, with such an unassuming manner, possibly be the economic architect for Indonesia's great developmental successes? Appearances can be remarkably deceiving in Indonesia, especially to foreigners. I quickly learned the intellectual power of this man; his energy; his skills at guiding all who came in contact with him; his capacity to spot the core of a problem or the weakness of an argument; and, above all, his humility.

Look at a few of the great triumphs.

Mobilizing bilateral and multilateral donors into the aid consortium (the Inter-Governmental Group on Indonesia as it was known in the old days). Escape from hyper-inflation and a return to economic growth much faster than the "experts" predicted. Successful resolution of the Pertamina debt crisis. Adept management of the economy in the 1980s to avoid a repeat performance when much of the rest of the developing world was mired in debt crisis. The all-out cabinet battles that must have been fought to jump-start the deregulation drive. The list could go on and on. While Widjojo was not personally responsible for each of these triumphs, ably backed up, as he was, by an extraordinary team of first-rate economists, no one then or now would question his leadership. *He set the direction; he set the tone; he was the master strategist.*

He still is. Indeed I vividly recall a meeting—not all that long ago—we had arranged for the Vietnamese, who were then beginning to embark on their own reform program. We all listened with rapt attention to Widjojo's account of the early days of the Indonesian reform program, and especially *the bold decision to open up the capital account. To be sure, it was risky, Widjojo said; but he saw it in strategic terms, as a vehicle to enforce fiscal discipline.* As it indeed turned out to be.

After thirty years, Professor Widjojo remains not only the Government of Indonesia's, but also the World Bank's "senior economic advisor." These days, his hair is thinner; grayer; the shoulders maybe a little more stooped, the glasses a bit thicker. But I would wager a sizable amount that if Bernie Bell were with us today he would testify that the intellect is just as sharp; that the questions are just as insightful; and that the dedication to the people of Indonesia is just as strong as ever.

In 1968, the World Bank came to Indonesia to advise the Government. Over the next three decades we became the students, Professor Widjojo, our teacher. We have all been honored to be a part of his team. ◆

46

From Hard Experience He and His Colleagues Often Repeated the Motto: " Good Times Make Bad Policies" and Worked Hard to Introduce Good Policies

James Q. Harrison*

W hen I first met Professor Widjojo in the summer of 1989, I was somewhat anxious. I had just arrived in Jakarta to replace Mark Baird as Lead Economist in the World Bank's Resident Staff in Indonesia (RSI). Together with Mark and Attila Sonmez, then Director of RSI, I was about to meet the man who had guided Indonesia's economic policies for more than two decades, decades when Indonesia had moved from hyperinflation and stagnation to stable, rapid growth; from famine to adequate rice production; from life expectancies of about 40 years to over 60 years; from 6% of the secondary school age population enrolled in secondary schools to over 45%; and from about 60% of the population living below the poverty line to 15%. Over these decades Indonesia weathered some serious crises, notably the debt crisis catalyzed by Pertamina in 1976, and the severe external shocks of the mid-1980s. By mid-1989, however, the economy was growing vigorously within an effective program of stabilization and economic reform, financed with substantial donor support.

In this first meeting, I was expected to review with Professor Widjojo a very ambitious agenda for future economic reforms. While this agenda had been developed as a collaborative effort by Professor Widjojo, his colleagues and Bank Staff, I was concerned that, after

* Dr. James Q. Harrison (US) is a Lead Economist in the Europe and Central Asia Region of the World Bank. From 1989 to 1993, he was Lead Economist in the World Bank's Resident Staff in Indonesia.

having achieved so much success, there would be little enthusiasm for the continued efforts needed to implement additional difficult reforms and that my first meeting with my most important client would be a disappointment for all concerned.

Of course, I should not have worried.

As we reviewed various elements of the reform agenda, Professor Widjojo made it clear that this was his agenda, referring to it as "our checklist". But this did not mean that he was satisfied with it. His gentle but shrewd probing was all directed at such questions as: was the reform agenda ambitious and comprehensive enough? Were we missing any important problems? What threats lay just beyond the horizon? What practical steps were needed to implement a particular reform most effectively? *Here was a mind with no room for complacency or self-satisfaction, a mind relentlessly seeking ways to fight economic problems, grasp opportunities, and safeguard the hardwon gains of the Indonesian economy and the Indonesian people.*

I left that meeting, as I was to leave many subsequent meetings over the next four years, inspired, excited, and with a long list of *PR (Pekerjaan Rumah,* or "home-work") to complete before our next meeting.

Over those four years, there was no major crisis, but there was an ongoing struggle to prevent one from emerging, while maintaining the momentum of economic reform that would enable Indonesia to grow and compete vigorously in the world economy. Already in 1989, the non-oil trade deficit was widening quickly, as the export spurt from earlier rounds of deregulation ran out of steam, and as imports rose rapidly in response to equally rapid expansion in domestic demand. The growing imbalance in the non-oil economy was partly hidden by unusually high oil export earnings in 1990/91 due to the high oil prices resulting from the Gulf War. These windfall oil earnings also generated a temporary bulge in budget revenues that threatened to overheat an already rapidly growing economy, rekindling inflation and widening the non-oil trade deficit.

During 1991, the economy was further endangered by massive commercial foreign borrowing being contemplated for several huge, capital-intensive projects whose priority and viability in a competitive market were questionable. If these projects had materialized, they would have raised Indonesia's debt to unsustainable levels and further overheated the economy. These challenges to economic policy arose over a period when the general perception of Indonesia's economy was increasingly upbeat, both in Indonesia and in the international capital markets.

For Professor Widjojo and his colleagues, however, this was no time for euphoria. *From hard experience they had adopted, and often repeated, the motto "Good times make bad policies". Accordingly, they worked continuously over this period to introduce good policies that would restore balance to the economy and put it on a sustainable growth path.* Additional phases of deregulation were introduced to revitalize non-oil export growth and increase the competitiveness of the economy. Monetary policies were gradually rationalized and tightened, bringing the growth of credit to more sustainable levels. Windfall oil revenues were carefully used to establish a development reserve while ensuring essential expenditure needs were met. And the risks of massive, uncoordinated foreign borrowing were contained by establishing a Commercial Off-shore Loan Team, which established borrowing ceilings and an orderly, prioritized approach to borrowing for large, quasi-public projects. These policies helped to continue the momentum for growth and reform, contain inflation, and reduce the non-oil trade deficit, so that by 1993, it was less than half its 1991 peak.

Professor Widjojo would no doubt stress that these achievements, and many of those of the past 30 years, are not his alone. Indonesia has been fortunate to have had a President who has recognized that sound economic policies are essential for the welfare of the people. And *Indonesia has also been fortunate to have had a superb team of clear-thinking, pragmatic economic policy makers who deserve much credit for what Indonesia has achieved. But I believe these same people would be the first to insist that Professor Widjojo's strategic vision has been, and continues to be, the guiding force that has helped focus their work and make it effective.*

Professor Widjojo is an inspiring example to anyone who would seek to be a good economist and a good citizen. I am grateful to have had an opportunity to work with him. ◆

47

Guru, Man of Strong Will, and Our Expectation toward Indonesian Youth

Toshihiko Kinoshita *

I t was in May 1983 when I met Prof. Dr. Widjojo Nitisastro for the first time. I will never forget this impressive meeting for the rest of my life. The late Mr. Okura, a former governor of the Export-Import Bank of Japan, paid a courtesy call on him, then Coordinating Minister and Chairman of Bappenas. I accompanied the governor as Chief Representative of the bank in Jakarta. The Indonesian government, just after the devaluation of its currency *(Rupiah)*, was due to announce an additional stringent policy, named *rephasing* of governmental projects, namely, freezing, postponing, or reducing the scale of some 30 projects which had been signed between the Indonesian government and foreign contractors (many of whom were Japanese firms to which the bank was to finance export credits) in order to adapt to the shortage of foreign reserves caused by weakening prices of primary products. Dr. Widjojo (and Dr. Ali Wardhana, then Finance Minister, at another meeting) told Mr. Okura that the government's measure to be announced soon might negatively affect foreign exporters, but that this measure was unavoidable. "We devised the word *rephasing*, as a common word for *rescheduling* (of projects), which is in this case misleading. We promise to pay our foreign debt on schedule by all means," he said. "Please understand our position and help us persuade Japanese exporters not to complain about this measure".

---

* Mr.Toshihiko Kinoshita (Japan) is Professor at the School of International Liberal Studies, Waseda University; Special Research Advisor, the Export-Import Bank of Japan.

Since around the middle of the 1980s, the Indonesian Government adopted a new economic policy—a package of deregulation of foreign direct investment, trade and financial sector—thereby stimulating its economy. No doubt Dr. Widjojo and other leading technocrats initiated such reforms. These policies were basically correct and the Indonesian economy began to recover gradually.

But around that period I had no special idea that destiny would lead me to develop closer relations with Dr. Widjojo, Head of "Berkeley Mafia", and his colleagues later in life. Upon my return to Tokyo in March 1985 after three and a half years of service in Indonesia, I was assigned Deputy Director General, Loan Department No. 1 which covered Indonesia and the rest of Asia. Let me introduce an episode from that time.

In the summer of 1986, the bank received an urgent request from the government of Indonesia as well as from the World Bank to support a big current account deficit which stemmed from the sudden and sharp drop in the international price of oil. Again, stringent measures were initially taken by the government such as devaluation of *Rupiah* and curtailment of fiscal expenditures. Dr. J.B. Sumarlin, then Minister of Finance, one of the Mafias, took the initiative. Dr. Widjojo, Advisor to President Soeharto, supported the measures.

The drastic fall in the oil price had a major negative impact on both fiscal revenues and the balance of payments, for the Indonesian economy excessively depended on oil, which accounted for around 60% of fiscal revenues and export at that time. This loan request aroused strong resistance from within Japan, for it was quite an unusual request to the bank and the concerned ministry. My colleagues and I thought we should positively respond to this request in consideration of the deep bilateral relations between Indonesia and Japan, and more importantly, to assist in the Indonesian government's effort to overhaul and reform its economy. Recalling the old proverb "a friend in need is a friend indeed", our team began to set up a strategy to persuade our Board members as well as the concerned ministry.

Because of the restraint of the bank's law prohibiting apparent balance-of-payment support loans, we considered that the only financial option available then was to finance the local cost portions of "ongoing" projects in Indonesia using an untied loan (not tied to Japanese goods and services). These had previously been exclusively used in the case of development of natural resources overseas under long-term supply contract of the resources with Japan as a destination. Frankly speaking, at the beginning we were not sure whether we could realize this unusual loan. What's more, our loan department had another difficult and urgent issue concerning how to deal with the Philippines, which just expelled the former President Marcos. The newly elected President Aquino also requested a new loan from the Export-Import Bank of Japan for rehabilitation of the country. The request came at the same time when negotiations on debt reduction (!) were to be conducted with foreign commercial banks.

Regarding the loan request from Indonesia and the World Bank, some argued that such a loan would be unwise for if the bank began to finance massively in such a way just to meet the local cost portions which any host government should generate by itself, the loan would virtually encourage easy fiscal policy of recipients, resulting in a disaster.

The argument had been orthodox for a long time. Thus careful study on the Indonesian economic policy over the past decade and the effectiveness of the new Indonesian government's policies to improve the situation as well as on the selection of good projects from over 50 on-going projects of the World Bank to which the bank was expected to finance were enthusiastically made by our team, including our representative office in Jakarta headed by Mr. M. Horiguchi. After the exhaustive studies for months, our team reported to Mr. K. Tanaka, then Governor, and other Board members that Indonesia's current financial crisis was not due to its policy failures but rather to a kind of *force-majeure,* and that the bank should and could support the government's effort to overcome difficulties most effectively by a timely *de-facto* balance-of-payment loan.

We added that "since the support is an emergency rescue, it would not be advisable to continue such a measure indefinitely". Some months later the Boards of the bank agreed to support the financial package, trusting in the technocrats in Indonesia who had been succesful in supporting President Soeharto by not having driven the heavily-indebted country into such overall debt overhang situation as widely seen in Latin America (plus the Philippines in case of Asia) in the 1980s. It was a nightmare referred to as "the lost decade". Thus soon after the bank committed a US$ 900 million untied loan for 21 ongoing World Bank projects in February 1987, most of the amount was disbursed to the government of Indonesia[1]. A US $ 300 million syndicated loan comprised of Japanese commercial banks soon followed. The above two were counted as the first two loans under the "Capital Recycling Program" initiated by the Japanese government[2]. In the following year, 1988, a yen credit of similarly quick disbursement type followed from OECF, a Japanese aid agency.

The assistance proved to be very successful. And all parties concerned then were happy to see the success. A few years later, fast growing manufactured good exports began to replace the position of reduced oil/gas revenue, and foreign direct investment in Indonesia began to soar at the end of the 1980s.

During the period and afterwards, I had the privilege as an expatriate to talk often with Dr. Widjojo both in Jakarta and Tokyo. *He enlightened me on what had happened in Jakarta, Washington, Davos, etc. We discussed the IGGI (now CGI), Bogor Declaration of APEC, NAM (Non-Aligned Movement), the socio-economic problem in general in developing countries and South-South socio-economic cooperation.* Occasionally, our common friends, Prof S. Asanuma, a former advisor to the Indonesian government (who later became Director of the World Bank), and Prof. M. Komatsu an advisor to the government until recently, a successor to Prof. Asanuma, joined the

---

1   For further information, see Masaaki Horiguchi, "Roles of Official Flows in Developing Finance their Concept and Introduction of Official Finance Development (ODF) *Journal of International Development Studies,* The Japan Society for International Development, Tokyo, Vol. 1 No. 1, November 1991.

2   For further information regarding the "Capital Recycling Program", see Toshihiko Kinoshita, *The End of the Cold War and Japan's financial contribution to international development* (S. Mansoob Murshed & Kunibert Rafter eds).

discussions. Dr. Widjojo, a man of strong memory, has always been well-informed of and sincere to any problem related to economic development issues. In such a way, I, for one, learned a lot from Dr. Widjojo and his close colleagues, who have treated me as their friend. I could not have studied well on the opportunities and challenges that developing countries encountered without the aquaintance of Dr. Widjojo and his group.

He is a true Javanese gentleman who is always calm, smiling, and seldom says "no". He loves his country from the bottom of his heart and has risked his life to support and improve its socio-economic situation. I gazed at his face when he said that he took a gun during the independence war and fought against the Dutch. It was no wonder that he did so, if you know his age. Yet, for years I had seen him as a born economist. Such a story as how he met President Soeharto for the first time enchanted me. He has many good friends all over the world. But, as I assume, not so many in the political field. There are exceptions, though. *He respected a Japanese politician, the late Mr. Takeo Fukuda, who has been famous particularly in the ASEAN region for the "Fukuda Doctrine". Dr. Widjojo wrote a short essay for him when he passed away a couple of years ago.* Former German Chancellor Helmut Schmidt also respected the former Japanese Prime Minister, famous for his sincerity, intellectuality, mental vitality and youthfulness in all his entire life. Dr. Schmidt described in his memoirs that Mr. Fukuda is special among all Japanese Prime Ministers whom he met. I believe that Dr. Widjojo found the same character of his own in Mr. Fukuda and enjoyed the discussion with him each time he visited Japan.

Now I regard myself as his "student", though symbolically. I once asked him whether he had an idea of writing a memoir for his fellow countrymen, policy makers, researchers and Indonesia watchers of the world. I said that many people strongly hope to see the *Guru's* memoirs. He said nothing but just smiled in quite a Javanese way.

Everyone has the ability to contribute to the world and his or her nation in his or her own unique way. Indeed, Prof. Dr. Widjojo has made a profound contribution to the Republic of Indonesia, particularly through the planning and implementation of development policies with his colleagues. He has also contributed to the international aid community at large as an advocate of better coordination between aid donors and recipients. What then has characterized his career? He has done, is doing and will continue to do his best and utmost. Since he is basically an optimist[3] he never gives up and always considers everything in his effort to reach a definite conclusion. He wishes to realize a better world and a better Indonesia. For that purpose he has dedicated all his time and efforts. Everyone who talks to him is impressed by *his wisdom and personal character: open-mindedness, intellect, modesty, strong will and his sense of humor. Everyone who knows him well fully understands that he never compromises on matters of principle.*

His painstaking efforts over the decades have earned him a world fame. He has received many awards nationally and internationally. Take Japan's case for instance, he was awarded "Grand Cordon of the Order of the Sacred Treasure" by the Japanese government in 1983. He was also given a special award as a major contributor to the economic development in Asia by *Nihon Keizai Shimbun* (Economic Journal of Japan) in 1996, which was recently established in that year (Dr. Manmohan Singh, former Finance Minister of India, became the second man to receive the same award, in May of this year).

Then, is Dr. Widjojo very popular in Indonesia? Naturally, yes. Everybody knows his name and his fame. However, it does not necessarily mean that the general public in Indonesia may be well-informed about what he is doing. His long-term friends and eminent economists on Indonesia, David C. Cole and Betty F. Slade wrote in their recent book that "the technocrats (in Indonesia) have also been remote from and little understood by the broader Indonesian public". It is probably due to their less frequent exposure in the press. Indonesian technocrats, Advisors to the President in particular, cannot shoot two birds at the same time. They are tackling difficult problems today quietly while dreaming of an improved situation for Indonesia tomorrow.

---

3 For instance, see Dr. Widjojo Nitisastro's address at the European Management Forum Davos Symposium: *In the Mutual Interest of Rich and Poor Nations,* January 30, 1982.

Indonesian youth have complained for almost twenty years that the era for the aged shall not last long. They have exclaimed "give us a chance". I can understand their logic. Should some of them be given high positions, then, will they dare to risk their lives to change the situation drastically through perenial fights with internal vested interests and so forth? And how? They would argue back, saying that "are you saying the current situation is good or tolerable for the intelligent" and that "we can not choose for ourselves". I have no intention of perpetuating a chicken-and-egg controversy on this issue here.

Let me conclude this short paper with a story from my own experience. Some twenty years ago, outside Japan, I became very well aquainted with a Korean banker, for whom I have great respect. One day, he asked me whether I could manage to get a series of certain Japanese historical books. It was a popular novel in Japan. I asked my friend in Japan to send them to me. Upon receiving several volumes, I delivered them to him. A couple of months later, he said that it took a long time to read through. That was due to his poor Japanese language. What he said was rather serious and provocative. "Mr. Kinoshita", he said, "You Japanese may not recognize. But you have been lucky, for each time when something critical to the nation happened, heroic people came up from somewhere and they risked their lives for the nation in various field. The tragedy of our nation of Korea is that there have been a great number of well-educated people in every historical period, but few of them really dedicated themselves to the nation in emergency situations. That has made a big difference between the two countries historically". I could not say a word.

I now recall his words. That has been true in Japan for a long time. But what about now? Everyone admits that now is the most critical period to Japan for its true rejuvenation for the next century, similar to the period of *Meiji Restoration* after the defeat in the World War II. Japan needs genuine reform (or revolution) in politics, business and education. Japanese must make their government slim and make it very efficient. Private firms must observe good corporate governance, make the decision-making process quicker and transparent with individual responsibility. Are there many leaders who are willing to risk their lives for those reforms? There is an old Chinese proverb saying that "when a household becomes almost bankrupt, a filial child appears, and when the country falls into a critical situation, a truly loyal chancellor appears". Will this hold true of Japan today? And what about Japanese youth?[4]

Today, unlike several decades or a couple of centuries ago, every Japanese is able to spend a rather complacent life without putting him or herself into a critical position by fighting with the vested interests, for instance. That's why many young people have become more conservative than their seniors. They tend to say that today it is the firm or individual that selects the country where they dwell, and not the reverse, and that, if Japan cannot change for the better, they might as well move to the US, Canada, Australia or elsewhere.

Well, then, whose responsibility is it to reform Japan? Those people would not be truly welcomed and trusted anywhere, because anyone who does not love his or her country and not try to improve— the condition of the country through his or her own capacity (except the politically abused) would and could not love his or her new place, be it New York, Paris, London or Sydney. Those places will be just good dwelling spots for them as decent places of convenience. Someone must keep the country or city in order. So, some day, President/Prime Minister or governors/city mayors would echo the theme of former US President Kennedy. "Ask not what your country (state or city) can do for you. Ask what you can do for your country". Then those who fled from their duties in their homeland would be the first to recognize what they should have done.

It may be improper to compare the above story to the current situation in Indonesia. However, I have observed that many Indonesians aspire to realize far more egalitarian, more affluent and freer society with more efficient government sometime in the 21st century. If that be the case, Indonesians must begin to really tackle reforming their socio-economic situation with all their might. Will many Indonesian youth respond positively?

Deep in my heart, I am worried about Indonesian youth, as I am about Japanese youth, most of whom keep silent now. They may begin to consider something big for the future. Hopefully, they will jump up sooner and show us their own picture of how to develop and manage their own country better and how to co-prosper with the rest of the world.

I believe Dr. Widjojo also really wishes to see this happen soon in his own country and in other countries of the world.

Long live *Guru Bapak* Widjojo. ◆

48

The Interaction between Economic Growth and Welfare is Summed Up in the 'Development Triad' of Growth, Stability and Equity

William C. Hollinger*

When I arrived in Indonesia as a graduate student in the early 1950s the first person I met was Widjojo Nitisastro. That was my very good fortune, continuing a precedent of good luck in making Indonesian friends: the very first two Indonesians I had met in the United States before coming to Jakarta were Professor Sumitro and later Professor Sadli. After my "generals" at the Massachusetts Institute of Technology I had joined the Indonesian team of a research project at MIT undertaking a comparative study on the economic development of Indonesia, India, and Italy. In the period of preparation before going to the field I had met Professor Sumitro when he visited MIT. A former United Nations advisor to the Ministry of Finance during his tenure in that office, the Canadian economist Benjamin Higgins was the leader of the Indonesian part of the MIT study. That same summer Professor Sadli was in Cambridge, Massachusetts attending a summer seminar being conducted by Henry Kissinger of somewhat later fame.

Sumitro, Sadli, and Widjojo! For an American graduate student hoping to become a professional economist it would be hard to think of a better start in becoming acquainted with the country.

* Mr.William C. Hollinger (US) was member of a Harvard team that advised the National Development Planning Board (Bappenas) on international trade, foreign exchange and investment, and oil and mineral policy (1968-1974). He advised the government of Indonesia in an independent capacity, fulfilling contracts with Bappenas, various economic ministries, as well as with the state-owned companies Krakatau Steel and Pertamina. He also advised other governments and private corporations, and helped to establish a private consultancy in Indonesia that offers advice in fields such as energy, environment, and manpower.

During Professor Sumitro's visit to MIT it had been agreed that I would teach two courses at the Faculty of Economics—International Trade and National Income Accounting—for no salary but for office space and research assistance. As a result I spent almost three years professionally based in FEUI. This gave me an extended opportunity to know and work with Professor Widjojo as fellow graduate students. This was both a pleasant experience and instructive.

In particular, I was always very grateful to Widjojo for the good spirits and perseverance with which he undertook the thankless task of helping me find some place to live in Jakarta. In those days the accommodations and rental prospects in Jakarta were a far cry from those of today. Apartments did not exist. The one good hotel in town, the Des Indes, was almost entirely occupied by individuals and business that set up permanent quarters in it. Finally, after a heroic effort we located a room over the laundry in the Hotel Dharma Nirmala—which stood where the President's office is now located—which I shared with three other men! Things did get better, much better, after a spell.

Many of the qualities that later marked Widjojo's career, such as single minded pursuit of the current priority objective, patience and good humor were in evidence in his performance of that lowly task. Looking forward, one would have to have had a degree of clairvoyance to have foreseen the historic role Professor Widjojo would come to play, but looking back, one can see that the qualities of mind and personality that shaped his performance as a manager of economic policy were clearly evident in Widjojo the graduate student. More of that later.

In addition to getting to know many of the future members of the "Berkeley Mafia" then still students, I was able to play the part of a fly on the wall observing the birth of the UI - Berkeley affiliation that in time produced the "Mafia". The MIT project which had brought me to Indonesia was made possible by a Ford Foundation grant. This resulted in a good deal of contact which in turn developed into a personal friendship with Mike Harris then the Foundation's representative in Jakarta. As a result of that relationship, I became a sort of case carrier cum errand boy for Mike and the various senior professors who came out to Jakarta from California to define the arrangements with Professor Sumitro in his role as dean of the faculty.

The early days of the California affiliation were interesting and exciting times for everyone in the Economics Faculty. There were some bumpy moments with the initial faculty arrivals from Berkeley, but soon people like Leon Mears and Bruce Glassbumer appeared on the scene, men who quickly established a constructive rapport with their Indonesian colleagues and who continued over the years to have an intimate and useful involvement with Indonesian activities as long as they were professionally active.

The field work phase of the MIT project ended and I returned to MIT in 1956. During the remainder of the Soekarno years when Professor Widjojo was first doing his graduate studies at Berkeley and then, per force, keeping a low profile at FEUI and Leknas there was a long hiatus in my direct contact with him. This must have been a tricky and frustrating time for Professor Widjojo and his Berkeley program colleagues. He did, however, make good use of this quiet interlude in his career. Fortunately for Indonesia the domestic political situation did not preclude his teaching economics at the ABRI command school in Bandung.

In 1966, at the very start of his tenure in office, Soeharto turned for help in developing and implementing the economic component of the New Order. Widjojo, in turn, mobilized the assistance of his fellow alumni of the FEUI-University of California affiliation and the "Mafia" was born.

Faced with the challenge of creating a relevant and effective Bappenas, Widjojo sought assistance once again from the Ford Foundation, and the Development Advisory Service (DAS) of Harvard University (now the Harvard Institute of International Development, or HIID) was commissioned to field a team to work for and support Bappenas efforts in preparing the First and Second Repelita. I was fortunate to be working for the DAS when this opportunity arose. At that time I was working with a Harvard team in Liberia. In addition to the prospect of working with old friends the choice between Jakarta and Monrovia was not very difficult. I returned to Indonesia in August 1968 and worked with the Harvard team in Bappenas until the Ford Foundation project ended in 1974. That was the period of my most active working relationship with Professor Widjojo. However, I did continue to work with various economic ministries or agencies until the late 1980s. This afforded me the chance to observe the remarkable achievements of Professor Widjojo throughout the full twenty five years of the First Long Term Development period.

The extent of those achievements is hard to overestimate. Indonesia's remarkable economic and social transformation during the quarter of a century following 1966 was largely the work of policies defined and implemented by Professor Widjojo and his colleagues in the Berkeley Mafia. While in an important sense that effort was a collegial effort Professor Widjojo was clearly the leader of the Economic Team—to give the group its more formal designation—and the main architect of their activities. He was the "Chairman of the Board".

Under Widjojo's leadership the Economic Team played a key role in bringing about Indonesia's long sustained economic growth and enhanced quality of life with its accompanying dramatic reduction in poverty. *Other countries have achieved higher growth rates in particular years, but no other country, as far as I know, has sustained high growth rates uninterruptedly for more than twenty five years.* This in one of the many remarkable "stabilities"—the consistency of policy direction and the tenures of key policy personnel are two other important ones—that characterize the Indonesian economic success story during this period.

The details of the role of the Team's policy performance and its contribution to that success story has been studied and recounted many times elsewhere. *What is appropriate on this occasion is to ask how it was that Professor Widjojo played the important part in the history of the period. The explanation is a combination of personality, talents, and perceptions.*

It seems to me that personality is an important component in this story. It was important on two different counts: in shaping the nature of the Economic Team; and it was important in shaping the team's relationship to the government and the process of running the country. It was important to the character of the Economic Team because the Team was not a group with an inherited structure or whose structure evolved over the course of time. It was essentially a group that came into existence on the spur of the moment at a watershed point in the nation's history. It consisted of contemporaries, all of whom knew each other well and all of whom were highly talented people, men of strong personalities.

It is easy for such a group to start as friends and colleagues but end as competitors and antagonists unless a leader who can achieve cohesion without generating rebellion emerges. Professor Widjojo was such a natural leader. He knew where he wanted to go and what it would take to get there. He was able to exert his leadership and maintain the unity of the group through the force of his personality, his drive, his commitment and the central importance he placed on loyalty to and within the group.

While many people—including, above all, President Soeharto himself along with many other members of the government and all the members of the Team—contributed to shaping the operational characteristics of macro-economic management throughout the New Order period, Widjojo's imprint is clearly to be seen. This is particularly true of the regime's pragmatism, the sure sense of timing, the emphasis on stability and continuity, the focus on issues of poverty reduction and the capacity to learn from mistakes or set backs. Above all his personality was critical in the unique relationship he and the Team had with the President. This relationship, of course, was critical to the Team's impact on policy and the overall success of its efforts.

Certainly the depth and longevity of Professor Widjojo's relationship with President Soeharto contributed hugely to the success of Indonesia's economic and social policies since 1966. This relationship was based on what appears to outsiders to be the unusually high level of compatibility of the two men. They both are deeply rooted in the culture and etiquette of their native Java. They both place great importance on politeness, decorum, and a proper respect for position and relationships. They both are good judges of people and both are men who like their thinking and analysis to be based on facts and details.

Given that this relationship provided the basis for Professor Widjojo's impact on developments since 1966, what is the explanation of the effectiveness with which he used that opportunity? Thinking back over the long record of Professor Widjojo's accomplishments, a number of characteristics of his performance come to mind. First is his ability to prioritize the issues with which he is dealing at any juncture and to focus his concentration on what he judges to be the key issue of the moment. His unusually long—and well organized—memory allows him to operate in this highly focused way without the other important issues becoming lost or overlooked when it becomes appropriate to move them to the center of the stage. I remember one occasion. I think it was in 1973, when he called me into his office and asked me if I could lay my hands on a memo I had sent to him about two years earlier. When I wrote the memo the issue it raised was not then a top priority for the Chairman of Bappenas, but its time had come!

Another characteristics that never fails to impress the observer, and which is also important in explaining the sustained success of the program is his astute and finely attuned sense of time. This feel for the right time to make a move or take an action operated in several dimensions: the economic, the political and the social. It is not only a question of when to make a particular move, but also the pace of actions and change that the political and economic systems will tolerate. When one observes the chaos and economic decline plaguing the former Soviet Union since 1992, one cannot help but wonder whether it would not have been better for Russia if the pace of change had not been more moderate. It is not just the pace at which reforms and policy initiatives took place, but Widjojo and his colleagues in the Economic Team showed a deft hand at usually getting the correct order in which things were done. It seems to me that this aspect of the Team's performance is, in part, the other side of the coin of the often mentioned pragmatism of Indonesia policy since 1966.

Other aspects of the regime's pragmatism have been the ability to learn from mistakes and the efficiency in modifying tactics as the domestic and international economic conditions alter without changing policy directions and objectives. The response to

Pertamina's financial difficulties that surfaced in the spring of 1974 is a good example of both the sense of timing and the ability to learn from adverse events in the domestic economy. That Pertamina had a financial planning and control problem was suspected earlier than March 1974, but until the foreign creditors of Pertamina began claiming default it was difficult to address the issue in any basic way. Once the foreign banks began to make claims on the government for obligations incurred by Pertamina actions to gain fiscal control and accountability in Pertamina in particular and the remaining state enterprises in general were swift and well designed. In fact, it was the response to the Pertamina crisis that provided the Republic with the opportunity to access private international financial markets with quite good terms from the beginning of its participation in those markets.

The responses to the oil shocks of both the 1970s and 1980s are good examples of the ability to adjust to unexpected impacts of international events. The response to the huge increase in resource inflows that resulted from the rise of oil prices starting in 1973 was responsible for making Indonesia largely immune to the so-called "Dutch Disease" that afflicted most of the other OPEC exporters. The response to the sharp fall in oil prices of the early 1980s, on the other hand, permitted the country's high growth rate to continue largely unscathed. The "rephasing" of large projects allowed resources to be husbanded for the social and economic development programs, while the process of restructuring and deregulation that was launched against the background of pessimism on future oil revenues laid the basis for the pervasive diversification of the economy and the rapid increase in non-oil exports. In all these developments Professor Widjojo played a key role.

Another trait of Professor Widjojo and his colleagues in the Economic Team that never failed to impress me was *their calmness in the face of serious difficulties*. This ability to keep cool was helpful in their handling of the Pertamina crisis and the later fall in oil prices. Perhaps their most impressive display of this *sang froid* came in implementing the decision to substantially free the rupiah exchange rate mechanism in the early 1970s at a time when foreign exchange reserves were quite low. From a relatively exposed position they promulgated what at that time was as free an exchange rate regime as you could find in many OECD countries and freer than any other developing country.

Many people familiar with the Indonesian development story are particularly impressed with Professor Widjojo's role in what may well be Indonesia's major contribution to the thinking about the development process: the centrality of the interaction between economic growth and welfare. This, of course, is summed up in the Indonesian context under the rubric of the 'Development Triad' of growth, stability, and equity. There are occasionally snide remarks that brush this concept off as empty sloganeering. It is not. It catches the essence and has shaped much of the actions adopted in the Indonesian pursuit of development. Professor Widjojo and his colleagues understood that without stability, economic reconstruction and later development, could not take root and be sustained and without growth it would not be possible to mount a significant attack on poverty, the main component of equity and conversely without poverty reduction it would be difficult to sustain the conditions allowing both growth and stability.

While the approach was central to President Soeharto's public policy, and political thinking, many people contributed to its articulation and implementation. Professor Widjojo was one of the principle architects of the Development Triad in action. His major contribution, in his successive roles of Chairman of the Economic Team/Chairman of Bappenas/Minister of National Development Planning/Coordinating Minister for Economic, Financial and Industrial Affairs, was as overseer and manager of economic policy initiatives seeking to achieve the goals of the triad. In addition, he played a more direct role in the intense attention he gave to the issue of a sound rice economy and adequate supplies of the basic commodities at stable prices that assured both the producer and the consumer that their interests were being served.

This was a part of Professor Widjojo's activities when his legendary powers of concentration on the priority issue of the day were most sharply on display. When a critical issue arose in the rice economy the lights in his office often burned through the night! This attention to issues of the rice economy was part of a broader concern with the equity component of the development strategy. Poverty reduction was never far from Professor Widjojo's thoughts.

One could go on and on enumerating things that one admired about Professor Widjojo as a person and about his accomplishments as a public figure. Let me draw this short personal memoir to a close by simply saying how much I have felt privileged, how much I have enjoyed, and how much I have learned by working for and with Professor Widjojo. The whole experience was greatly enhanced by his unfailing courtesy. ◆

49

My Mentor and Indispensable Person For Indonesia and Japan

Masaaki Komatsu *

I first met Prof. Widjojo in 1984, when I became a member of the financial advisors (called the Advisory Group, which consists of three investment banks i.e., Lehman Brothers, Lazard Freres and SG Warburg) to the Government of Indonesia. Since then Prof. Widjojo is my mentor.

At that time Prof. Widjojo was an advisor to the Indonesian Government and his office was at Bappenas. It was not easy to meet him and we used to wait for hours at his waiting room. There were a number of people waiting in queue, who told us that they were also waiting for even longer time. Once Prof. Widjojo received us he spent hours with us asking many questions and guiding us to the imminent economic issues which the Government should tackle. Chairs in his meeting room at Bappenas were old and springs were sticking out. But, our discussions were always stimulating and his guidance was thoughtful and precisely to the point. When we came out of his room after the long meeting, our bottom was sores but we all were so excited and filled with the mission.

Despite Prof. Widjojo's high position and our age gap, he makes me feel so much at ease by his great warmth and kind personality. For those who know him, in addition to his professional capabilities, it is his personality that makes people feel affected toward Indonesia. He is a gentle, warm and caring person. He is a clear-headed

* Prof. Masaaki Komatsu (Japan) is Professor of the Graduate School for International Development and Cooperation Hiroshima University, Japan.

economic thinker, policy architect and statesman. He is not only a seer economic intellectual. He is a man of action filled with a firm sense of mission. Despite his eminence and seniority he always analyzes issues in detail by his own, and thrashes out a solution to the problems for a number of policy makers and senior government officials. He also meets with young government officials even at director (*kachou*) level. With whoever he met, he made a deep impression and became good friends. I often saw him carry an old typewriter at the lobby of Hotel Okura in Tokyo. After the series of meetings with Japanese policy makers and officials, he used to sit in front of the old typewriter and tried to improve the documents by incorporating what he had discussed during the meetings before. I have never met any other minister working like Prof. Widjojo.

It is wrong to think that Japan is the one who helps the Indonesian Government unilaterally. It is true Japan has been providing a substantial amount of economic assistance to Indonesia. The relationship is, however, always mutual and two-way. Prof. Widjojo helped Japan and the Japanese senior officials at various occasions, particularly at difficult time. He helped Japanese officials to understand Indonesia better. He gave advises to Japanese politicians and senior officials how to proceed with Indonesia at a crucial point. He also carried many difficult messages back to Indonesia from Japan and tried to convince his colleagues, senior policy makers in Indonesia. He possesses an amazing capacity to listen to outside views and opinions. He always listens carefully and patiently even to what the Indonesian Government does not normally wish to hear. And if he agrees that it is of crucial importance to Indonesia-Japan relationship, he is the one who carries the difficult task bravely and carefully with a strong will.

Because of his educational background he is often considered to be pro-American. I would like to say, however, among many Indonesians, who are considered to be close friends of Japan, Prof. Widjojo understand Japan most and he is the best friend of Japan. People tends to forget their true friend who helped them at difficult times. Prof. Widjojo is indispensable for Japan-Indonesia relationship at difficult times.

It is considered that Prof. Widjojo is always cautious with large capital intensive projects. It is clear that Prof. Widjojo's objective is not only to make development projects successful, but to achieve Indonesia's economic development sustainable. With strong oppositions from more powerful business interests in both Indonesia and Japan who narrowly focused on their own affairs, Prof. Widjojo had to fight without rest in order to maintain prudence in Indonesia's economic management, but he did not always succeed.

Ironically, no project can be successful, if there is no brave policy actions led by Prof. Widjojo. Success of an individual project depends upon the success of Indonesia's macro management. Too many projects and too much borrowings without screening would lead to overheating of the economy and balance of payment problems, thus viability of all the projects would also be negatively affected. For those who invest in Indonesia, it is their presumption that the prudent economic management is to be maintained; therefore there would not be too much borrowings and too many projects except their own. This is clearly a fallacy of composition. There is no doubt that the creditworthiness of Indonesia would have been much worse and foreign investments as well as domestic investments would have been much less, if there were no "Widjojonomics". Not many foreign investors, including the Japanese, have realized this fact.

His contribution is not limited to the management of Indonesia's economic development. He is also dedicated in helping the development of the Third World. His contribution to the Third World development is not only the intellectual quality but the quiet work behind the scene. Prof. Widjojo makes efforts to disseminate benefits of economic success in Indonesia to other developing countries including Sub-Sahara Africa. He seeks to promote development in these countries by offering valuable advises on the basis of his own country's experiences and achievements. He also encourages the Japanese Government to take an initiative to extend more substantive assistance to developing countries, particularly to the poorest countries like Sub-Sahara Africa, which are compatible with Japan's economic strength. Prof. Widjojo tries to forge a common vision of economic development and international cooperation between developed and developing countries.

Now turning myself to teaching at a graduate school of Hiroshima University starting from this year, I try to review what I learned from Prof. Widjojo over the last number of years. He is always against narrow economic nationalism. He distrusts protectionism as a means of economic development. He distrusts the use of economic sanctions to solve economic conflicts.

He accepts the reality in Third World development that there are no simple and quick solutions. He trusts the goodwill of people, believes in the importance of freedom and free markets and trusts people's wisdom to overcome difficulties that lie in front of us. He is confident that problems facing the Third World can be overcome, at least step by step, through concerted action taken together by the developed and developing countries.

And those are the themes I wish my students understand deeply in their heart. ◆

50

A Towering Figure on the World Economic Scene, a Scholar, a Teacher and Writer as Well as a Statesman

Eric Roll*

I t gives me very great pleasure to have this opportunity of taking part in a tribute to Professor Widjojo Nitisastro on the occasion of his 70th birthday. Professor Widjojo *is a towering figure on the world economic scene, a scholar, a teacher and writer as well as a statesman*. I had heard of Professor Widjojo as a Professor at the University of Indonesia when I was first becoming acquainted with the post—war and post—colonial history and development of his country in the sixties when I was the United Kingdom Executive Director of the World Bank and the International Monetary Fund in Washington. I had also around that time heard about him and the development that Indonesia was then embarking upon from my old Harvard friend, Professor Edward Mason, who together with a team of American economists was at that time advising the Indonesian authorities.

My own opportunity of making the acquaintance of Professor Widjojo came exactly 30 years ago in 1967. He had just been made Chairman of the Economic Team and I had just left my public service

* Lord Eric Roll of Ipsden (UK) was educated on the Continent and at the University of Birmingham where he received a Ph.D. He had a long public service career and an ealier academic career before entering banking activities. In 1963 he became Head of the U.K. Treasury Delegation, Washington and also Executive Director for the U.K. International Monetary Fund and International Bank for Reconstruction and Development. From 1964-66 he was Permanent Under-Secretary of State, Department of Economic Affairs. From 1971-80 he was an independent member of the NEDC and from 1980-83 Director of Times Newspapers Ltd. He was Director of the Bank of England from 1968-77 and Chairman of S.G. Warburg & Co.Ltd. from 1974-1983. He was Joint-Chairman of S.G. Warburg & Co. Ltd. from 1983-87. In addition he was Chairman of Mercury Securities Ltd. from 1974-84. From 1987-95 he was President of S.G. Warburg Group plc and he is now Senior Adviser of SBC Warburg. He passed away in 2005.

career after many years and after an earlier academic career and was entering the City of London as a member of a United Kingdom merchant bank. I met Professor Widjojo as I remember very vividly, though I do not know whether he will remember it, in 1967 at a conference in Geneva organised by a number of international industrial and financial leaders, very largely from the United States and very much under the general guidance of David Rockefeller, designed to meet the "new" team of those who were then taking the leadership of Indonesia's development.

Professor Widjojo played the most important part in that group and in that gathering. He was the leader of the economic component of what was clearly going to be a major new thrust of development after the early trials and tribulations of political independence and the turbulent immediate political sequelae of that development.

A few years later I had the opportunity of getting to know Professor Widjojo more closely and on an individual basis when I was negotiating primarily with Bank Indonesia. But obviously it also involved all the economic ministries and Bappenas—the National Planning Agency—of which Professor Widjojo was then the head. They were assigned as advisers on international economics with greater emphasis on financial matters.

As this relationship is continuing now and clearly involves business matters as well as current high policy issues, it would be inappropriate to dilate upon it here. However, what can be said is that it has given those of us who are privileged to be involved in the specially valuable possibility to observe the practical applications of principles and experiences of planning and development at close quarters and in an environment of exceptional opportunity.

The achievements of Indonesia in this last quarter of a century or so are of course remarkable and Professor Widjojo and the relatively small number of people associated closely with him in this work have written a page of economic development which will remain outstanding and of model value in the history of modern economic development theory and practice.

The literature of economic development is very large and still growing. Professor Widjojo has made many distinguished contributions to it. However, what is particularly impressive in my opinion is not only the elaboration of principles of economic development but more particularly the marriage between these principles derived ultimately from basic economic tenets to the actual practical problems of a particular nation state at a particular time.

Indeed Indonesia has many unique features. The size and geographical uniqueness of its structure, its large population, its endowment with large and important natural resources, its possession of a population of considerable talent both in work and in thought already having achieved a substantial development in a cultural sense and with a long history which has among other things given it experience in varying circumstances, political and economic, offers a specially difficult field for the application of principles of economic development in practice.

To be really successful, economic development has to rely not only on sound economics, its analysis, particularly in relation to problems of the stages of economic development, but it also has to be very carefully and meticulously adapted to the history and current situation in every possible respect, political, cultural, demographic as well as national structure and international circumstances of the day and of the country concerned. The best economic development principles will not succeed if they do not take into account the constraints which history and current circumstances impose upon their application. Here, Indonesia has been remarkably successful and here Professor Widjojo has shown a unique talent in producing a coherent and successful marriage between principles and practical possibilities.

At the outset of the period during which I have had the privilege to observe more closely the development of Indonesia's economy and finances, the main problems I suppose could be classified as lying primarily in the field of balance of payments policy, the management of the country's reserves, the utilisation to the fullest extent of the export and foreign exchange earning possibilities in international trade of Indonesia's large resources, notably oil. This required a great deal of subtle and yet practical planning of Central Bank policy in regard to foreign exchanges to the exchange rate of the rupiah itself, to the encouragement of maximum export earnings and import saving possibilities. Needless to say arising out of this were also very important consequences for internal monetary policy in regard to interest rates, credit control and so forth, with its wider implications for the development of the banking system and capital markets.

Very soon the still wider implications of all this became evident and led to the tackling of fiscal, that is to say budgetary, problems as well as the broader planning of the development of technology, the encouragement of particular types of industry and the organisation of the corporate sector both private and public, in so far as it was or remained in public hands. In short the whole gamut of economic and financial issues that confront a modern state.

Alongside these developments the administrative apparatus in so far as the state and its authority had to be brought into play was being adapted so as to make it more effective and more efficient in fulfilling its tasks. Not surprisingly, although titles and organisations and their attributions were changed from time to time, a core of personnel, a sort of stage army if I could call it that, remained in being throughout the period and with it Professor Widjojo very much at the head and at the centre.

I should mention that apart from my relationship through the specific advisory contacts with the Indonesian authorities I had many opportunities of meeting Professor Widjojo in international organisations and conferences. One that I think deserves particular mention, which gave me great pleasure, was to be privileged to sit alongside him in a group of what were known as "eminent persons" brought together by the United Nations under the leadership of Helmut Schmidt, the former German Chancellor, and containing a number of former Prime Ministers, Central Bank Governors as well as academics from North America, Europe, Asia, and Africa, of which Professor Widjojo was a very prominent member. I also belonged to that group whose task was to produce a report on the best way of maintaining in the long term a flow of funds to the developing countries both on a bilateral and multilateral basis, through individual countries as well as from international or supranational sources, so as to ensure the continuity of the assistance which countries at a certain stage of development still required could be guaranteed.

Our group produced its report. I myself believe it was a good one and each of us had the task of submitting it to our respective head of government or state in certain cases. This was duly done. As so happens with reports of this kind, it was widely acclaimed and regarded as a major contribution to a highly important subject and to the solution of the problems with which it was concerned, but I personally would find it very difficult to point to any very practical steps which followed from it. I do not know whether Professor Widjojo shares this impression but if he does, I am sure he will feel as I do that this is the sort of fate that is not uncommon for some of the best reports of this character.

This is not the place to embark upon an elaborate analysis of the problems of economic development of Indonesia or indeed of development more generally nor of the details of the present achievements and still remaining problems of this country to which Professor Widjojo has made such an outstanding contribution. What I can perhaps repeat to conclude with is a point which I have made earlier, namely to stress the very intricate process of combining good economics with good policy and good policy with good application to practical problems. Here the secret of success in my view, and by success I mean not only short-term practical success but acknowledgement of a lasting achievement, lies in not abandoning the wisdom accumulated over centuries of economic analysis to pressing exigencies nor, on the other hand, of ignoring these immediate practical urgencies and the constraints which they impose for the sake of upholding and maintaining abstract economic principles. This secret, this very difficult balancing act, is not frequently achieved by economists who venture out into the field of statecraft. Professor Widjojo Nitisastro is an outstanding example of such achievement: very unique and deserving of the highest praise and recognition. ◆

51

We Three Investment Banks Have Advised Many Governments and Many Officials, but No One Has Held Our Affection and Admiration as He Has

*William G. Bardel**

I t is a privilege to be asked to write in connection with the celebration of Professor Widjojo's 70th birthday.

I worked with and for the Professor as a member of the Troika, the team of three investment banks which have advised the Government of Indonesia since 1975. *We three banks—Lehman Brothers, S.G Warburg, and Lazard Freres—have advised many governments, and many public officials, since we began our collaboration in Indonesia, but not one has held our affection and admiration as has the Professor.*

On many Saturday mornings we sat with him in his office at Bappenas—a bit dark and cool, spare, not too recently redecorated, totally without pretension—and explored problems and opportunities, not only relating particularly to Indonesia, but also to developing economies every where. With a question, several nods, and typically a smile of sympathetic understanding, we were led, as in a tutorial, through the material which interested the professor and then, inevitably, were given several assignments for our next meeting.

As we left, we invariably felt encouraged to do our utmost to justify a return visit as soon as possible. Professor Widjojo has the special ability to draw out the best from his colleagues and advisors,

---

*   Mr. William G. Bardel (U.S). was a former managing director of Lehman Brothers, the US investment bank, where he was the head of the firm's government advisory group. In conjunction with two other banks, Lehman Brothers has been a financial advisor to the Indonesian Government since 1975.

always curious and open-minded, never defensive or dogmatic. And, as a tutor, he was far too considerate ever (well, rarely) to reveal any disappointment with the efforts of his students.

Most importantly, perhaps Professor Widjojo throughout his career has had the ability to identify good colleagues, to encourage their best work, and without prejudice or personal bias, to translate ideas into effective policy. Who, in recent weeks, looking at economic policies and the exceptional financial disturbances in Southeast Asia could not be pleased—indeed proud—of Indonesia's response so in contrast to certain of its neighbors. This, as we all know, is in large measure because of the outstanding contribution of Professor Widjojo—and his exceptional compatriot Professor Ali Wardhana—to Indonesia policy over many years.

I no longer have occasion to visit Indonesia as I once did, and from afar, as I respect Professor Widjojo, I also miss the friendship and thoughtfulness which he showed to me and my companions on so many occasions.

Best wishes to him for the happiest of birthdays. ◆

52

May Others Follow His Example

*Helie de Pourtales**

I am a modest but keen observer of human behavior, in particular that of people in power, having been close, as a financial advisor, to more than thirty governments, over the past twenty years. I have seen the ambitious, the brutal, the Machiavellian, and more rarely the visionary, the good, the humane.

Professor Widjojo Nitisastro was one of the first Ministers I met in Indonesia, in 1974, together with Professor Sumitro Djojoha-dikusumo, Professor Ali Wardhana, Professor Rachmat Saleh and later on Professor Sumarlin. The Ministers decided in early 1975 to select our investment bank as one of the three financial advisors to the Government.

1975 was a year of crisis, one of the biggest financial crisis of the time in the world. One from which most Governments would shy away, and abandon all to multinational institutions. No foreign exchange reserves at all, high level of debt, few elements of decision available, a mountain of unpaid promissory notes signed by Pertamina, Bank Indonesia funds blocked by determined profiteers, everything that could happen, did so.

* M. Helie de Pourtales (France) has been responsible for International Operations at Lazard Freres since 1979; he created the International Capital Market Division, the International Merger and Acquisition Department and the Government Advisory Division. In this capacity, he has been acting as Adviser to many Governments and Central Banks throughout the world, particularly in connection with the implementation of economic stabilisation measures and debt renegotiation or reduction programmes. He is General Partner at Lazard Freres et Cie, Bankers in Paris, New York, London and Tokyo since 1979.

Within the tempest there was good, solid, but inspired judgement from the above team, with Professor Widjojo Nitisastro *calming the muddied and furious waters with an elegant and clear mind, a dedication, a patience to listen.* This is an inimitable style, one which we, Europeans, like to define as Asian, for the good reason that we have no such harmonious minds over here.

Then the seemingly inevitable rescheduling of the Republic's external debt was avoided, profiteers were sent home, creditors were impressed, and Indonesia was on its way.

I think that *harmony is the right word when we think of Professor Widjojo, and then he has the virtue of giving more than he receives.* We have always felt better about people after having had the pleasure of seeing him, working with him as we have now done for twenty two years.

I have always thought that *he has shown us that it was possible to be morally clean, and in power.* We did not really know that this was possible, or possible to that extent. Perhaps Gandhi would have taught that to us too. To give energy to other people with the most polite attention, with dignity as deep as a well, and never, but never letting anything of importance go unheeded, that could benefit the country.

The lesson we learnt, we have recited in other countries, sometimes, but rarely with success. *It is not easy to be a visionary with economic power, and not to fall to compromise.*

Indonesia as a whole is an example to the world. Professor Widjojo Nitisastro has been one of the pillars used to create Indonesia. May others follow his example. ◆

53

An Exceptional Figure Who Combines Statesmanship, Vision and Wisdom With Decisiveness

Herman C. van der Wijck*

It is a privilege and pleasure for me to have the opportunity of taking part in a tribute to Professor Widjojo Nitisastro on the occasion of his 70th birthday.

In the nearly forty years I have been involved in industry, investment, and banking, there have been fortunately gratifying occasions, albeit all too rare, *to meet and work for an exceptional figure on the world scene who combines statesmanship, vision and wisdom with decisiveness, a brilliant analytical mind of an outstanding human qualities.* Professor Widjojo Nitisastro is such a figure.

My initial experience with Indonesia following a long family tradition was that of a schoolboy, spending golden and exciting years in Bandung. It was therefore one of the most challenging and exhilarating moments in my life to be given the opportunity in 1975 to return to my roots and serve the Government of Indonesia, under the aegis of Professor Widjojo Nitisastro, Governor Rachmat Saleh, Professor Ali Wardhana and their ministerial colleagues as a member of a team of financial advisors, retained by Bank Indonesia and constituted by a consortium of three investment banks. This team, the Advisory Group - known in Indonesia as the "Three

---

* Mr. H.C. van der Wijck (Netherlands) joined S.G. Warburg & Co.Ltd. in 1969 and was appointed Director in 1973. Since 1975, he has been closely involved with Indonesia as a senior member of a team of financial advisers - The Advisory Group - retained by Bank Indonesia. The Advisory Group has served the Indonesian Government for more than twenty two-years. Prior to joining Warburg, Mr. van der Wyck spent nine years with the Royal Dutch / Shell Group of Companies, where he was first associated with marketing operations in a number of Far Eastern countries and later at the London head office with joint production, refining and marketing in French speaking countries.

Houses" was appointed by the Government in the wake of the Pertamina debacle, at the time one of the most serious external financial crises to be faced by any country.

The crisis was resolutely met and solved; and not only was rescheduling avoided of the mountain of Pertamina debts, for which the Indonesian Government had courageously assumed responsibility, but the sound principles on which the country's economy had been rebuilt since 1966—namely stringent fiscal and monetary policies, the balanced budget principle and a freely convertible Rupiah—were preserved. Without the leadership and judgement of Professor Widjojo Nitisastro and the technocrat Ministers this could not have been achieved.

However, crisis management is only successful if solid foundations have been established for the management of the economy and it is here that Indonesia owes an immense debt of gratitude to Professor Widjojo Nitisastro. His wide grasp of sound macro-economic principles, his ability to adapt these to Indonesia's cultural and social environment and his masterful handling of a succession of domestic and external challenges and shocks have been essential elements in the spectacularly successful and sustained rise of the country during more than three decades to a leading economic power.

Indonesia's impressive growth record, the country's increasingly diversified and deregulated economy thereby reducing its initial dependence on oil and gas exports, the establishment of a strong rural sector with self-sufficiency in rice, the vigorous inflows of capital and the Government's willingness to embark on a comprehensive programme of structural reforms and timely policy adjustments all bear witness to Prof. Widjojo Nitisastro's guiding hand.

In the twenty-two years that we have been associated as financial advisers with these achievements, I have had the unique privilege of not only observing Prof. Widjojo Nitisastro as a leader and mentor but also as an exceptional human being. *Invariably calm, courteous and patient whilst radiating confidence and dignity Prof. Widjojo Nitisastro always makes those who work for him feel that their lives have been morally and intellectually enriched through his presence, the intensity with which he listens and his gift to go to the heart of the matter.* It is therefore natural that Prof. Widjojo Nitisastro is held in the highest esteem not only in his country but also far beyond its borders. His understanding of Indonesia's place in the world and in the international fora of which he is a prominent member, as evidenced by his deep involvement in the continuing North South dialogue, enables Prof. Widjojo Nitisastro to provide the leaders of his country with wise counsel on the consequences of economic policy initiatives and to consider those in a true global perspective.

There is a saying in my country that the love of one's country is instilled in everyone. This is probably Prof. Widjojo Nitisastro's secret; his ability to combine his passion for the country of his birth with a deep feeling for those priorities which lead to the increasing well-being of its people. Indonesia can rightly be proud of one of her greatest sons. ◆

54

A Policy-Economist with a Warm Heart and Cool Head

Isamu Miyazaki*

In Japan, an old word used to express a seventieth birthday is "Koki". This word roughly suggests that man seldom lives to be seventy years old and therefore is used for honoring longevity. I am very pleased that despite reaching his seventieth birthday, Professor Widjojo remains healthy. What is more astonishing to me is that he has long been and still contributing to the development of both the Indonesian and Asian economies.

Confucius, an ancient Chinese philosopher, insisted that people over 70 should be modest in their behavior. Professor Widjojo is such a person.

I have no clear recollection of the day when I first met Professor Widjojo. While I worked at the Economic Planning Agency (EPA), I made economic plans or carried out economic analysis under the late Mr. Saburo Okita (Former Minister of Foreign Affairs). In 1968, soon after the Soeharto Government took office, Mr. Okita went to Indonesia and met President Soeharto and Professor Widjojo. This was where Mr. Okita's friendship with Professor Widjojo began.

When Professor Widjojo came to Japan, I was introduced to him by Mr. Okita. In those days, Professor Widjojo was the leader of an economic advisory committee set up by President Soeharto. The committee consisted of young economists who are graduates of the University of California at Berkeley. Hence came the nickname

* Mr. Isamu Miyazaki (Japan) was Deputy Minister, Economic Planning Agency (1979-1981); Chairman of Daiwa Securities Research Institute concurrently Chairman of Daiwa Institute of Research Ltd. (1982); Minister of State for Economic Planning (1995); Special Advisor to Daiwa Institute of Research Ltd. (1996).

"Berkeley Mafia". Mr. Okita sent some talented economists of the EPA to Indonesia. These economists, who were jokingly called the "Okita Mafia", included Mr. Koichi Baba (now professor at Nigata University) and Mr. Shinichi Ichimura (now professor at the University of Kyoto). I discussed, in particular, the methodology of economic planning and the North-South problem with Professor Widjojo who was the Chairman of Bappenas (the National Development Planning Agency) from 1968-1971. Since then Professor Widjojo has been in several important development-related posts. Because of this career path Professor Widjojo's opinions were based on the realities of the Indonesian and Japanese economies, though he also respected economic theory. His ideas often stimulated us at the EPA.

After completion of several important postings, Professor Widjojo became an economic adviser to President Soeharto. Even after leaving several important posts, Professor Widjojo often came to Japan for various events and meetings. When I was invited to such events, I had many opportunities to speak with him.

My most vivid memories of such events are those of the Inter Action Council (IAC) meetings of former Heads of Government. I sat with Professor Widjojo on the same board (the Policy Board), and Professor Widjojo and I had a pleasant talk with the late Mr. Takeo Fukuda (Former Prime Minister). Mr. Fukuda was then the Chairperson of IAC.

IAC was a council for former presidents and prime ministers, and was initiated primarily by Mr. Fukuda and Mr. Helmut Schmidt (former West German Prime Minister). When he was Prime Minister, Mr. Fukuda had a deep interest in international problems, particularly in the North-South problem and the energy problem. These problems partly motivated him to set up the IAC. In addition, when he officially visited Asian countries as Prime Minister, Mr. Fukuda announced the so-called "Fukuda Doctrine" in which his opinion about ASEAN was firmly stated.

The lively discussion between Mr. Fukuda and Professor Widjojo on the Fukuda Doctrine still remains impressed in my memory. Motivated by this discussion Mr. Fukuda started to promote 'Heart-to-Heart Communication' between Japan and ASEAN by inviting

many students from ASEAN countries to study in Japan. On Mr.
Fukuda's official visit to ASEAN countries, for which I was in
attendance, I saw that Professor Widjojo made a significant
influence on Mr. Fukuda's opinion. This is also the reason for my
deep respect to Professor Widjojo.

When Mr. Fukuda passed away Prof. Widjojo conveyed words of
condolence, in which he highly praised the Fukuda Doctrine. The
Doctrine may be summed up as follows:

> **First,** Japan rejects the role of a military power and is
> resolved to contribute to the peace and prosperity of
> Southeast Asia.
> **Second,** Japan consolidates the relationship of mutual
> confidence and trust based on "heart-to-heart" under-
> standing with the countries of Southeast Asia, not only in the
> political and economic fields but also in social and cultural
> areas.
> **Third,** Japan is an equal partner of ASEAN and its member
> countries and cooperate to strengthen their solidarity and
> resilience, while fostering a relationship based on mutual
> understanding with the nations of Indochina, thus con-
> tributing to the building of peace and prosperity throughout
> Southeast Asia.

Through IAC activities, former presidents and prime ministers
are able to propose various measures concerning various problems
from an objective, international long-term point of view, while
leaders now in office are compelled to focus on short-term problems.
Optimizing their position, IAC members discuss and offer
suggestions mainly about the following four issues: 1) promotion of
world peace primarily through nuclear nonproliferation and a
reduction in armaments; 2) enlivenment of the economy of each
country without causing either inflation or deflation backed by
strengthened international cooperation; 3) cementing relationship
between developed and developing countries to facilitate economic
and social development of the developing countries; and 4) a
balanced increase in world population growth and equitable

distribution of food and energy together with the conservation of nature and the environment.

Feeling strongly about the lAC's ideals, Prof. Widjojo joined the IAC's Policy Board in which he offered constructive opinions. Mr. Robert McNamara and Mr. Van Lennep were also board members and my participation on the board enlightened me very much.

In the summer of 1995, I took part in former Prime Minister Murayama's coalition cabinet and worked for a while as an economist from the private sector. Even then, Prof. Widjojo came a long way to see and encourage me. At that time, the yen was appreciating unabatedly and we talked much about various problems stemming from the strong yen. Prof. Widjojo was, in particular, concerned about an adverse impact of the strong yen on countries which were granted loans from the Japanese government. 1 was very impressed with his wide point of view because his concern was not limited to his own country, but encompassed the development of all of ASEAN as well as the Japanese economy.

The 21st century is drawing near. Although World Peace is not far away with the end of the Cold War, it is not yet guaranteed. In economic terms, we have not yet reaped the "peace dividend". Fortunately, most countries in the world have adopted reforms and open-door policies, which have been building a firm foundation for mutual prosperity under mutual dependence. The living standards in the Asian region in particular have been developing remarkably in recent years.

However, there are various hurdles still to be cleared, further enlivening economies, narrowing the gap between rich and poor countries, controlling population, the fair distribution of food and energy, a better symbiotic relationship between human beings and nature, etc. Every issue requires creative thinking and the ability to take the necessary steps.

I believe that Prof. Widjojo is a man of great ability who can properly handle these issues. Now that he reaches the age of seventy, we sincerely hope that he will take care of his health and continue to do the great job we have come to expect. ◆

55

The Man For The Challenge

Ennio Rodriguez[1]

"... I am I and my circumstances ..." Ortega y Gasset

1. Towards Modernization

The circumstances of Professor Widjojo's contribution to Indonesian development have been most extraordinary, and likewise he has been the most extraordinary man for his circumstances. This paper is thus a reflection upon the extraordinary.

As is well known, Indonesia comprises of 17,000 island archipelago extending more than 3,000 miles, with numerous ethnic groups, religions, and many languages. From this tremendous diversity, there was an attempt to unify a nation while simultaneously embark on a fast course of modernization. Indeed, if there has been a miracle in East Asian development, Indonesia is this miracle.

Modernization was conceived and undertaken as part of the wider political process of strengthening national unity. Modernization entailed a change in the direction of development strategy along with the promotion of national unity via the development of a sense of belonging and participation on the part of

---

1 Professor Ennio Rodriguez (Costa Rica) was Former Minister of External Finance and Debt, Republic of Costa Rica, Professor University of Costa Rica, currently Principal Economist at the Inter-American Development Bank. Met Professor Widjojo in the Non-Aligned Movement Ad-Hoc Group of Experts on Debt.

different cultures and groups within a nation that offered hope to all, in spite of regional differences in the level of development.

Today, with the benefit of hindsight, an assessment can easily be made. Indonesia's wider political objectives could not have been achieved without changing the direction of their development strategy. Uninterrupted growth and progress was clearly the result of shifting from self-sufficiency and autarchy to economic openess and full participation in world markets. However, in the late sixties, when this decision was made, it took both great foresight and courage. Courage, in particular, because this move ran against Indonesia's recent history, and seemed to contradict some longer lasting cultural traits, including communal participation and decision making.

The form of modernization was tailored to Indonesian society. Otherwise, wider political objectives would, very likely, not have been achieved. The longer term objectives of economic reform were clear, however the sequence of the reform, its speed, and the need to incorporate 'non-economic' elements. These could not be taken from a text book on development economics. Today we realize that well grounded economists and social scientists were instead able to read from the book of Indonesian living history and dream of the achievable, in order to construct the possible.

Indonesia's history of social, political and philosophical exchange between its incredibly diverse culture and religious groupings, can only be rooted in a spirit of great tolerance. Indeed, Indonesia could not have survived as a unified society if tolerance was not a central cultural trait. Political activities thus require considerable consensus building skills. As a consequence, the exercise of leadership, and political reform itself, has to be based upon consensus building processes.

2. Indonesia's Economic reform

One observation stands out when analyzing Indonesia's economic reform. This is the clarity of the long term objective of resource allocation being increasingly based on well behaved markets. Indonesia's route was one of gradualism. Economic liberalization was not undertaken for its own sake, but rather in the sectors and circumstances where markets were ready to produce better than *dirigiste* results. Moreover, occasional policy reversals were undertaken or were allowed when the circumstances were not deemed right, maintaining adherence to the long term objectives over a longer time horizon.

Although the international circumstances are now different, it is perhaps unfortunate that the Indonesian case was not studied more carefully as it could have shed more light on the transformation of Eastern Europe.

Another salient feature of Indonesia's reform process has been prudence in the conduct of economic policy. Today the economic profession agrees that careful fiscal and monetary policies are more conducive to sustain high growth rates. However, this has not always been the case. Development economists previously saw imbalances as an unavoidable element of development. Indonesian policy makers never fell into this trap.

The sequence of Indonesia's reforms also deserves a special note. As implemented, the reforms avoided incurring large transition costs by carefully timing the markets to be liberalized based on the maturity of conditions, thereby avoiding negative spillovers into other markets and ultimately the viability of the process. Again textbook recommendations were not simplistically followed.

Indonesia's long term economic strategy has been guided by a three-pronged objective of simultaneously pursuing growth, equity and stability. When trade-offs emerged one objective operated as a constraint for the achievement of the others, but, more interestingly, the positive feedbacks were actively pursued.[2]

The process of privatizing the economy to increase the rate of growth and consolidate stability never followed a 'big bang approach', but was rather based on creating the conditions for markets to operate effectively without inducing a concentration of ownership, which would have contradicted equity considerations among individuals, regions and ethnic groups. A clear example was the slow removal of controls and interventions affecting agriculture in what was a predominantly rural society.

---

2 Hollinger, W.C. *Economic Policy under President Soeharto: Indonesia's Twenty Five Year Record.* The United States-Indonesia Society. Background Paper Number 2, 1996.

The sequence of the reform also responded to this triad of inter-related objectives. First, macroeconomic stability was achieved before any market liberalization was attempted. Thereafter, stability became a condition of economic policy. Second, in order to promote greater economic dynamism and growth, the investment climate was improved by selective liberalizations. Third, in turn foreign exchange markets were opened up. Fourth, foreign trade was deregulated. Fifth the tax system was reformed. Sixth, once the preceding reforms were in place (in 1983) financial reform was started.[3] Seventh, it is worth emphasizing that in spite of criticism by external observers, agricultural policies have included farm gate price stabilization and subsidized fertilizers.

Equity considerations and practical knowledge of rural Indonesia have justified these policies. The overall results have been positive, which reveals an able management of these major policy interventions. These results contradict similar attempts in other parts of the developing world, in which managerial and/or political weaknesses have resulted in flawed interventions leading to increasing fiscal deficit and inflation.

Moreover, poverty reduction and equity concerns led to a comprehensive human resource development plan, including extensive networks of social and physical infrastructure.[4] It is interesting to note that the multiple policies of this program have contributed to the redefinition of Indonesia's comparative advantage, and have created growth opportunities in the more skill intensive sectors of the late nineties and the next century.

A very interesting feature of the modernizing reforms is the inclusion of communal participation, in itself a strength of Indonesian society. The economic significance of communal participation include, for example, the management of the otherwise difficult issue of water allocation in irrigation projects. Non-economic benefits include the organization of community based

---

3 The costly failure of the Chilean experience of the seventies comes to mind, in which there was a simultaneous liberalization of trade and financial markets.
4 Hollinger, *Op. Cit*

family planning, which also is related to wider economic development objectives.

3. The Economic Team Leader

The role of the economic team in the modernization of Indonesia is widely recognized.[5] The importance of its relative permanence over a long period of time is a key to understand the continuity of policy reforms. Different individuals occupied different positions over time, but on the whole, it seems that a shared vision and group loyalty have prevailed.

Rather than 'technocrats', the economic team has been an ideal combination of clear headed analysts and skillful politicians. They have been able to accurately diagnose the political reality, propose realistic courses of action, convince higher political authorities, and implement the policies.

The recognized leader of the economic team has long been Professor Widjojo. Providence situated him in the right places at the right times. He was able to meet, share experiences and build trust with the younger team members while teaching at the Army's Staff and Command School in Bandung and the Faculty of Economics at the University of Indonesia.

Professor Widjojo's leadership emanates from many of his outstanding characteristics. An interesting fact is that he is not only a trained economist but he is also a demographer. As a demographer he was free to include non-economic elements in the development strategy, such as family planning, but perhaps more importantly, as an economist he was free from the arrogance that sometimes afflicts the profession. In him, common sense and the ability to carefully weigh different options were not obscured by any dogmatic adherence to economic theories. All this has made Professor Widjojo an excellent economist, with a global view on the many elements involved in the challenge of modernizing Indonesian society.

Professor Widjojo is, by personality, a team player. He listens and promotes respectful exchanges of opinion. He distinguishes himself as a consensus builder. In this respect, he has helped to accomplish

---

5   *Ibid*

two things: on the one hand, his consensus building skills glued the economic team together, and set its working style; while on the other, he is rooted in the Indonesian political tradition, which has enabled him both to understand political realities and encounter the best methods of change, and act effectively in the political processes of the country. Professor Widjojo is the quintessential Indonesian, a paradigm of tolerance and respect for others; a consensus building leader.

Professor Widjojo's humble unassuming personality has given him the strength of a leader who can be trusted. Indeed, President Soeharto's trust in him created the necessary space for the presentation of policies and recommendations by the economic team. Fellow team members could work more effectively with a trusted leader whose example always sheds light on Indonesia's common good above group or personal gain. Professor Widjojo's transparency in his intentions provides the foundation for his quiet leadership. He is the wise man who has learned to disentangle petty personal or group interests from the larger common good, be it of Indonesia or the developing world.

Professor Widjojo, drinking from the fountain of the foundations of Indonesian society, grew strong and wise, and was able to guide his economic team in providing solutions tailored to the needs of Indonesians.

Professor Widjojo, the humble man from Java, has grown into a giant from Indonesia, spreading his influence overseas, yet remaining at heart the affable, caring and humble man from Java. In a most extraordinary country, living in extraordinary times, Professor Widjojo has been a most extraordinary man, rising to the challenge of helping to steer a young nation towards a future of shared prosperity. ◆

56

He Combines Profound Scholarship with That Pragmatic Touch of the Man of Affairs That Marks Him Out as A Leading Political Economist in the Third World

*Pius Okigbo**

I have known Professor Widjojo Nitisastro closely since 1987. We both have served as Members of the South Commission until 1990, on the Advisory Board of the South Centre, Geneva from 1990-1995 and, since then, on the Board of the Centre with Mwalimu Julius Nyerere as Chairman of each of these bodies. *Quiet, self effacing, keen and sharp with that final quality of humility*, Widjojo has been of outstanding help to all of us on the Commission and the Centre. I have come to understand how he rose to such a commanding height in the economic administration of Indonesia. One of the members of the original group of Indonesian economists to be trained in the University of California at Berkeley (as leader of a group to be later named the "Berkeley Mafia"), Widjojo has led his team to transform the economy of Indonesia from the near bankruptcy of 1965 to a buoyant thriving status of the last twenty years. *He combines profound scholarship with that pragmatic touch of the man of affairs that marks him out as a leading political economist in the Third World.*

As Widjojo turns seventy in September, I know he will continue to work for the growth of the Indonesian economy, to contribute to

* Dr.Pius Okigbo, MA, PhD. (Nigeria) was Former Lecturer in Economics, Northwestern University; Former Economic Advisor to the Federal Government of Nigeria; Former Ambassador to the European Economic Community; Member- South Commission; Member-Board of Governors, South Centre-Geneva; Vice Chairman, African Institute for Policy Analysis, Cape Town; Chairman - Council of African Advisers, African Development Bank, Abidjan, Cote D'Ivoire. He passed away in 2000.

the development of South-South Cooperation and for economic justice globally. It has been a privilege for me to know Widjojo and a bonus to have been so closely associated with him these past ten years. ◆

57

A Recollection of his Work in the South Commission

*Carlos Fortin**

I had the privilege and the pleasure of working with Professor Widjojo in the years 1989 and 1990, after I became Director of Programmes of the South Commission in Geneva, of which he was a member. That this should have been possible was not evident at first. Due to his heavy and important commitments back home he was Economic Adviser to the Government of Indonesia—Professor Widjojo had not been able to participate actively in the work of the Commission by the time I joined the Secretariat in mid-1988. There were indeed doubts whether he was in a position at all to combine his commitments in Indonesia with the demands of the work of the Commission, which were increasing as progress in the preparation of the major Report envisaged proceeded.[1] This was a matter of concern for us in the Secretariat. We felt that Professor Widjojo's vast experience in the development field would be invaluable in providing the link between analytical rigor and practical policy content that the Report was striving to achieve. That was precisely the combination of skills at which Professor Widjojo had excelled throughout his public service career.

The Challenge to the South. It was subsequently published in all official languages of the United Nations.

---

* Dr. Carlos Fortin (Chili) is Assistant Secretary-General, United Nations Conference on Trade and Development (UNCTAD), Geneva. The views expressed here are the author's and do not necessarily represent those of the United Nations in general or UNCTAD in particular.
1 The Report was published in English in 1990 by Oxford University Press with the title

Fortunately, the concerns dissipated in 1989, when, no doubt through major personal effort, Professor Widjojo was indeed able to combine his duties in the Government of Indonesia with full integration in the work of the Commission. He attended all subsequent meetings and was regularly in contact with the Secretariat in the intersessional periods, providing advice, commenting on drafts, pointing to important issues that needed treatment or expansion. This he did clearly but kindly. His comments were always knowledgeable and thoughtful, his criticisms constructive and forward-looking, and his praise informed and sincere.

Three aspects of Professor Widjojo's contribution were especially noteworthy. The first one was on the issue of the relative importance of the economic growth dimension both in the definition of development and in the identification of policies to bring it about. Here, Professor Widjojo took a clear stance alongside those who felt that economic growth was an essential element of development: a pre-condition, to be sure not sufficient, but certainly necessary to generate the kind of fundamental change in people's lives, attitudes, expectations and prospects that we associate with the process of development.

With some hindsight, this might not appear as a particularly controversial proposition. But almost a decade ago, when the South Commission Report was being prepared, this was a hotly disputed matter in some influential quarters of the international development community, notably academics and NGO and grassroots development activists. The second half of the seventies had witnessed the discovery in earnest of the social and the environmental aspects of development. Many analysts had come to the conclusion that sustainable development could not be a mechanical by-product of accelerated economic growth, and that in some contexts there could even be trade-offs between the two[2]. From this unassailable finding, however, stemmed more debatable views that argued that economic growth was not only not coterminous with development, but that by

---

2 For an early, seminal discussion of the distinction between development and economic growth, see Seers,' D., "The Meaning of Development", *International Development Review* Vol. II,No.4, 1969.

and large it was inimical to development. The zero-growth approach-whose origins went back to the sixties and to the notion, associated with the work of the Club of Rome, of the unsustainability of economic growth because of the exhaustion of natural resources[3]-found new exponents among those especially concerned with issues about the quality of life in developed societies.

It is not surprising that a Commission composed solely of citizens of developing countries would have found calls for zero-growth less than persuasive. Professor Widjojo was able to bring to bear his formidable experience as a top economic policy maker in Indonesia to show the need for rapid economic growth—provided it was of the right sort—as a condition for sustainable development. He would come back to this topic after the completion of the work of the Commission, and I shall refer below to a more recent contribution by Professor Widjojo that touches precisely on this important topic.

But at the same time Professor Widjojo was acutely sensitive to the need to introduce the social and human components in the making of economic development policy. This was a second *leitmotif* of his contribution to the South Commission. In particular, he emphasized the need to place the eradication, or at least the alleviation, of poverty at the centre of the agenda of national and international policy makers. And he certainly agreed that poverty eradication would not be an automatic by-product of rapid growth. For one thing, the kind of growth that was to be striven for should be that which would have maximum effect on poverty alleviation, through providing the poor with opportunities to integrate in the national economy. For another, there should also be provision for assisting the disadvantaged to enable them to face the challenge of new opportunities, and to come to the aid of those who otherwise found it difficult to avail themselves of those opportunities. The topic has also remained central to Professor Widjojo's analytical and policy concerns, and the more recent contribution mentioned above elaborates on the issue from the Indonesian experience.

Thirdly—and, again, not surprisingly—none of the above would in any sense detract from Professor Widjojo's concern for the

---

3   See *Meadows, DH et al..* The Limits to Growth: A Report for the Club of Rome's Project on the Predicament of Mankind, *New York, Universe Books, 1972.*

international environment as another precondition for successful development policy in developing countries. In particular, his view was that, while primary responsibility for the eradication of poverty lies with the government of the country concerned, the external environment can either help or hinder—sometimes seriously—the achievement of the goal. It is the duty of the international community to put in effect policies that assist the development efforts of developing countries and particularly their efforts at dealing with poverty, which in many cases call for substantial investment of resources. In particular, he felt that the creation of an appropriate external environment included as a central component the strengthening of South-South cooperation.

Thus, Professor Widjojo's contribution to the work of the South Commission touched on all fundamental elements of its remit[4]. His subsequent work retained this comprehensive scope, while in some respects paying special attention to the question of the appropriate international environment. He was a major figure in the process of reflection and introspection that the Non-Aligned Movement undertook during the Indonesian presidency, and which resulted in major steps forward in defining an agenda for both South-South economic cooperation and for reopening the North-South dialogue on development. In this effort he enlisted the cooperation of the South Centre, a small but highly capable and dedicated secretariat that continued to operate in Geneva after the disbanding of the South Commission. An especially noteworthy example of this collaboration is a text on Non-Alignment in the 1990s, which addressed directly and creatively the issue of the role of the Non-Aligned Movement in the post-Cold War context[5]. Professor Widjojo was also closely associated to other important publications of the NAM on the international debt issue[6].

I have already mentioned that Professor Widjojo, after the completion of the work of the South Commission, was able to further

---

4 The importance of economic growth is discussed in *The Challenge to the South*, Chapter 3, pp.82-83; economic growth and poverty, in Chapter 2, pp. 36-39; people-centred development, in Chapter 3, pp.79-82; South-South cooperation is devoted a full chapter, 4; and the North-South environment, notably the debt issue, is discussed in Chapter 5, especially pp. 226ff.

5 The South Centre, Non-Alignment in the 1990s: Contributions to an Economic Agenda, *Geneva, 1992*

6 *Non-Aligned Movement*, The Continuing Debt Crisis of the Developing Countries, 1994; and Report on the NAM Meeting on Debt and Development, *1994*.

elaborate on the issues highlighted above at various occasions. A particularly illuminating contribution is his presentation at the IMF-World Bank Conference on *Fifty Years after Bretton Woods: The Future of the IMF and the World Bank,* which took place in Madrid in September 1994[7]. The theme of the presentation was "Reduction of Poverty: The Indonesian Experience." *In characteristically modest fashion, he opens his remarks with the disclaimer that "as to poverty reduction, I am familiar only with the experience of Indonesia. Therefore, my contribution to this conference will be limited to poverty reduction in Indonesia only". It is soon, of course, clear that his comments, while strongly anchored in the Indonesian case, are of more general interest.* After substantiating the proposition that poverty in Indonesia has fallen rapidly over the preceding 25 years, he asks the question, "What explains this sharp drop in poverty?" His answer both confirms and elaborates the views he brought to the work of the South Commission, and which I summarized above:

The most important factor seems to be sustained economic growth, which was broadly based and labor intensive. The effects of this growth were reinforced by an array of policies that improved the health and education of the poor, reduced population growth to manageable levels, and provided infrastructure. In economic terms, the rate and pattern of growth generated a strong demand for labor, while the policies in education, health, and infrastructure enabled the poor to take advantage of this demand to improve their incomes.

He elaborates afterwards on more specific aspects of the policy. *The starting point was an effort directed towards establishing a strong rural economy and an extensive network of social and physical infrastructure, including in education, sanitation and health, transportation and irrigation. In particular, there was a rapid growth of rice production due to a combination of spread of irrigation, provision of inputs and high yielding varieties,*

---

7   Boughton, J.M. and K.S. Lateef (eds.). *Fifty Years After Bretton Woods,* Washington, D.C., International Monetary Fund and World Bank Group, 1995.

supplemented by investment in rural infrastructure, public procurement and price stabilization policies that redistributed income towards the farmers. In his own words, "this early emphasis on agriculture played a decisive role in breaking the downward cycle of poverty, population growth, and environmental degradation".

In the second half of the 1980s a new phase was entered into. This was in a sense a natural corollary of the first phase, but was also a concomitant of the economic reforms and structural stabilization necessitated by the external difficulties that the Indonesian economy was undergoing because of the debt burden and the fall in international oil prices. The second phase was marked by a rapid growth of exports of labor intensive manufactures, which produced a strong growth of manufacturing employment.

The story exemplifies the central points of Professor Widjojo's approach to equitable growth and development. Economic growth must be rapid and decisive, but must also be of the kind that will serve the needs of the majority of the population. The emphasis on agriculture and on labour intensity testify to this policy concern. And the international environment must be conducive to the success of the efforts[8].

It is an approach that has served Indonesia well and that can provide a model for other developing countries. We are all grateful to Professor Widjojo for having had a decisive role in implementing it in his own country and for his willingness to share it with the citizens of the developing world, through the South Commission Report and through many other Third World efforts and endeavours. ◆

---

8 Professor Widjojo provides detailed evidence of the pernicious effects that an inhospitable external environment can have. He refers in particular to currency volatility, which "could have wiped out Indonesia's endeavours in poverty reduction"; to market access, especially in textiles and garments, where export of developing countries are still facing non tariff barriers; and to the debt burden, which Indonesia was successful in easing its debt burden through a special arrangement with the Paris Club creditors based on a study by a German banker. "Unfortunately", writes Professor Widjojo, "the Paris Club said that this was a unique case that could not be used as a precedent for other developing countries".

58

A Special Tribute for His Vital Role to South-South Global Institution Building

Branislav Gosovic*,
Ann Zammit**, and Henock Kifle***

W e wish to pay Professor Widjojo a special tribute for his vital role in the establishment and consolidation of the South Centre, and thus a major contribution to South-South global institution-building.

Our contribution to this volume of tributes to *Pak* Widjojo is a token of our appreciation of his advice, support and friendship over the years, and of his readiness, in spite of his other important duties, to devote time and attention to the needs of the Centre. We wish to place on record some of his actions that represented major building blocks in the continuing process of consolidation of the South Centre.

His first major contribution came in the summer of 1992, when the former members of the South Commission met to review the work of the South Centre, which had been established as a two year follow-up office and was thus supposed to wind up its work. The general consensus was that efforts should be made to transform the Centre into a permanent institution. *Pak* Widjojo was one of the articulate supporters of this idea, pointing to the potential usefulness of the Centre, by referring to the work it had undertaken, in particular the policy paper prepared for the Group of 77 on the eve of the Rio UN Conference on Environment and Development.

* Dr. Branislav Gosovic (Montenegro) was with the South Centre, Geneva.
** Ms. Ann Zammit (UK) is with UNRISD, Geneva; formerly with the South Centre.
*** Dr. Henock Kifle (Ethiopia) is Chief Economist of the African Development Bank, Abijan, Cote d'Ivoire; formerly with the South Centre.

Indeed, the very next day he invited the Centre to prepare a paper on an economic agenda for the Non-Aligned Movement (NAM) for the 1990s, to serve as an input for the forthcoming Jakarta Ninth Summit of NAM. The Centre convened a small working group to help it in this task and the resulting text was printed and distributed at the NAM Summit. *Pak* Widjojo also arranged for the staff of the Centre and the experts to be invited to the NAM Summit, where, from behind the scenes, they provided advice and helped in drafting some resolutions and the programme of action for the follow-up to the Summit. In a sense, the NAM Jakarta episode put the South Centre on the map, gained its political and technical legitimacy among developing countries, and demonstrated its potential usefulness to a wider circle.

Once the Summit was over, *Pak* Widjojo was instrumental in enlisting the assistance of the South Centre to help develop and execute the Economic Agenda for Priority Action 1992-1995 of the Non-Aligned Movement. The Centre was thus requested to help Indonesia in organizing and servicing the NAM Ad Hoc Expert Group on External Debt, with *Pak* Widjojo directly involved in guiding this important undertaking, working particularly closely with his long-standing friends Drag Avramovic and Gamani Corea. Towards the end of the exercise, he decamped to Colombo, Sri Lanka, where, in close consultation with Gamani Corea who was the Chairman of the Expert Group, and from his hotel room in which he spent more than a week working around the clock, he personally fashioned the final version of the report.

This report was eventually endorsed by a NAM ministerial conference in Jakarta following which, under *Pak* Widjojo's direction, a major effort was mounted by the Indonesian Government to publicize its content and recommendations, and to introduce it into the proceedings of the World Bank, IMF and the United Nations. It can be argued that the carefully drafted contents of the NAM Expert Group Report and the subsequent diplomatic offensive played an important role in generating the political pressure and in bringing about the Bank/Fund multilateral debt relief initiative for highly indebted developing countries. This demonstrated, once more, the usefulness of having an institutional mechanism, such as the Centre, to back up the collective policy action and negotiations of the developing countries.

With *Pak* Widjojo's full support and involvement, the Centre was also commissioned by Indonesia to carry out for NAM a series of studies, including those on the UN reform, trade in commodities, South-South trade, the Uruguay Round and the TRIPS. These were submitted to the 10th NAM Summit in Cartagena, Colombia. In the light of subsequent discussions, some of these studies were revised, edited and published, thus making them more broadly available.

In addition to providing NAM and the countries of the South with useful analyses and policy recommendations on important topics, this work enhanced the Centre's image and it helped strengthen its network of collaborating institutions and individuals.

The Centre's involvement in the NAM follow-up, and the financial support provided by Indonesia, in its capacity as the chair country of NAM, to help cover the Centre's operating costs during the three year period 1992-1995, facilitated the Centre's consolidation and helped give it an early sense of direction. *Pak* Widjojo's confidence in the Centre's ability to deliver and his personal and direct involvement in the Centre's work made us feel that he was almost one of the staff, so that perhaps we approached him too often for advice and assistance, which he was always glad to give.

And, when the vital issue arose regarding the continuation of the Centre's legal status in Switzerland, once more we sought help from *Pak* Widjojo. And indeed, Indonesia acted in its capacity as the Chair Country of NAM: President Soeharto addressed a letter to the Swiss authorities on the subject, and the then Coordinating Minister for Economy, Finance, Industry and Development Supervision for International Economic Relations, Radius Prawiro (another close friend and supporter of the Centre), visited Berne to recommend the extension of its legal status. This was granted and the Centre was able to concentrate on building itself up.

Professor Widjojo maintains his close and direct involvement in the work of the Centre, and is also a member of its Board. It is to be hoped that, as one of its caring parents, he will continue to participate in the Centre's growth and evolution for many years to come.The South Centre is but one small episode in Professor Widjojo's long and illustrious career. However, it is illustrative of his vision and commitment to the South-South cooperation and solidarity and it was of great importance for South institution-building at the global level, where no major progress had been recorded for decades. Today, there is a South Centre, based on an intergovernmental agreement, with presently 45 member states, with a growing global network of collaborating individuals and institutions, and with intellectual output which is beginning to provide useful backup for the collective action of the developing countries.

The countries and peoples of the South are greatly indebted to Professor Widjojo for his contribution to making all this possible. In this, he worked alongside two other indefatigable and committed persons. One was Amir Habib Jamal, Permanent Representative of Tanzania to the United Nations in Geneva and Personal Representative of Mwalimu Julius K. Nyerere, who played a vital role in this institution building from the very inception of the South Commission and then as the Honorary Executive Director of the South Centre until his death in 1995. The other is Gamani Corea, former Secretary General of UNCTAD and member of the South Commission, who from the Centre's beginning has worked extremely closely with the staff, spending long periods of time in Geneva and chairing meetings, providing continual policy and intellectual guidance, and writing a number of papers and contributions himself. This illustrious trio have provided invaluable assistance to Mwalimu Nyerere in his efforts to transform the South Centre into a useful and viable institution.

The countries of the South and the South Centre look forward to Professor Widjojo's continuing championing and actively promoting South-South solidarity and cooperation. ◆

59

A Highly Respectable Personality in the World of International Economic Diplomacy

V.R Panchamukhi*

Two qualities of Dr. Widjojo Nitisastro impressed me immensely when I first met him in Geneva at a Workshop organised by the South Centre: *his simple and balanced disposition and his clarity in thoughts and expressions. I have yet to see a person with such rich credentials of high academic status and also holding a high influential position in the policy world who is so modest and humble.* I also discovered that his humble expressions were stoutly fortified by his commitment to and consistency in the pursuit of the cause dear to him. I feel that these attributes distinguish Dr. Widjojo Nitisastro as *a highly respectable personality in the world of international economic diplomacy.*

I had the privilege of being a member of the Working Group on the economic agenda for the Non-Aligned Movement set-up by the South Centre, Geneva, in 1992, on the advice of the President of Indonesia in his capacity as the Chairman of the Tenth Non-Aligned Movement. The tasks of the Working Group included, among others, preparation of a background documents of the summit and also to assist the office of the Chairman to prepare the text of the Jakarta Declaration and the final document of the Tenth Non-Aligned

---

* Dr. V.R. Panchamukhi (India) was Director, Research and Information System (RIS) for the Non-Aligned and Other Developing Countries, when he was invited by the South Centre, Geneva to participate in a meeting preparatory to the Xth Non-Aligned Summit scheduled to be held in Jakarta, Indonesia in 1992. Dr. Panchamukhi continues to be the Director of RIS for the Non-Aligned and Other Developing Countries, New Delhi, which is an autonomous body set up with the financial funding by the Government of India. Dr. Manmohan Singh is Chairman of RIS.

Summit. This Working Group was chaired by Dr. Gamani Corea, former Secretary-General of UNCTAD and Dr. Widjojo Nitisastro was one of its distinguished members. This Working Group prepared a document, entitled "Non-Alignment in the 1990s: Contributions to an Economic Agenda" which provided a valuable basis to the deliberations at the various technical sessions of the Summit. The functioning of the Working Group was greatly facilitated by the valuable help and support given by Dr. Widjojo Nitisastro. I recall that our working in close association with the highest policy circles in Indonesia was a source of immense joy and education.

The range of subjects covered by Dr. Nitisastro in his lectures, writings, and discussion meetings has been very wide covering issues such as poverty alleviation, population control, liberalisation and globalisation, debt problem, foreign assistance, commodity problem, international economic order, environment and development, as also the recent issues before WTO. He is very candid in expressing his views very clearly and forcefully, but always with a focus on the real practical issues and policy actions. It is way back in 1982, when he addressed the Davos Symposium giving his reflections on the emerging issues in the world economy, he had almost envisaged the various critical issues that are likely to take a place of prominence in the world debate on development strategies and international economic relations about a decade later. While accepting the role of the market forces in regard to the trade and investment flows, he had underscored the critical role of the State in providing the most crucial facilities of physical and social infrastructure. He had rightly pointed out that "... no private enterprise can be expected to build irrigation canals or mount a program to eradicate illiteracy or malaria, for the simple reason that there is no private earnings in those type of investments." He had also reiterated the views of Willy Brandt that the development process in the developing countries requires both foreign aid and foreign private investment. Dr. Nitisastro has been quite consistent in reiterating these very perceptions even during the later half of the 90s when the world has been undergoing radical structural changes in the field of international economic relations.

In the above mentioned lecture, he had also expressed his views that the problem of debt burden and debt settlement should be resolved in such a way that the problem does not repeat again and it does not, in any way, adversely effect the development capability and credit worthiness of the debtor country. He had endorsed the principle that the settlement of debt should be related to the ability of the country to pay and that it should be a one time settlement rather than postponement of the debt burden on a continuing basis. It is commendable to find that these very perceptions expressed in the 80s by Dr. Nitisastro have provided the basic principles for the recommendations made in the comprehensive report on debt prepared by the Non-Aligned Movement Adhoc Advisory Group on Debt in 1994 when the President of Indonesia in his capacity as Chairman of the NAM had set up an Expert Group on Debt. It may be noted that Dr. Widjojo Nitisastro was also one of the distinguished members of this group.

It is useful to reiterate here the various principles that were laid down by this NAM Expert Group for dealing with the debt problem. These principles were derived from the paper prepared by Dr. Nitisastro on the Indonesian Debt-Settlement Example. These include: i) a once-and-for-all arrangement for settling all outstanding debt; ii) the application of debt reduction to all categories of debt including multilateral debt; and iii) the application of the above principles as well as an adequate degree of debt-reduction for all countries, although within such an overall framework, there will necessarily be a case-by-case approach in dealing with the debt of individual countries.

The burden of debt still continues to be a major problem for many developing countries. It is often argued that foreign direct investment is a better option for the developing countries for capital inflows to supplement the domestic savings for investment activities. The world is now obsessed with the debate on multilateral disciplines for flows of goods, capital and services. The problem of debt burden and the need for evolving comprehensive approach to deal with this problem on the basis of the general principles stated above are receding to the background. In fact the close nexus that exists between the FDI flows and the accentuation of the debt burden in a future period deserves special attention at the analytical and policy levels.

The recent experiences of some of the countries which have had massive inflows of foreign direct investment in the past few years bring out that, at least in the initial few years, the high import intensity of the FDIs coupled with their inadequate export orientation causes adverse effects on the balance of payments which could be the source for further increase in the debt burden of the indebted countries. Even if one assumes that FDI flows would be of great help in reducing the debt burden, it is observed that the countries which are having high debt burden are precisely the ones which fail to attract sufficient flows of foreign direct investment in view of their low credit rating by the international credit rating agencies.

The debt burden and the growing emphasis on FDI have kept the topic of Official Development Assistance (ODA) to the background. In fact the ODA has a special role in the context of the present world economic situation, because it is only through ODA that some crucial sectors like education, health, and infrastructure could be developed with a view to improving the capabilities of the indebted countries to absorb the additional capital flows from the rest of the world. The approach of ODA could be an effective modality for the developed countries to maintain the framework of development cooperation for achieving sustained development the world over.

The phenomenon of large volumes of flows of financial capital, across the globe, with significant speed and diversity has inducted new dimensions to the challenges of debt management in the developing world. On the one hand, financial integration across the different economies and facilitation of flows of financial capital are expected to generate additional resources in situations where such resources are required. However, the volatility of capital markets and the dangers of the quick reversals of the flows—as in the case of Mexico in the recent period—introduce unprecedented uncertainties in the development profile and in the domestic saving and investment activities.

The perceptions presented by Dr. Nitisastro and the comprehensive analysis provided in the NAM Expert Group Report could be used as a basic framework for reviewing the problem of resources for development in the developing world. The various new issues such as FDI flows, volatility of capital markets, renewed role of ODA stated above, deserve special attention in this context. I am sure that the various fora with which Dr. Nitisastro is connected at the national and at the international levels would be persuaded by his charismatic style to undertake more studies on these issues and come out with useful guidelines for international action.

Reduction of poverty and the problem of increasing gap between the rich and poor have been some of the several concerns which have found prominent place in the writing and lectures of Dr. Nitisastro. In his address to the IMF and the World Bank Conference entitled "Fifty Years After Bretton Woods: the Future of the IMF and the World Bank", Dr. Nitisastro chose to speak on the theme *of Reduction of Poverty: The Indonesian Experience*. By bringing the issue of sustainable poverty reduction to the central place of debate in the Conference, Dr. Nitisastro affirmed his economic philosophy that the primary goal of the process of development is to improve the living standards of the millions of the world community who are often left behind in the process of rapid growth and structural changes.

The forceful and clear presentations by Dr. Widjojo Nitisastro in regard to the issues and the policy actions based upon the Indonesian Experience have been extremely rewarding contributions to the debate on the subject of poverty alleviation which still remains as a major issue of concern not only to the developing countries, but also to the world community as a whole. By dealing with the success story of Indonesian experience in reducing poverty in a short period during the eighties, he brought out the need for adopting special measures of poverty reduction along with the process of high growth and emphasis on labour intensive structure of production. He has brought out clearly that the initial conditions before the launching of the structural adjustment programmes in terms of the social and the physical infrastructures are extremely important for achieving sustained progress in poverty reduction even during the structural adjustment. He also categorically stated that the government in Indonesia protected the budgetary expenditures on poverty related sectors even in the midst of rapid structural adjustments and policy reforms. Emphasis on labour intensive forms of technology and also concerted efforts in controlling population growth have been pointed out to be the important factors for Indonesia's success story.

The perspective remarks made by Dr. Nitisastro on the challenges of structural adjustment have been corroborated by the massive literature that is now flowing in the analysis of the experiences of the different countries in the world economy in regard to the standardised programmes of structural adjustment imposed on them by the mandarins of the World Bank. The fact that the experiences of structural adjustment are diverse and that there are more failures than successes bring out that the scope and the content of the structural adjustment programmes cannot be standardised. Even the World Bank itself has now been engaged in intensive rethinking on the design of the structural adjustment programmes. They have introduced the concept such as phasing, sequencing, timing of liberalisation and the imperatives of taking into account the initial conditions of the economies in designing their structural adjustment programmes are being recognised. However, there is considerable scope for educating the policymakers in the different developing countries to design their own structural adjustment programmes in a manner which best suited their national interest. Further, many initiatives are required for intensive debate and dialogue among the developing countries to learn from each other's experience in regard to the reforms and the structural adjustment programmes.

Indonesia has been considered as one of the case studies of success in regard to the implementation of the policies of reforms and structural adjustments. It has achieved consistently high growth in an environment of reasonable inflation rate and manageable debt burden. Its achievements in maintaining high savings and investment rates, reduction of poverty, control of population growth, evolution of a strong and disciplined civil society speak very highly of the approach of economic management pursued in Indonesia. While these achievements are obviously the result of the team work reflecting the commitment and the steadfastness of the leadership, the fact that intellectual underpinning of these processes are provided by the experts and analysts cannot be ignored. It is here that the contributions of Dr. Widjojo Nitisastro who has been consistently positioned at a very high place of influence in the machinery of economic decision making stand out distinctly as the lubricants for the rapid moving wheels of growth and development.

Indonesia, as the Chairman of the Non-Aligned Movement during 1992-95, had taken many bold initiatives to set up expert groups and organise meetings on many issues of current relevance to the developing world. The fervour with which Indonesia had functioned during this period had inducted a new dynamism in the Non-Aligned Movement. I would like to take this opportunity to suggest that persons like Dr. Nitisastro should persuade the Government of Indonesia to continue to be actively associated with the subsequent Chairman and the Coordinating Bureau of the Non-Aligned Movement and ensure that NAM would remain as an effective forum for meaningful cooperation among the developing countries.

Dr. Nitisastro's commitment to the philosophy of Non-Alignment and its relevance even in the changed world after the end of the cold war period have been amply clear by the contributions he has made to the deliberations of the Tenth Non-Aligned Summit organised by Indonesia as the Chairperson of the NAM during 1992-95. The various booklets brought out as the background documents of the Non-Aligned Summit and also subsequently, as a follow-up of the recommendations of the Summit, brought out with the support of the Government of Indonesia bear the clear imprint of Dr. Nitisastro not only in regard to the choice of the themes and of the organisational pursuits for setting up of Expert Groups and the preparations of their reports, but also in regard to the underlying philosophy, perceptions and policy guidelines.

Dr. Nitisastro has provided consistent support to the activities of the South Centre, which was established by Dr. Julius Nyerere, Chairman of the South Commision after the completion of the South Commission report. Dr. Nitisastro himself was a distinguished member of the South Commission and his consistent involvement in the activities of the South Centre obviously reflect the deep commitments that Dr. Nitisastro has possessed, to the cause of the developing world. Despite all the efforts initiated at the national and at the international levels, the challenges before the developing world continued to be diverse and complex as in the past.

I do hope and pray that Dr. Widjojo Nitisastro would be blessed with hitherto more zeal and vigour to enable him to continue his missionary work in regard to the tasks that still haunt the developing world. ◆

60

Some Reflections on His Ideas

Eneas da Conceicao Comiche*

1. Professor Nitisastro's Contribution

I came to know Professor Dr. Widjojo Nitisastro when we were both members of the South Commission from 1988–1990, and I was able to meet him again during the Non-Aligned Countries Ministerial Meeting on Foreign Debt and Development held in Jakarta in August 1994. *He made an enormous contribution to the thinking on the developing world's central problems: the protectionist trend in the industrialised countries, the increasingly unfavourable terms of trade and the heavy burden of foreign debt.*

Prof. Nitisastro's ideas were, for him, a weapon of struggle, and he fought for a world in which both the South and the North would be winners. He argued that the prevailing forms of North-South relations were unsustainable. Economic progress can only be sustainable if the effort at national level is backed up globally.[1]

He criticised the high degree of protectionism of the in-dustrialised countries, which prevent or hamper the entry of products from developing countries through fixing tariffs and quotas. This is aggravated by the unfavourable trend of developing countries' export prices in comparison with their imports, which reduces their purchasing power on the international market. The non-oil producing developing countries were the worst hit by the

---

* Dr. Eneas da Conceicao Comiche (Mozambique) was Minister in the President's Office for Economic and Social Affairs and Governor of the Central Bank of Mozambique.
1 Nitisastro, Widjojo, 1982. *In the Mutual Interest of Rich and Poor Nations,* Address by Prof. Dr. Widjojo Nitisastro, Minister Coordinator for Economic, Financial and Industrial Affairs of the Republic of Indonesia at the European Management Forum: Davos Symposium 1982, 30 January 1982. Abbreviated (p.l)

international rise in oil prices at the beginning of the 1970s, and by the beginning of the 1980s their situations were extremely difficult.

These countries had only just emerged from colonialism, and had the challenging agenda of raising general living standards and promoting development. The reduction in their purchasing power meant that they sought alternative ways of injecting foreign exchange: they went into debt. By the 1980s the debt problems were serious. In many sub-Saharan African countries the debt stock started to be greater than the Gross Domestic Product (GDP), and the debt service was higher than the value of their feeble exports.

The paradox identified by the South Centre could be observed:

> ...the phenomenon of a net flow of external resources not from the developed to the developing countries, as called for by the imperative of development, but in the reverse direction from the developing to the developed countries.[2]

Instead of promoting development, foreign debt was and continues to be an enormous obstacle to success for many countries, including Mozambique, that are working to promote economic growth and reduce poverty. The foreign debt is umbilically linked to the prevailing international economic order, which is unfavourable to developing countries: the South accumulates deficits in its external accounts while the North accumulates surpluses. This is why both Professor Nitisastro and the other members of the South Commission argued for the need for a definitive solution to the developing countries foreign debt problems.

Rescheduling debt, the mechanism adopted by the members of the Paris Club, has already shown itself to be ineffective. Many countries remain with unsustainable debt stocks and flows after negotiating various rescheduling. Many highly indebted countries have the lowest per capita incomes in the world, and fall behind with their payments. The Non-Aligned Movement's Ad Hoc Advisory Group of Experts on Debt recommended a substantial reduction in debt.[3]

---

2   South Centre, 1993. *Non-Aligned Movement in the 1990s: Contribution to anEconomic Agenda*. Geneva: South Centre

3   *The Continuing Debt Crisis of the Developing Countries,* Report of the Non-Aligned Movement Ad Hoc Advisory Group Experts on Debt. Jakarta: August 1994

In August 1994 in Jakarta, the Non-Aligned Countries Ministerial Meeting on Foreign Debt and Development, after studying the Expert Group's report, concluded that the solution must come through a substantial reduction in debt stock. At this meeting Prof. Nitisastro spoke about the case of Indonesia, which is a rare example in the developing world of resolving the foreign debt problem once and for all. This requires a commitment from both sides: the creditor countries and the debtors.

2. Mozambique's Position

These concerns have been at the centre of our attentions. Since 1987 Mozambique has been implementing economic reforms as part of its Economic and Social Rehabilitation Programme (PRES). Despite the war and natural disasters, the results achieved so far are encouraging, though the living standards of the majority of the population continue to be low. The Mozambican economy has experienced growth since 1987, averaging 7 percent annually. In 1996 the inflation rate fell to 16.6%, against 54.1% in the previous year. By June 1997 accumulated inflation was 3.7%, measured by the price index of Maputo City.

However, Mozambique has an unsustainable foreign debt. At the end of 1996 the foreign debt stock guaranteed by the Government was US $ 5.7 billion, three times the size of GDP. From 1992-1995 the ratio of programmed debt service to exports of goods and services was an average 125%. Over the same period the debt service absorbed 25% of exports and 25% of State budget current expenditure.

Faced with this difficult situation, Mozambique has undertaken a vast range of actions:

1. Five reschedulings have been negotiated with the Paris Club since 1984. The most recent, in November 1996, was on the basis of the Naples terms, i.e. a 67% flow reduction.
2. By December 1991, with finance from the IDA and other donors, the Government had concluded a buyback of debt owed to 34 banks and financial creditors, which accounted for 64% of the total commercial debt outstanding.

3. The Government is negotiating and signing agreements with bilateral creditors outside the OECD to gain rescheduling terms that are comparable to those achieved with the Paris Club.
4. The Government has been selective in contracting new loans, giving preference to grants, or highly concessional debts.

These measures have resulted in reducing the debt stock growth from an average of 15% per year in 1985-1990 to 2.5% during 1990-1996. Nonetheless, the debt continues to be unsustainable, which suggests the need for a different approach. Successive rescheduling merely postpones the problem. Although the multilateral debt is on highly concessional terms, its weight is increasing. In 1996 46% of the debt service was to multilateral institutions.

In the difficult agenda of promoting growth and eradicating poverty, a prerequisite for success is a once and for all solution to the foreign debt so that more resources can be channeled to priority areas for development and more investments can be attracted. Thus:

* Mozambique needs and deserves the earliest possible debt relief from the HIPC Initiative, with its decision point by mid-1997 and its completion point as soon as possible thereafter, possibly two years later;
* Mozambique needs targets for debt sustainability at the bottom of the intended ranges; namely debt service/exports ratio of 20% and present value of debt/export ratio of 200%.

3. Perspectives for the New International Economic Order

Recent international developments show that the struggle conducted by Prof. Nitisastro and the Non-Aligned Countries is winning some victories. The HIPC initiative, which seeks to resolve the debt problem of highly indebted poor countries, is undoubtedly a result of the pressure that has been brought to bear and the search for the involvement of all the interested parties: creditors and debtors.

However, notwithstanding the good examples much still remains to be done. The economic interests of the North may hinder commercial exchanges in an increasingly free environment. *And in the case of the debt initiative there are two worrying aspects: (i) the case by case treatment and (ii) dealing with flows, and not with stock as argued for by the Non-Aligned Movement.* ◆

61

A Fellow Warrior

Layashi Yaker*

T he anniversary of the birth of Widjojo Nitisastro is the anniversary of a very dear friend. His struggle for global justice, equity and economic development has not ended and is unlikely to end. The world of today shows growing disparity between rich and poor, across nations and within nations, it shows fragile economies and turbulent markets and hearths of potential and actual conflict.

Widjojo Nitisastro fought through the United Nations Conference on Trade and Development, the body that seeks "development for all men and for mankind as a whole". When I was serving my country, Algeria, as Minister of Commerce from 1969-1977, I could not fail to be impressed by Widjojo Nitisastro who brought to the debate in Nairobi elements for international policy, that would benefit national economic development (UNCTAD IV). At that Conference he was the coordinator of the Group of 77 for Asia while I had the honour to be the Group of 77's coordinator for Africa. In an environment of unbending believe in a just world economic order, together with the late Manual Perez Guerero and UNCTAD's Secretary–General Gamani Corea, a milestone in North-South relations was established when the Common Fund for Commodities was agreed upon.

Our paths kept crossing, while the struggle went on. I could again admire the intellect, foresight, experience and moderation of my

* Mr. Layashi Yaker (Algeria) was Minister of Commerce (1969-1977); Ambassador to the US(1982-1984);Ambassador to the USSR (1979-1982);Member South Commission;Member Brandt Commision; Under-Secretary-General of the United Nations.

brother in arms as a fellow member of the South Commission under the chairmanship of Mwalimu Julius Nyerere. While the basic issues of development remained the same, technological development had changed the face of the globe. While television reached viewers globally, large numbers of people were still living below the poverty line. While the North moved into cyberspace, bringing basic health and education to all, this was still a priority for a large number of countries of the South. How to combine catching up within the new parameters of sustainable development, globalization and liberalization with the basics of human and economic development had become the main challenge for the developing countries. *Indonesia had its debt settled and therewith freed itself to concentrate on development and poverty alleviation. Linking this with broad-based labour intensive economic growth proved a formula of success. A model that could be emulated, provided there were a true commitment from policy makers.*

These were the themes Widjojo Nitisastro kept advancing: true commitment and the development of individual and institutional capabilities, to identify problems and opportunities. While first and foremost each country has to make its own homework, the international community has to provide for an enabling external environment.

The Conference in Budapest of the North, the South and Eastern Europe held in cooperation with the Council of Europe, which I initiated, provided yet an opportunity to cooperate for economic empowerment. Serving subsequently the United Nations in its UNESCO and its Economic Commission for Africa and now the Independent World Commission on the Oceans, Widjojo Nitisastro and myself continued exchanging ideas to accelerating growth and to eradicate poverty.

We are linked, as we expressed in *The Challenge to the South*[1] by the primary bond that links the countries and peoples of the South, that is by the mutual desire to escape from poverty and underdevelopment and secure a better life for our citizens and a better world. This is our shared aspiration and the foundation of the

---

1 The Report of the South Commission, 1990.

South's solidarity and of South-North cooperation, which is expressed through organizations such as the Group of 77 and the Non-Aligned Movement.

The future demands intensified action, to be based on a holistic approach to development. In this respect I may take one part of the globe I have particularly been involved with recently, the World Ocean. There must be a shared stewardship between all countries in order to assure that the uses of the oceans and its resources are fairly distributed among peoples, both rich and poor and among different generations. For developing countries the important issues is how to both exercise their rights and responsibilities accorded to them under the Law of the Sea. To manage the assets provided by the oceans wisely for themselves and in a responsible manner for the international community they need adequate means and resources. The oceans which provide living resources such as fishstocks, are a source of biological diversity and play a major role in regulating the natural cycles that affect our lives, make tourist and communication services possible and are being used for waste disposal. The challenge will be to see how, with growing populations and increasing incomes these resources can be sustained without putting the whole World Ocean and therewith our entire planet, at risk. These issues, pertinent to the oceans, are valid for development in general.

Future and immediate action is needed. I firmly believe that this requires a readiness to look beyond the at times self-imposed limitations, be they geographical, technological, social, political, cultural or religious. Geographical for me implies not only land boundaries, but more the spatial delimitations between land, water and outer space. Optimal use of resources demands recognition of the inseparability of the different parts of our planet and therewith a responsibility to consider the implications of each single activity on earth and on other parts of our planet. Technology poses opportunities and challenges. While technically communication is possible with many people at the same time with practically no limitations of distance and it is possible to reach individuals through various media world wide, communication among persons still poses a major challenge. The importance of human communication and of communication processes for development is still underestimated. If participatory development has to take place, communication for development must be redefined and integrated in the political process, even more so in this so-called the age of communication. In realizing equality among men and women nationally and globally, major hurdles have yet to be taken in many societies in North and South. For the potential of 50% of the world's population to be tapped successfully, action to fully empower women must be taken sooner rather than later. The growth of the private sector world wide creates a unique opportunity for women to demonstrate their talents and abilities in business - provided an accommodating environment exists.

The high cost of unresolved political differences makes it mandatory to think beyond the here and now in selfish terms and/or for short term gains rather than to look towards peace, stability and development.

As was stated in the Report of the Non-Aligned Movement *Ad Hoc* Advisory Group of Experts on Debt[2], the issues that have figured on the agenda of the North-South dialogue need to be resolved. Hence, the reactivation of the North-South debate was imperative. In the world of today, ways and means of effectively involving new major players in international affairs such as the private sector and NGO's in this dialogue, must be devised. The United Nations and its most universal forum, the UNCTAD, must therefore be given a greater role to play in action oriented dialogue for development, in cooperation with the other global institutions within and outside the United Nations system.

The challenge will be to undertake action, agreed upon internationally, at the national and local levels. To ensure such an osmosis the role of regional cooperation must be energized.

As development requires primarily solidarity of the South, strengthening the institutions of the South remains, more than ever, a priority.

These are the idea and noble objectives Widjojo Nitisastro has been promoting so ably and I am proud to have him as one of my best companions. I wish him all the best.

---

2 The continuing debt crisis of the developing countries, 1994.

62

Your Intellectual and Human Qualities have Won the Respect and Admiration of Us All

Qian Jiadong *

Accordng to Chinese custom, it is a big event in one's lifetime to be 70. Very soon it will be your turn to mark the important anniversary. On this auspicious occasion, I would like to extend to you my warmest congratulations and best wishes for good health, long-life and happiness.

Though a bit belated, it is my honour and privilege to have made your acquaintance. We missed you in the South Commission in the beginning and were pleased that you joined us later. The Commission was inspired by your participation. It was also made more colourful with *your knowledge and experience in international affairs and your dedication to the cause of the South, you enhanced our deliberations and strengthened our Report. Your intellectual as well as human qualities have won the respect and admiration of all.* I wish you further successes and greater achievements in the years to come in your untiring efforts to advance the well-being of your country and the Third World as a whole. I also wish that the good relations now existing between your country and mine will continue to grow.

The members of the South Commission will be meeting in Kuwait in November. I shall be going and hope you will come too.

Looking forward to seeing you again. With my best personal regards. ◆

---

* Mr Qian Jiadong (China) was Ambassador-Permanent Representative to the UN in Geneva; Special Research Fellow of the China Institute of International Studies.

63

A Well-Informed Strategic Thinker

Yves Guerard *

M y first visit to Indonesia goes back to January 1985. I had been asked to spend a few weeks in Jakarta to discuss the concept of a proposed Pension Law still being drafted and provide comments to a few officials on related issues. I should have realized that there was a strategic thinker pulling the strings because among the reasons given to convince me to undertake the long trip to Indonesia were the fact that they needed an actuary having experience with funded pension plans in the North American style but familiar with a civil code legal environment as is the case in Indonesia. Only a well informed person would know that Quebec, the French speaking province in Canada offers such combination!

I did not need to wait many days to discover that the strategic thinker and the well informed person was Professor Widjojo whom I met in his quiet Bappenas office. I realized also that he had done his homework and understood the key issues that would require strategic policy decisions. Professor Widjojo was not wasting time in details, his objectives were clear and he was determined to achieve them. He wanted to provide future retirees with financial security in retirement to prevent them becoming a burden for future generations.

He saw private Pension Funds as a better alternative than public Plans such as an enlarged Astek that create entitlements and high dependency on taxes and intergenerational transfers.

---

* Dr.Yves Guerard, FSA, PICA, FCA, Ph.D (h.c.) (Canada) is Chairman, Ernst & Young (Canada) Actuaries and Consultants Inc.

Nowadays the demographic shift and the aging of populations have become kitchen words. But in 1985 few people beyond actuaries, demographs and other specialists, understood the adverse consequences of the anticipated demographic evolution. Many reports, articles and publications that have since made the headlines, including the well known World Bank publication "Averting the old age crisis" published in 1994, were yet to be written. Professor Widjojo had understood that funded plans would be more easily sustainable in a country where the family policy embodied in *Dua anak cukup* would accelerate the aging of the population. Thus he wanted funded pension plans that would mobilize the savings necessary to support the growth of the economy and build the capacity to produce the goods and services a larger and older population would require.

I was pleasantly surprised that he was aware of alternative financing mechanisms such as pay-as-you-go or book reserves but was fully committed to a funded approach and to the prudent conservation of the resulting assets until they could be used to pay the retirement benefits. He was also supportive of a voluntary approach and we coined the expression "Freedom to promise but obligation to deliver".

The Government objective was to promote Pension Funds by giving them a clear legal and fiscal status, prudential governance requirements and full protection of assets from the claims of creditors by making Pension Funds a legal entity separate and distinct from the sponsoring Employer or group of Employers. Although funding was part of the original objectives, this requirement was deemed onerous by some and repeatedly challenged; suggestions that two classes of Pension Funds one funded and the other unfunded, be allowed to co-exist had to be thought back. Ultimately, the challenge was useful because it led to a much stronger definition of what types of arrangements would fall under the Law. Of course, offering an escape road from funding requirements, would likely have decreased rather than increased the funding levels prevailing in the existing Yayasans, and thus the availability of long term investments contrary to a primary national objective.

Professor Widjojo was a fast learner and in the course of a few sessions, he had digested the basic principles underpinning the major pension policy decisions: funding and solvency requirements, diversification of investments, vesting and other minimum standards, the need of actuarial reports for Defined Benefits program, the complementary role of Defined Contributions programs and especially of individual accounts which were to become the Financial Institutions Pension Funds, the phasing out of lump sum settlements in favor of life annuities, the regulatory challenge, etc.

The actual development of the Pension Law was done within the Ministry of Finance and the Pension Law would not have been born without the constant support of a number of Ministers (Ali Wardhana, Radius Prawiro, J.B. Sumarlin) and key Directors (Oskar Surjaatmadja, Marzuki Usman, Bambang Subianto) but I always suspected that Professor Widjojo was the ultimate source for the common inspiration that guided them all towards the national objective. I also presumed that his tall shadow helped the Pension Law survive unscathed in Sekneg and almost unscathed in Parliament, deserving a very positive appreciation by the World Bank.

Although over the years my contacts with Prof. Widjojo became much less frequent as the emphasis shifted form strategy to implementation, I felt personally comforted by the knowledge that *there was in a key place a well informed strategic thinker that understood and appreciated the work being done* and towards whom I could turn should unforeseen insuperable hurdles suddenly appear. That feeling was a decisive factor in motivating me to accept the initial challenge and to persist until Prof. Widjojo could look at the pension legislation and say "Mission accomplished". ◆

64

Economic Cooperation from the Days of the North-South Dialogue to Today's Globalised World

Helga Steeg*

I t is a great pleasure for me to join friends and colleagues to pay tribute to Professor Widjojo Nitisastros's 70th Anniversary in September 1997. Here is a man who has not only been instrumental in forming and implementing Indonesia's economic policy but at the same time been a highly esteemed partner in deepening bilateral economic relations between Germany and Indonesia. Furthermore he has been an excellent partner in multilateral conferences and dialogues since the beginning of the seventies.

These were the times when the North-South Dialogue between industrialised and developing countries was highly confrontational on almost all economic issues: finance, trade, investment, commodities to name the most important ones. Prof. Widjojo while presenting his country's position was constantly working for a better understanding between the two groups of countries. He was able to do so, because of his command of economic issues. Always trying in his calm but at the same time sound way he helped in no small way to bridge controversies. He was able to do so because he did not only preach economic policy but practised it at home, in a country which had no lack of extremely difficult problems. We, representatives of

* Dr.Helga Steeg (Germany) was the Executive Director of the International Energy Agency in Paris (1984-1994); entered into the Federal Ministry of Economics in Bonn, as administrator in the Department of Money and Credit (1955); Alternate German Director, the World Bank (1965-1967); Division Chief for Foreign Export and Investment Insurance (1968-1970); Deputy Director General for Development Assistance in the Ministry (1970-1973); Director General, Head of the Department for Foreign Economic Policy in the Ministry (1973-1984); Executive Director of the International Energy Agency, Paris (1984-1994); Lecturing on International Energy Law and Politics at the Ruhr-University Bochum (since 1994).

the industrialised countries, not only listened to him with great care but also often thought whether his arguments could assist in finding common ground. I remember with joy the many talks the two of us had in this respect.

Prof. Widjojo is an outstanding example of someone who can bring nations and countries closer together. I can still see him—in his modest way—smile and bring forward his point of view. One can surely regard him as a pioneer in making his interlocutors understand national and international economic correlations.

While saying this, I am not suggesting that the world of today has solved all problems. This is of course not the case. It would be naive to make the readers believe that differences of interests, positions and policies would vanish. They have not and they will not. The globalised world of today is characterised by competing and bargaining partners who seek their own best results. The so called global market place in which partners can operate demonstrates this every day. In order not to resort to a policy of a "Manchester" type capitalism there is a need for national and international rules to set the framework for the functioning of the market as well as bilateral and multilateral cooperation.

We have all made our experiences with successful and unsuccessful policies. What is important is that policies react flexibly to changing international cicumstances and also pursue policies for those citizens of our societies who need particular assistance. In other words economic policies without social policies would be condemned to failure. In Germany we call thisn"*Soziale Marktwirtschaft* (social market economy). There are clearly quite a number of similarities between two Professors Widjojo and Ludwig Erhard. The latter was the first Economic Minister of Germany after World War II. Social policies however must not become another synonym for protectionism on the international scene.

The globalised world poses challenges and chances. When I read the twenty-five year record of Economic Policy under President Soeharto I find that Indonesia with the openly assisting hand of Prof. Widjojo has done extremely well to achieve—in a period of dramatic change—economic stabilisation and poverty reduction. I am confident that this process will continue in Indonesia.

Other contributors to this important birthday are better qualified to comment on Indonesia's success story. Let me only say this. Considering where Indonesia started, with a population of about 200 millions people today and where she has arrived, it could be called a *Wirtschaftswunder* (economic miracle). But as Ludwig Erhard constantly insisted, that the recovery of Germany was not a miracle. As in our case the success in Indonesia must be attributed to good policies, hard work of the citizens and a climate of confidence and optimism in the country. I would like to pick up only a few points. Having moved to an open economy, among others in trade and investment as we find Indonesia today, we in Germany had always hoped for this development. We are impressed by the extent of the success.

I remember well the debt rescheduling exercise by Hermann Abs, when he presented his concept to the Ministries in Bonn. He brushed away all what he called " bookkeeping arguments" against his plan. He was already at that time convinced of the Indonesian success story. *Later when working in the Executive Board of the World Bank I watched the constant progress of Indonesia. The country was presented as an example of progress and economic development in Asia. Another outstanding example of Indonesia's forward looking policy is the reduction of population growth. If only other countries could follow similar paths, the future of the world would look brighter.*

Indonesia's role in the North-South Dialogue to which I already referred, has been one of a moderator. I am strongly convinced that in the end Indonesia did not only bring about a better understanding but it also led to a decrease of tensions and a greater convergence of positions.

Prof. Widjojo and I did not always see eye to eye or agree on all subjects. I cannot resist the temptation to mention the commodity issue, where I profoundly disagreed with the positions of the "Group of the 77", however well founded was the request of commodity producing countries to participate to a larger extent in processing productions either at home or in consuming countries. The way to achieve this is by opening up both industrialised countries manufactures sectors as well as creating an open investment climate in producing countries for foreign investors. I hastened to add that on both sides of the table work remains to be done.

This must be a two track approach. Indonesia, it seems to me, is on the right track. One final issue in this respect where I agree one hundred percent with Professor Widjojo is that for a number of developing countries private investment is not enough. The mixture of private investment and aid must continue. However, numerical targets have not really been the most promising way to achieve the goals. In my view these options were either unrealistic or outdated by new developments, like the protection of the environment with its global implications. Public financial funds must definitely be transferred to the really poor countries to assist them.

As to the bilateral German-Indonesian economic relations, I regard these as examples of ever intensifying cooperations. Many sectors could be mentioned here. They were not always without problems. The Indonesian steel sector was one of them. But companies with the assistance of the two governments have solved them amicably and give mutual benefit. In recent contacts with German companies I was told that Indonesia continues to be regarded as a very interesting country for their future business. All in all there seems to be a bright future for integrating German and Indonesian interests.

My more recent contacts and cooperation with Indonesia have been in the energy sector. The country is an important producer of many raw materials, including fossil fuels. Most important of all is its membership in OPEC, where Indonesia was involved in the top management of this organisation.

The beginning of the nineties, I believe, can now be characterised by the disappearance of confrontation between OPEC and IEA. Conferences and discussions between producers and consumers started after a long period of confrontation, misunderstanding and, worst of all, absence of talks. The concepts of the two organisations differed fundamentally for historical, political and economic reasons. In my responsibility I regarded the Indonesian representatives as instrumental to identify points of common understanding to move to an exchange of views, when the political scene lent itself to opening up the talks.

Without belittling the vital role of Professor Subroto to start this process from the OPEC side, I am quite sure that the Indonesian concept for a modern economic and energy policy was helpful. The political and economic change in the former command economies accompanied by their move to international cooperation has led to a variety of contacts such as seminars on various energy issues. The IEA conducted its first seminar with Russia in 1992 on the topic of energy and mining regimes. Participants were, apart from Russian representatives, delegates from IEA member countries and from energy companies. Also invited was Professor Widjojo as a representative of an oil producing country outside the IEA.

I remember vividly the intervention he made on Indonesia's practice, the production sharing regime. The response of the audience was very positive, not only by the Russians but also by companies and country representatives. Some Western company spokesmen were very supportive of the Indonesian option.

Professor Widjojo speaks with authority on economic issues based on profound knowledge and practical experience. It is always rewarding to listen to him. I am happy to have had the opportunities to meet him and exchange views with him. For his students and above all for his country, I hope he can contribute for many years to come. I extend all my good wishes to him. I am grateful to know such an outstanding man. ◆

65

Finding The Optimal Balance: Globalization, Technology, Govemance, Competition, and The Urban Question

*Louis Emmerij**

1. Introduction

One of Professor Widjojo Nitisastro's permanent professional interests lies in the relationship between efficiency and equity and in bringing together the concepts of distribution and poverty. Indonesia has been one of the countries that has brought down considerably the percentage of people living in poverty and Professor Widjojo's wise stewardship has been decisive in this success.

I am sure that he will agree with me that the world economy has changed almost beyond recognition during the last 15 years or so. To sustain success countries must take account of new factors. Several of these factors are highlighted in this article written in his honour.

The past 40 years have seen considerable developmental-policy changes. The emphasis is again very much on growth itself rather than on the redistribution of the income from that growth; on free trade, whatever the robustness of the national economy; on the market approach, whatever the ensuing distortions in the economy and in the society; on global markets, whatever the societal implications; and on privatization, whatever the importance of the firm or the enterprise in question for the strength of the nation. It can be objected that in the 1970s too much emphasis was given to redistribution, protectionism, the state, nationalized enterprises, and

* Mr. Louis Emmerij (Netherlands) was Special Advisor to the President, Inter-American Development Bank, Washington, D.C.

parastatals. Although this matter does invite debate, no one would deny that an effective approach does not consist of swinging from one extreme to the other. It follows that a proper balance is of the essence. In every developmental undertaking, a judicious mixture must be found of the best of the "old" and the best of the "new" policy ideas; of "hard" and "soft" issues of international and national policies; of public and private sectors, and so forth.

In the world economic and social scene of the mid-1990s, the following five major policy issues stand out, each of which we shall discuss in turn:

- globalization and its effects on the nation-state, with particular reference to the social sectors: moving beyond the dichotomy of free market and the (welfare) state,
- employment creation and productivity increases: going beyond the dichotomy of growth and redistribution,
- global markets and global governance: moving beyond the dichotomy of private versus public power,
- the paradox of competition: going beyond the dichotomy of black lamb and grey falcon[1], and
- the urban paradox: moving beyond the dichotomy of the best of times and the worst of times.

2. The Paradox of Globalization: Global Wealth and National Poverty

Globalization is a phenomenon driven by the private sector. Global enterprises undertake their multivarious activities in those geographical locations in which it is most cost-effective for them to do so; this truism applies also to the payment of taxes. Globalization sharpens competitiveness, and therefore, ever-greater efficiency and cost-effectiveness are required on the part of individual enterprises. Companies' ability to produce bits and pieces of their final product nearly anywhere in the world, their successful attempts to minimize payment of taxes, and the increasing footlooseness of their production units are some of the reasons that many national governments are becoming relatively impoverished, both in terms of decision-making power as well as financial income.

---

1 Rebecca West, Black Lamb and Grey Falcon - A Journey through Yugoslavia, (Penguin Books, 1994, 907-15). Basically the title refers to an old Serbian poem about the conqueror and the vanquished.

Other problems related to globalization are also mounting and intensifying, such as unemployment and underemployment, drug trafficking and drug use, crime, and political and economic refugeeism. Such problems themselves are taking on global characteristics: the employment problem has become worldwide, drug trafficking has itself become a global enterprise, refugees are covering ever-larger distances, and so forth. Questions that arise in this context and that need urgent further examination are the following:

* What are the exact relationships between the rise of globalization and the rise and intensification of other phenomena such as unemployment, drug use, and crime? Clearly, these relationships are real; there in fact exists a growing body of literature spelling this fact out.[2]

* What are the costs and benefits of globalization in the economic and financial spheres? How can the benefits be maximized and the costs minimized? Given the relationship between globalization (economic and financial) and increased social problems, should one not think of imposing special taxes on global economic and financial activities in order for the nation-state to be better armed to tackle the social issues? An example here is the so-called Tobin tax, named after economist James Tobin, Nobel prize winner.[3]

* Considerations such as the foregoing raise all the important issues of today—namely the relationship between state and market; the relationship between free trade and protection; the relative emphasis to be given to economic versus social considerations; and the relationship among international, regional, and national activities and policies.

The paradox of globalization illustrates the degree to which an active world level private sector has placed passive and impoverished nation-states on the defensive.

---

2 For an excellent summary, see UNRISD, States of Disarray: The Social Effects of Globalization (Geneva, 1995).

3 See the UNDP Human Development Report 1995 (Oxford University Press), and for more details Haq, Kaul, Grunberg, eds. The Tobin Tax: Coping with Financial Volatility (OUP, 1996).

3. The Paradox of Technological Progress: A Curse and a Blessing

It is under the topic of technological progress that the issues of employment and unemployment arise. The blessing of technological progress is, of course, that it enables people to produce more with less effort. But it is amazing to observe how this blessing has been turned into a curse through lack of insight and organization skills on the part of human beings.

In the case of industrial countries, the core problem is that economic and technological changes have not been accompanied by the needed societal changes. Labor markets, educational systems, pension schemes, and the like continue to be organized and structured in the same way as they were decades ago. They have not kept pace with the new economy that has emerged during the present period.

This lag in societal change has given rise to the curse of high levels of open and hidden unemployment in industrial countries in general and in Europe in particular. The blessing has indeed been turned into a curse. We do now produce more with less effort and fewer hours, but these advantages are distributed in a terribly misguided fashion. We are faced with a new distribution problem— namely, how to distribute the "less work" and "fewer hours" in a more rational fashion that avoids pushing 25 percent to 30 percent of the population into the margins of the economy and of society.

Old-style full employment most probably is no longer attainable and is not even desirable. We have to move toward a new-style full employment, based on a different societal structure in which people can move in and out of school, job and (creative) leave in a recurrent fashion rather than a sequential one. This approach will lead to qualitative changes in the economy and in society and to a different form of full employment that can be combined with a more creative life.[4]

As long as the employment problem in industrial countries remains unresolved, the latter will remain on the defensive with respect to East and South. The solution of the employment problem

---

4   The present author has written extensively on the necessity of changing the concept of full employment. There are indications that finally European thinking and practice are coming around to such a concept, which brings the societal structure in line with the economic and technological changes that have taken place in recent years.

in the West is therefore of crucial importance for developing countries and for countries in transition.

The problem in developing countries is not different in essence but needs a different policy treatment because of the degree to which the difficulty presents itself. The emphasis in these countries must be much more on identifying the right mixture between high-tech production in the export sectors and equally high-tech but more labor-intensive production in the domestic sectors. The main issue here is not to redistribute the available work in a smarter and more creative fashion but instead to create additional employment opportunities and also to increase the productivity of those presently employed at low levels of productivity and income.[5]

4. Global Markets and Global Governance

As mentioned earlier, globalization is basically a phenomenon driven by the private sector. Today's regionalization, on the other hand, is a state-driven phenomenon. As usual, the public sector is running one lap behind the private sector.

At the national level and regional level alike, we can observe a growing imbalance between the private sector and the public sector. At the global level, this public-private imbalance becomes a chasm.

Just as there should be a balance between the state and the private sector at both the national level and the regional level, so should there be a public-private balance at the global level.

At present there exists at the global level no equivalent to the state. Even worse, at the very moment such an equivalent is most needed, the weak institutions we do have (such as the United Nations and the Bretton Woods Institutions) are coming under increasingly severe attack, as might well be expected in the political and ideological situation that has emerged during the past 15 years.

What is needed now is a very sensitive and subtle approach, because it is easy to go overboard and to come up with utterly unrealistic proposals. Basically, we are concerned here with revitalizing the institutions currently existing at the global and regional levels, in order to make them relevant and effective in

---

5   See UNDP, Human Development Report 1996 (OUP 1996)—in particular, Chapter 4.

addressing the new situation of global markets and global enter-prises—in short, in addressing today's global private power.

5. The Paradox of Competition

Globalization tends to push competition to an extreme intensity worldwide. Nobody would deny that a degree of competition is positive. Healthy competition—at school, at work, in research, as well as in the economy—helps a society or an individual to progress and to remain innovative. The Latin root of the verb *compete* is *competere*, which means "to seek together".

But the intense competition in today's global era is a far cry from this old ideal. Competition has become a weapon to wipe out the adversary. It has become an ideology and an imperative, and some even speak of the gospel of competition.[6]

Competition in short has come to be seen as an answer to almost all economic ills. Is there a worsening unemployment problem? Then what is needed is to become more competitive. Is there a growing poverty problem in certain countries? Then what is needed for them is to become more competitive. Education and training must be geared more and more to the panacea of competition. The discussion is reminiscent of the proposals concerning a "flat tax" in the United States during the presidential campaign of 1996. In both cases a single proposed remedy is supposed to cure every ill in society.

Competition is in the process of becoming viewed as the only solution to the problem of globalization. The result is that the world's societies are increasingly engaged in a ruthless economic battle. Reports abound with such titles as "Winning in a World Economy," and the cult of competition even has its own "scientific" instrument—namely the World Competitiveness Index, published every year by the World Economic Forum, which ranks countries' competiveness in much the same way that the ATP classifies professional tennis players.

Competitiveness taken to such an extreme has undesirable effects, such as distortions in national economies. It also has negative

---

6　See the Group of Lisbon, Limits to Competition (MIT Press, 1995).

social repercussions, such as growing unemployment and downward pressure on salaries and income—and hence, growing inequality.

Such an extreme system is bound to flounder. Indeed, extreme competition diminishes the degree of diversity existing in a society and contributes to social exclusion: individuals, enterprises, cities, and nations that are not competitive are being marginalized and eliminated from the contest. This approach is unacceptable morally and inefficient economically. The more a system loses its variety, the more it will lose its capacity to renew itself. But above all, the ideology of competition devalues cooperation, and seeking together. It wipes out solidarity, and therefore we are not surprised that this era is also witnessing heavy attacks on the welfare state.

The question could reasonably be asked, what will the declared "winner" of this competition rat race actually do after leaving everybody else in the world so far behind? But the most important weakness of this "competition fundamentalism" is that it is incapable of integrating social justice, economic efficiency, environmental sustainability, political democracy, and cultural diversity.

6. The Urban Paradox Today

The facts are well known: one-half of the world's population lives in urban conglomerates; 75 percent of the population of industrial countries and of Latin America lives in cities; the increase in the urban population since 1965 has been 1.5 billion; over the next 10 years, there will be another 1 billion more people living in the city, most of them in the developing countries; and 17 out of 21 megacities are to be found in the Southern Hemisphere.

Behind these cold figures are increasing problems common to industrial and developing countries alike, problems that have given rise to the "urban question." The growing inequality observed between and within nations over the past 15 to 20 years is most starkly reflected in the city. There exist growing urban dualism and growing informalization, which have given rise to the specter of cities divided against themselves.[7]

---

7 "Every city or house divided against itself will not stand" (Mattew 12:25).

The essence of the urban problem is social in character: the poverty and the marginalization have become structural. Simultaneously with the globalization of the economy and of the financial system, we observe a global social problem: old-age pensioners, one-parent families, the unemployed, the disabled, and certain ethnic varieties are becoming increasingly marginalized by the to-them impenetrable new economy that is appearing before our eyes. On top of that, we observe in many urban centers more and more street children, child prostitution, child labor, and drug addiction.

In consequence, we see an increasing lack of social cohesion, leading to the phenomenon of divided cities. Most cities are losing the battle against poverty, and different urban groups are growing rapidly apart.

The urban explosion of course also has a sunny side, which is well captured in the words of Lewis Mumford: "The city is the most precious collective invention of civilization...second only to language itself in the transmission of culture." Indeed, the city offers better quality and more choice in education, material comforts, medical care, employment opportunities, and self-expression. It provides a wide variety of skills, services, culture, delivery systems, and the like. People are not fools when they let themselves be attracted by the bright city lights. They will eventually find their universe within this mass of steel and glass.

Or at least so they hope. But many of them run straight into their cities' dark side. The megacities of the South, and increasingly those of the North, are "Romes without empires." They have been boosted artificially; they are too expensive (for example, in terms of infrastructure investments) they tend to foster open unemployment and squatterism; they breed crime; and they waste resources (for instance, in terms of workers' daily commute to and from work and of the necessity to pump city dwellers' drinking water from farther and farther away).

The urban question clearly has many dimensions, including poverty, housing shortages, unemployment and underemployment, slum areas, crime, drugs, and the plight of street children. But one of the urban question's more baffling aspects is that it amounts to more than the sum total of these different specific problem areas. It is difficult to express just what this synergistic negative "value added" is, but it certainly has a lot to do with the quality of life—or more precisely with the lack of quality of life—in many urban settings. This phenomenon harms not only the poor; the rich also are negatively affected by the deterioration of the urban situation, and they have to move farther and farther away from the city center and to live in increasingly bunkerlike bungalows.

In the industrial countries, cities have started to grow again. A cycle—from the center to the suburbs to even more-distant "developments" and then back again to the city center—is now coming full circle. But one of the paradoxes here is that in many instances the downtown areas have indeed started growing again, as have the suburbs, but the slums have continued to deteriorate.

In industrial and developing economies alike, we can observe issues common to urban conglomerates worldwide. These include the following:

* growing inequality, dualism, and informalization, leading to the phenomenon of "cities divided against themselves"
* the social character of the urban problem, with poverty and marginalization now being structural in nature

These problems are reflected not only in the growing numbers of people who have no entry into today's globalizing and liberalized economies but also in the magnitude of the street children issue, child prostitution, child labor and drug addiction. Bangkok, with its rate of economic growth of 10 percent, is a spectacular illustration of global wealth harboring individual misery at the urban level. Within many of the world's cities, we observe a spreading social divisiveness, a losing fight against urban poverty, and a rapid drifting apart of the different urban groups, with a new apartheid looming on the horizon.

In general terms, current trends in globalization and competitiveness are intensifying the world's social problems (such as unemployment, downward pressure on income levels of parts of the population, and skewed income distributions). These problems are becoming themselves globalized, as are the related ills of drug trafficking, crime, and the whole's range of urban difficulties.

These intensified social problems (intensified by the global financial and goods markets) are left on the doorstep of nation-states that are themselves already facing problems of public finance and that hence are cutting back their welfare systems at the very moment these systems are needed most. There exists now a growing imbalance between the power of the free market and the influence and weight of the state. Nowhere is this public-private imbalance more visible than in the social arena and in the lack of the equivalent of the state at the global level.

The world economic and social scene is evolving very quickly, and change is in the air with respect to socioeconomic policies and institutions, in the light of huge and mounting social problems that have remained unsolved and that are becoming increasingly serious. It is indeed time to take stock of these problems and to examine the new policy ideas that are now emerging as ways of effectively addressing them.

Life starts at 70 and I would invite Professor Widjojo—whom I warmly congratulate at this occasion—to devote his attention and his mind to the solution of these emerging problems and to the examination of new policies to solve them. ◆

66

He Worked Hard Also to Set an Example for Others

*Guy Pauker**

Professor Widjojo Nitisastro and I have been friends for exactly forty years. During three long decades my admiration and respect for him have constantly increased. Undoubtedly, many highly qualified professionals will discuss his remarkable contributions as planner, as policy maker, scholar and teacher. My relation with Widjojo was personal, not professional, and I am therefore better qualified to comment on his character and personality than on the technical aspects of his work, though knowing, of course, how much Indonesia's economic development and successful campaign against poverty owe him.

My first exposure to Indonesia was in 1955, when I spent most of the year there as part of the joint MIT-Harvard research team on Indonesia's economic and political development problems under the leadership of Professor Benjamin Higgins. I do not recall whether I got acquainted with Professor Widjojo during that year. I returned to Indonesia for a second year of research in 1957, after having transferred from Harvard University to the University of California, Berkeley, where I took charge of the new Center for Southeast Asia Studies.

---

* Guy J. Pauker, Ph.D. (US) Harvard University 1952, was a Lecturer on Government there till 1956, teaching courses on Southeast Asia. He then joined the faculty of the University of California at Berkeley where he advanced to Professor and was also Director of the Center for Southeast Asia Studies. In 1963 he joined the RAND Corporation as a Senior Staff Member in charge of Southeast Asia Studies, from which he retired in 1982. Prof. Guy J. Pauker passed away in 2002.

The University of California had established a successful relationship with the University of Indonesia Medical School. Ford Foundation wanted to establish similar relations between the University of California, Berkeley's Economics Department and Economics Faculty of the University of Indonesia.

The project was approved, and Berkeley economists were scheduled to teach in Jakarta and Indonesian graduate students to come to Berkeley for advanced studies.

Widjojo and I met in Jakarta a few times, during 1957. I returned to Berkeley at about the same time as his arrival. Other Indonesian graduate students who later had distinguished careers, such as Professors M. Sadli and Emil Salim, to name a few, started their studies at the same time.

During the years Widjojo was in Berkeley we saw each other occasionally and had good conversations and enjoyed a few families social occasions, but in general Widjojo was not available. During my whole academic experience I had never encountered anybody who studied as hard as he did. The other Indonesian graduate students commented almost in awe about his study habits and considered him as undisputed leader of their small community. Widjojo in turn told me once that he worked so hard not only for his own needs but also in order to set an example for the others.

When the Berkeley-trained economists returned to Jakarta in the early 1960s and joined the faculty of their Economics Faculty, they were completely ignored by President Soekarno. They were not only incompatible with his ideological leanings and his anti-Americanism, which was not unjustified, but also with his views on economic development which seemed to rely more on mystical numerology than on economic analysis.

That the policies and management by the economists have been successful needs no further proof than the condition of Indonesia thirty years later, as recognized by the World Bank, the International Monetary Fund, the industrial nations which provide aid and the foreign investors. But it is my strong personal opinion that these achievement would not have been possible without Professor Widjojo's wisdom, subtlety, diplomacy, strength of character and thorough honesty. First of all he gained and retained the confidence of President Soeharto, early gauging very accurately his position in the power structure without compromising his professional standards. Furthermore, he understood better than most the limitations imposed on abstract rational planning by the needs of powerful interest groups, especially the military with their extra-budgetary requirements and to a lesser extent the civilian bureaucracy. Under less thoughtful leadership the best intentions of the economists would not have survived politically.

Yet these potentially formidable political obstacles did not result in major distortions of the economic plans as long as Professor Widjojo remained entrusted with the management of the Indonesian economy and major resources were not diverted and possibly wasted for ideological reasons. Needless to say, the economy of the prosperous Indonesia of the late 1990s can tolerate with less pain policy mistake that would have been disastrous in the early years of the Soeharto regime. What the President and his Economic Team achieved in the past are still providing a solid foundation for the future despite present difficulties of political in nature.

During my yearly research trips to Indonesia in the 1960s, 1970s and 1980s I always visited Widjojo at his Bappenas office and he was invariably helpful to make me understand his country economic problems and Indonesia's relations with the rest of the world. Despite his strongly realistic and sharply critical mind, the dominant personality trait I recall from those conversations is his cheerful, robust optimism. This impression was revived and reinforced when after an absence of eight years I visited Jakarta again in September 1996 and had again a long talk with Widjojo. He proudly gave me the latest data on public education, public health, family planning, agricultural development and other results - without any indication of envy that others were now running Bappenas and managing the economy.

Widjojo's team was nicknamed by others, long time ago, the "Berkeley Mafia". Many may interpret this as meaning that this first generation of American-trained economists were captives of American economic doctrines. Nothing could be further from the truth.

The current generation of students at the University of Indonesia and elsewhere were small children when President Soeharto's Economic Team took over a desperately poor country, with a rate of inflation of over 600% and food scarcities.

Most of them have probably no idea what the first generation of pioneer Indonesian economists achieved and how this has affected the young generation's prospects. I believe the volume honoring Professor Widjojo should be made required reading for all students. ◆

67

The Next Challenge in Development: Tertiary Education and Technological Infrastructure

Frederick E. Balderston*

1. Introduction

From his early days of study in economics at the University of California, Widjojo showed exceptional commitment of purpose: *to gain mastery of the systematic methods of social science, and to focus these upon the leading problems and policy needs of Indonesia.* As a quite junior professor at Berkeley, I was assigned to be an advisor and liaison for Widjojo and the others in a small group, supported by the Ford Foundation, who came to study economics.

Widjojo wrote a path-breaking doctoral dissertation analyzing Indonesia's population and the underlying demographic trends. This became the first of many topics for which his analytical contributions were substantial—and to these efforts of analysis he joined a gift for designing important economic policies and priorities that could be, and were, implemented in the Republic of Indonesia.

Within the country, he and his colleagues identified a few critical, interlocking issues for the reduction of poverty and the advancement of the people. As Widjojo summarized it, the strategy for Indonesia's reduction of poverty was implemented ... First, through sustained, broad-based and labor-intensive growth based on rapid growth of agriculture, and then through rapid growth of labor-intensive manufacturing export. Second, the poor were able to participate in

* Professor Frederick E. Balderston (US) was Assistant Professor of Business Administration at the University of California at the time when he first worked with Professor Widjojo in the late 1950s. The author also met with Professor Widjojo both in Jakarta and in Berkeley from time to time over the years. Frederick E. Balderston is now Professor Emeritus in the Haas School of Business, University of California, Berkeley.

that growth because of substantial improvements in education and health and investments in infrastructure. Third, population growth fell sharply." [Widjojo Nitisastro, "Reduction of Poverty: the Indonesia Experience", presentation at IMF-World Bank Conference, Madrid, 1994.]

Widjojo's own work as founding head of Bappenas was channeled toward systematic progress in these interlocking areas. Each of these required of the government and the society a strong, patient commitment to the long view, and to resistance against short-term palliative. The record of achievement is remarkable.

2. Continuing Focus on the Importance of Education

The Indonesian national interest in the priorities for widespread education, as stated above, has more recently included attention to higher education. Many view this sector as crucial to the next wave of advance for the nations that have broken out of mass poverty and are now already growing players in the regional and global markets for manufactured goods and services.

Long active in the Faculty of Economics of the University of Indonesia, Widjojo induced me to focus on some issues of Indonesia's university system. I was in Jakarta for portions of each year from 1986 through 1989 to work with people in the Ministry of Finance on problems of financial regulation. Widjojo found that I had headed a research project on management problems of US Universities and, in the 1970s, had written a book about university management and planning. He staged a meeting for discussion with Professor Sukadji Ranuwihardjo, then Director-General of Higher Education. As with so many matters of policy significance, Widjojo initiated discussion of an important area of national concern and elicited the participation of others who could help to work on worthwhile issues. This led to further involvements.

At Professor Sukadji's request, my late wife, Dr. Judith Balderston and I arranged a management seminar to be held in Berkeley for key people from various Indonesian universities. This included intensive discussions with university administrators and faculty leaders at several universities. A number of the participants later assumed senior responsibilities in Indonesia.

In April 1991, again at the request of Dr. Sukadji, we arranged for a three-day conference at which Indonesian leaders in higher education presented papers on the significant topics of growth and change in Indonesia's university system. American scholars from Berkeley and other institutions contributed their views, as did education experts from the World Bank. Judith Balderston and I then edited a volume of proceedings, which were published under the title: *Higher Education in Indonesia Evolution and Reform* (1993, Center for Studies in Higher Education, University of California, Berkeley).

Participants presented papers on topics in several broad areas of concern: the quality of education and issues of national integration; the role of higher education in national economic and social development; and the role of graduate education, research and industry.

3. The Next Phases of Development: University and Technical Education on Widening Scales

It appears evident that nations in transition (and, in a real sense, all nations will be in various stages of change) will have to cope actively with the growing interdependence of the world economy. They face the necessity of contributing to, and adapting to their needs, the widening base of scientific and technical knowledge as well as cultural and humanistic understanding.

All this will require that an increasing fraction of the young population be provided appropriate opportunities for education beyond secondary school. In 1994, Indonesia provided such education for about eleven percent of the 19-24 years age bracket, as against 8.5 percent in 1989. At the same time, the number of those completing secondary school continues its substantial annual increase in accordance with demographic trends. Continuing rapid growth in tertiary education will be necessary, and very substantial public and private investments will be required. For some fortunate young people, educated overseas at universities in the US and elsewhere will enable them to bring back home new skills and intellectual capabilities.

The national economy, in turn, will need to supply employment opportunities to capitalize on the skills that young people acquire through the tertiary education system. Productive work experience will then help them to advance toward eventual positions of leadership in the society. Many factors influence the domestic and international flow of investment capital for continuing economic growth, but surely one important factor is the presence of a vigorous, well-educated population that can be counted on to be productive and adaptable to rapid technical change.

There is a continuing issue of macro-policy, for no one knows what fraction of the youth population should be provided a tertiary education. Indonesia is not alone. Nearly all nations face serious issues of how much to invest of the government's development capital, and how in private sector resources—not to mention the expenses borne by the parents of the young ! But it is clear that for a long time to come, an increasing fraction of the youth population will be destined for tertiary education. It will be a struggle to enhance the quality as well as to expand the quantity of education that the universities and the polytechnics provide.

Thus, what Indonesia accomplished at an earlier stage with its investments in universal primary education, rural health, and population policies will now, very probably, need to be matched in scope by investments in tertiary education and technological infrastructure. This appears to be the next, and challenging phase of Indonesia's development. ◆

68

The Mark of a True Scholar and Gentleman

Bram Peper*

As far as this writer is concerned, the most intense encounter with Professor Widjojo Nitisastro was the first, in 1965, before any face to face meeting actually took place. In that year, with all a young man's rapacious zeal and greed for knowledge, I threw myself into the study of population growth on Java in the 19th century, specifically in the period 1800 to 1850. As part of my quest I regularly borrowed rucksacks full of books from the splendid library of the Tropical Institute in Amsterdam. Having some doubts about the then undisputed 'given' that 19th century Java had a particularly high rate of population growth—in excess of 2 per cent a year, making it an exception in the so-called non-western world at that time—I badly needed determinants of birth and, especially, death. Investigating the true natures of these determinants—health status, economic development, and public order and peace (Pax Neerlandica)—I concluded that there were insufficient grounds to assume that the Netherlands exerted a major, positive influence in the period 1800 to 1850. Moreover, it was relatively easy to demonstrate that the basic population growth figures (1815) taken from Raffles' *History of Java* (1830)[1] had pitched the estimated size of population far too low. This alone was an independent factor for excessively high calculation of population growth in my period.

---

* Dr. Bram Peper (Netherlands) was Mayor of the City of Rotterdam; President of Eurocities and Minister of Home Affairs.

1 T.S. Raffles, *The History of Java*, 2nd edition, 2 vols., London, 1830.

I found powerful and welcome support for my view that, unintentionally, the writing of the history of Java was Euro-centric, as manifest in the exceptionally high population growth. That support came from the masterly thesis of a then quite unknown Professor Widjojo[2]. I discovered a photo-copy in the Amsterdam University Library. My own thesis was completed in 1965, but it was most rewarding that much later, in 1975, it appeared in Bahasa Indonesia.[3]

Later on I would encounter Professor Widjojo on several occasions. By then I was no longer a post-graduate student, but the Mayor of Rotterdam, and he has become—in the meantime—the economic architect of President Soeharto's New Order (Orde Baru). It is the mark of a true scholar and gentleman, that he extends the same help and courtesy to a struggling student as to one somewhat older, and presumably wiser. And indeed, so it was with Professor Widjojo - but this time face to face. Now he has reached 70, the age *of true strength, an*d this small contribution[4] is dedicated to him in gratitude, respect and friendship. ◆

---

2 Nitisastro, Widjojo, 1961, Migration, Population Growth and Economic Development in Indonesia, Ph. D. Thesis, University of California, Berkeley.
3 Peper, Bram, 1967, Grootte en Groei van Java's inheemse bevolking in de negentiende eeuw, Publikatie Nr. 11, Afdeling Zuid- en Zuidoost-Azie, Antropologisch-sociologisch Centrum, Universiteit van Amsterdam, Amsterdam. An abbreviated version was published as: Population Growth in Java in the 19th Century, A New Interpretation, in: Population Studies, vol. xxiv, No. 1, pp. 71-84, March 1970.
4 An article: "Integration and tolerance in a multi-ethnic society experiences from the Netherlands" in *Pembangunan Nasional: Teori, Kebijakan, dan Pelaksanaan*, edited by Moh. Arsjad Anwar, Aris Ananta, and Ari Kuncoro. Jakarta. Fakultas Ekonomi Universitas Indonesia, 1977.

69

Some Food for Thought in Revamping Indonesia's VAT to Meet the Requirements for the 21st Century

Sijbren Cnossen*

1. Introduction

Indonesia's unparalleled economic success during the Soeharto Presidency owes much to the inspiring vision and leadership of Professor Widjojo Nitisastro. He and his colleagues planned and implemented the now-famous policies that led to economic stability, rehabilitation, and high sustained growth. These policies are textbook *examples of sound macroeconomic management that, in less than 25 years*, propelled Indonesia from being one of the world's bread basket cases *to South East Asia's economic giant*.

Following the successful institutionalization of the country's macroeconomic policies, a task largely accomplished in the 1970s, Professor Widjojo and his colleagues turned their attention to other areas of concern. Thus, in the early 1980s, they embarked on a fundamental ref*orm of Indonesia's antiq*uated tax system. The reform was designed and brought to fruition by Professor Ali Wardhana, Finance Minister from 1968 to 1983. But as *Coordinating Minister of Economics, Finance, and Industry, fr*om 1973 to 1983, Professor Widjojo was closely involved in the reform and functioned as an indispensable sounding board. As a true example of *'golongan karya,'* his work was taken over by Professor Wardhana who was Coordinating Minister until 1988.

* Prof. Sijbren Cnossen (Netherlands) is Professor in the Faculty of Economics Erasmus University, Rotterdam; advisor to Ministers of Finance, Frans Seda and Ali Wardhana, 1967-1969; Member of Harvard Tax Group for Indonesia (1981-1983) and for more than a decade he organized educational programs for Indonesian tax officials.

By far the most successful item in the tax reform was the introduction, in 1985, of the value-added tax (VAT). The VAT replaced an outmoded, cumulative manufacturers sales tax, which was complex, highly distortionary, and yielded little revenue. In less than three years, the new VAT doubled its share in non-oil domestic revenues, rivaling the share of the income tax and enabling the Government to continue to finance its rapidly rising expenditures in a non-inflationary manner. Currently, VAT revenues are approximately 4.5 percent of Gross Domestic Product (up from one percent in 1984), an outstanding performance among developing economies.

Indonesia's VAT has many commendable features, including a consistent tax credit mechanism (which minimizes economic and competitive distortions), the use of a single tax rate (which greatly simplifies administration and compliance), the exclusion of un-processed foodstuffs (which mitigates the regressive impact of the VAT), the imposition of higher excise-type VAT rates on luxury products (which imparts an element of progressivity to the burden distribution of the tax), and the exclusion of small firms (which saves on scarce administrative resources).

The VAT has a number of aspects, however, which may have to be re-examined as Indonesia's economy, moving into the 21st century, continues to grow and diversify. The VAT, initially, was imposed at the manufacturers level. Although subsequently extended to the retail stage, the VAT lacks a unified concept of taxable persons. Manufacturers, wholesalers and retailers are still treated separately. Its origin at the manufacturers level also means that services are not taxed comprehensively. In addition, perhaps more can be done to tax public sector bodies more widely and to provide for more even-handed treatment of immovable property. Beyond this, some other features call for comment, including the treatment of capital goods and internationally traded services. The issues are reviewed in light of the experience of other countries with a VAT.

2. Extension of tax coverage through to the retail stage

Like Indonesia, many countries that started with a VAT at the manufacturers stage (M-VAT) have extended their VATs through to the retail stage (R-VAT). These countries found that M-VATs are highly distortionary (luxury products, services and imports tend to be favored); that M-VATs cause the VAT burden to be distributed unevenly, accentuating the regressive impact of the VAT with respect to consumption expenditures; and that M-VATs involve numerous valuation problems (when manufacturers sell directly to retailers and consumers, or establish their own distribution firms) and definitional issues (arising from attempts to delineate manufacturers from distributors).

In sharp contrast, a well-designed R-VAT has none of these problems. Neutrality is ensured because the tax is imposed as close to the consumer as possible. Discount mechanisms (required under an M-VAT if manufacturers sell directly to retailers or consumers) or uplift mechanisms (desirable if large retailers integrate backwards by assuming marketing functions usually performed by wholesalers and manufacturers) are not necessary. Manufacturing or distribution does not have to be defined, and taxable values are nearly always identical to actual prices. The usual argument in favor of the M-VAT —that the number of taxable persons is smaller than under an R-VAT and accounts are better maintained—is fallacious, because an appropriate exemption removes most small retailers from tax coverage, yet include department stores and supermarkets. In other words, it is not the stage at which the VAT is imposed which determines the number of taxpayers, but the size of the small-business exemption. Moreover, the exemption is not costly in terms of revenue foregone, because exempt small businesses (whose value added usually is small relative to consumer price) would still pay VAT on purchases.

Indonesia has taken commendable steps to adopt an R-VAT. Thus, in 1989, the VAT's coverage was extended through to the wholesale stage and in 1992 very large retailers were also made taxable. These desirable features were "added on," however. No attempt was made to formulate a unified concept of taxable persons;

rather, manufacturers, wholesalers and retailers continue to be separately defined. Moreover, separate small-business exemptions apply to manufacturers and wholesalers, on the one hand, and retailers, on the other hand. Particularly, the large exemption for retailers (Rp 1,000 million) should induce them to split up their operations and may induce wholesalers to masquerade as retailers. Furthermore, the manufacturers-wholesalers exemption differs between firms selling goods (Rp 120 million) and firms rendering services (Rp 60 million). Although understandable because the taxable value added content is usually greater in the case of services, the distinction nonetheless complicates the operation of the VAT. In due course, it may be advisable to introduce a unified concept of taxable persons with a single small-business exemption, at the level of, say, the current exemption of Rp 120 million.

3. Comprehensive inclusion of services

The move through to the retail stage permits the inclusion of services, often rendered by retail-type of establishments, in the tax base. This enhances the VAT's neutrality and revenue potential and reduces administrative problems. In Indonesia, taxable services probably constitute 25-30 percent of GDP. Taxing them removes the discrimination against goods and, given the required yield, permits a reduction in the VAT rate. The taxation of services should also lessen the regressive impact of the VAT, because taxable services tend to be more elastic with respect to income than are goods. Furthermore, administrative problems are fewer, because the taxation of services removes the incentive to substitute goods by services (cars can be bought but also leased). In any case, no satisfactory borderline can (or should) be drawn between goods and services on philosophical, economic or legal grounds.

In taxing services, Indonesia has followed a selective approach. Originally, only construction services were included in the tax base. Subsequently, in 1989, a wide range of service categories were made taxable, including telecommunications, domestic air transport, repair and maintenance, leasing of movable and immovable property (except hotels), and various professional services. A list of services not subject to the VAT was also issued. It included health care, education, banking, insurance, and various social services. River and land transport became taxable in 1994.

The implication of the selective approach to the taxation of services is that services that are not mentioned are not taxable. The selective approach is understandable in light of the start of the VAT at the manufacturers level which, by definition, does not readily permit the inclusion of services in the tax base. Other countries with a well-designed VAT have adopted a comprehensive approach; that is, they tax all services except those enumerated as being exempt. Taxing services comprehensively accords with the notion of equal treatment, promotes tax neutrality, and obviates the need for fine legal distinctions that add to administrative complexity.

4. The treatment of capital goods and input tax credits

It is widely recognized that VATs should allow a full and immediate credit for the tax on purchases of capital goods. Disallowing the credit on capital goods violates the neutrality of the VAT. First, the VAT on fixed assets enters into price, thus causing uneven effects on consumer prices, depending on the capital intensity of the production process. Second, the noncreditable VAT on fixed assets, unless it can be fully shifted forward to consumers, deters investment—which hampers technological change. (Forward shifting is unlikely, however, if competing imports can be sold without the element of tax on capital goods.) Third, the non-creditable VAT acts as a disincentive to exports, because exporters facing world prices will have to absorb the tax. Fourth, in the face of inflation, the real value of the tax credit, if allowed in 'installments,' declines rapidly, becoming equivalent in effect to a tax on fixed assets. Last but not least, capital goods must be defined.

Under its VAT, Indonesia has always allowed a credit for the VAT on capital goods, although any excess of input tax over output tax must be carried forward and, generally, is refundable only after the close of the financial year. On the other hand, the VAT on imported capital goods used in manufacturing products for export may be deferred and suspended on the philosophy that a tax credit or refund would have to be given anyway. This situation invites two comments. First, the carry forward of tax credits to subsequent tax periods means that the value of the credit is eroded through inflation. Second, the deferral and suspension of the tax on imported capital goods discriminates against domestically produced capital goods and may involve some tax leakage.

In some other cases, firms may be allowed input tax credits as a percentage of output tax, or firms may elect to be taxed on a gross basis. Firms choosing to be subject to tax on the calculation norm, for instance, are permitted to use a formula that sets the input tax credit at 70 percent of the output tax for taxable goods, and 40 percent of the output tax for the delivery of taxable services. Furthermore, domestic air transport firms are authorized to use an input tax credit figure of 30 percent of the output tax. In these examples, therefore, VAT is paid at tax rates of 3, 6, and 7 percent of turnover, respectively. Similarly, taxable retailers may elect to pay VAT at an effective rate of 2 percent of turnover. All of these presumptive types of VAT calculations violate the basic structure of the tax. Hence, regularized treatment is recommended. Presumably, in light of the high level of the small-business exemptions, these firms have adequate records for keeping track of input tax credits.

5. Re-examination of the taxation of immovable property

Newly created immovable property, including residential property, is taxed by all countries with a sophisticated VAT. Rents and rental values of owner-occupied property are usually exempt. As a result, rents and rental values are taxed indirectly, because the VAT on new residential property may be viewed as the capitalized VAT on the future stream of exempt housing services.

Countries differ, however, in their treatment of commercial immovable property. Under the exemption method, in use by countries following the example of the European Union, the lease or sale of used commercial property is exempt, just like the lease or sale of residential property. As a result, increases in the value of commercial property (and hence in the value of the services rendered by the property) are not taxed. To be sure, optional registration and payment of VAT is available in respect of commercial property, but it causes differential effects. Under the tax method, on the other hand, applied by New Zealand and Canada, all leases and sales of commercial immovable property are subject to VAT. Thus, increases in the property's value are included in the tax base, distortions are fewer, and change-of-use rules are simpler to apply.

Through the use of the tax method, Indonesia is taxing immovable property on a wider scale than are most other developing countries. The renting of residential property, moreover, is also included in the tax base. Hotel accommodation, on the other hand, is not taxed (because local governments tax hotel occupancies). In due course, all used residential property should actually receive the same treatment (that is, be exempted), while transient forms of accommodation might be taxed (even if this means that they would be taxed twice).

6. Wider taxation of public sector bodies

Another issue that is currently being discussed concerns the most appropriate treatment of services provided by public sector bodies, including government departments, state and local authorities, and public sector enterprises. Should such services always be subject to VAT, the approach adopted in New Zealand, or should public sector services only be taxed if their exemption would cause "significant distortions of competition," the criterion used in other countries?

To be sure, economic services, such as the supply of water, gas and electricity, telecommunications, transport of goods and passengers, port and airport services are taxed under both approaches. Furthermore, the payment of social benefits is exempt in all countries. What remains are services by public sector bodies that fall somewhere between economic and social services. The most important categories in this grey area are health and education. Exemption causes distortions, e.g. input VAT regarding hospital research for a pharmaceutical company cannot be passed on. Exemption also induces exempt institutions to self-supply inputs, such as food, cleaning and administrative services. This frustrates the natural division of labor.

So far, the debate on the wider taxation of public sector bodies is inconclusive. It does not seem to make much sense to tax government departments, for example, if they have no or hardly any involvement with the private sector. Some legal services, for example, may be obtained from another government department but also from the private sector. If, overall, departmental expenditures on such services are small, full taxation of departmental activities would seem to be a form of "overkill." However, when cascading and in-house provision reach major proportions (private clinics or training courses), inclusion in the VAT base seems indicated.

In due course, Indonesia may wish to take another look at the taxation of public sector bodies. In the meantime, many of these bodies are involved in collecting the VAT as withholders. Tax due to the supplier is withheld by the customer and paid directly to the Government, rather than the customer paying the amount to the supplier who, in turn, would pay it to the Government. Designated withholders are government agencies, various government-owned corporations (including Pertamina), and state and regional development banks. This unusual feature, aimed at preventing tax leakage, causes operational complications, because suppliers may not know if the VAT has been withheld or whether they should collect and remit it. More fundamentally, the technique violates the basic structure of the VAT.

7. Problems with internationally traded services

The place of services is often difficult to locate, particularly when they enter international trade. Whereas goods are supplied at the place where they are located and tax on them can be charged (or refunded) when they physically cross national borders, services are often intangible and recognize no national frontiers. To avoid economic distortions and provide for parity of treatment, most countries with a VAT have issued a number of rules to govern the place of supply of services. The main rule is that the place of supply coincides with the place where the supplier has established his business. Important exceptions are made, however, for services supplied across borders, related to immovable property (which are deemed to be supplied where the property is located), transport services (supplied where the transport takes place), physical per-formances (supplied where carried out), and various intangible services, e.g. of lawyers, accountants, banks, and insurance companies (which are deemed to be supplied where the customer is located).

The gist of the main rule and its exceptions is that services supplied mainly to consumers are deemed to be performed where the supplier has his place of business, while services supplied mainly to businesses are deemed to be supplied where the recipient of the services has his main place of business. Viewed in an international context, therefore, cross-border purchases of consumer services are taxed on an origin basis, but business services are taxed on a destination basis. So far, this arrangement has prevented major distortions. However, the growing importance of intangible services (telecommunications is a good example) has put this hitherto workable arrangement under stress. VAT administrations find it increasingly difficult to enforce the compliance with the VAT on "imported" (and "exported") services for which there is no tangible control. Order, invoice, payment, or use of the service may take place in different countries, for example. Clearly, greater international cooperation is called for if over- or undertaxation is to be prevented.

8. Concluding comment

The VAT has come of age and with it an increased awareness of its potential and limitations. Basically, the VAT is a revenue workhorse. Properly designed and administered, it can raise more revenue with less operational and economic cost than can be raised by other broadly based taxes. Indonesia's VAT compares well to the VATs in many other countries. The tax is broadly based and levied at a single rate. Some features and practices, however, may call for further review. Basically, these revolve around the fact that the VAT started at the manufacturers level and was not redesigned when the coverage was extended to wholesalers and retailers. *In the spirit of Professor Widjojo's foresight, this contribution offers some food for thought in revamping the VAT to meet the requirements for the 21st century.*

A major drawback of the VAT is that it, like all taxes, cannot make the poor richer and it is not very good at making the rich poorer. Its benefits for lower-income groups lie mainly with the expenditure programs which it can finance in a noninflationary manner. Thus, VAT's revenues make it possible to establish, in Professor Widjojo's words (Address at the IMF-World Bank Conference in Madrid): "a network of social and physical infrastructure, such as primary schools leading to universal primary education; integrated centers for health, nutrition and family planning; rural networks of roads, irrigation facilities, and support for flood control." These programs have contributed to a reduction in absolute poverty from 60 percent of the total population in 1970 to 15 percent in 1990. Surely, this is the true measure of Professor Widjojo's contribution to Indonesia's social and economic development. ◆

Team of Editors

Mohammad Arsjad Anwar. Born in Kuningan (West Java) in 1936. He achieved his MBA in Operation Research from the University of California, Berkeley, USA and completed his Doctoral Degree in Economics from the University of Indonesia (1983) with a dissertation titled *Pertumbuhan Pertanian Dilihat dari Pertumbuhan Produk Domestik Bruto di Indonesia* (*Agricultural Growth Viewed from the Growth of Gross Domestic Product in Indonesia*) 1960-1980. Appointed full professor of the Faculty of Economics University of Indonesia, he presented an oration titled *Transformasi Struktur Produksi, Pertumbuhan Ekonomi, dan Perencanaan Pembangungan* (*Transformation of the Production Structure, Economic Growth and Development Planning*) in 1985.

In addition to many activities within the University of Indonesia, especially with the Faculty of Economics, he was also involved in many other activities with a number of government agencies: Trade Department, Education and Culture Department, National Research Council, Badan Pusat Statistik (the Indonesian Statistics Office), and Bappenas (The National Development Planning Agency). He was the Director of CPIS (Center for Policy and Implementation Studies).

Besides teaching at the University of Indonesia, he was also Director of the Institute for Economic and Social Research, Associate Dean for Academic Affairs, Dean of the Faculty of Economics, and Coordinator for Economics of the Graduate Program of Economics University of Indonesia. From 1994 to 1999 he was named Chairman of Economics Consortium in Indonesia.

From 1998 to 2001 he served as Assistant Coordinating Minister of the Economy, Finance and Industry for Finance Division. Since 2001, he has been serving as Advisor to the Minister of National Development Planning and Head of Bappenas.

Aris Ananta. Born in Klaten (Central Java) in 1954. Apart from studying economics, he also studied demography. In 1983 he achieved his Ph.D. in economics from Duke University in the USA, with a dissertation titled: *An Economic Model of Fertility Behavior in Developing Countries: an Indonesian Case.* He was inaugurated full professor of the Faculty of Economics, University of Indonesia in 1995, presenting an oration titled *Transisi Kependudukan di Indonesia: Beberapa Masalah dan Prospek Perekonomian* (*Demographic Transition in Indonesia: Several Economic Problems and Prospects*).

Since 1983 he had been teaching at the Faculty of Economics University of Indonesia and serving as a Senior Researcher at the Institute of Demography of the Faculty of Economics University of Indonesia. From 1995 to 1997 he was named Associate Director at the Institute following his previous posts (Head of Research Division in 1988-1991, and Head of the Demographic Information Division in 1992-1995). He was named Coordinator for Economics of the Post-Graduate Program of the University of Indonesia (1996-1998).

In 1999 and 2000 he was teaching and carrying out research as a Senior Fellow at the Department of Economics, National University of Singapore. Since 2001 he has been a Senior Research Fellow at the Institute of Southeast Asian Studies (Singapore), carrying out various research activities on Southeast Asia, with a focus on the economic, social and political developments in Indonesia.

Ari Kuncoro: Born in Jakarta in 1962. In 1994 he achieved his Ph.D. in Economics from Brown University in the US with a dissertation titled *Industrial Location Choices in Indonesia*

He has been a lecturer at the Faculty of Economics University of Indonesia since 1988 and senior research associate at the Institute for Economic and Social Research of the Faculty of Economics, University of Indonesia since 1994. Hew was the Secretary for Economics at the Graduate Program of Economics, University of Indonesia in 1996-2000 and the Associate Dean for Academic Affairs, Faculty of Economics, University of Indonesia in 1998-2001. He is a leading scholar in applying economic models to issues of governance and corruption in Inodnesia. In particular his research covers how politic and rent-seeking activities as well as social relationship among various interest groups shape policy-making in Indonesia. He writes extensively in international journals and books. His latest publication is "Understanding Economic Reforms in Indonesia: 1983-2000," published in *Understanding Market Reforms; volume 2; Motivation, Implementation and Susceptibility*, edited by J.M.. Fanelli and G. McMahon, Swansea, UK: Palgrave Macmilla, 2006.

Index